First Workshop on South East Asian Language Processing 2023

Nusa Dua, Indonesia
1 November 2023

ISBN: 978-1-7138-9008-9

Printed from e-media with permission by:

Curran Associates, Inc.
57 Morehouse Lane
Red Hook, NY 12571

Some format issues inherent in the e-media version may also appear in this print version.

Printed with permission by Curran Associates, Inc. (2024)

For permission requests, please contact the Association for Computational Linguistics at the address below.

Association for Computational Linguistics
209 N. Eighth Street
Stroudsburg, Pennsylvania 18360

Phone: 1-570-476-8006
Fax: 1-570-476-0860

acl@aclweb.org

Additional copies of this publication are available from:

Curran Associates, Inc.
57 Morehouse Lane
Red Hook, NY 12571 USA
Phone: 845-758-0400
Fax: 845-758-2633
Email: curran@proceedings.com
Web: www.proceedings.com

IJCNLP-AACL 2023

The First Workshop on South East Asian Language Processing

Proceedings of the Workshop

November 1, 2023

The IJCNLP-AACL organizers gratefully acknowledge the support from the following sponsors.

Platinum

Gold

Silver

Preface

This volume contains the proceedings of the First Workshop in South East Asian Language Processing, held in conjunction with the 13th International Joint Conference on Natural Language Processing and the 3rd Conference of the Asia-Pacific Chapter of the Association for Computational Linguistics (IJCNLP-AACL 2023).

South East Asia (SEA) is one of the most linguistically diverse regions in the world, with over 1,200 languages spoken by 680 million people. However, the diversity of South East Asian languages has long been at risk due to the emphasis on national languages as the lingua franca in South East Asian countries at the end of colonization, and the increasing prominence of English due to the necessities of globalization.

This year is the first year we are conducting this workshop with the aim of bringing together practitioners from academia, government, and industry interested in the research and development of language technologies for SEA languages. The workshop also aims to build an inclusive community of everyone passionate about SEA languages, increase community awareness of works that have been developed to date on these languages, and foster collaborations that will strengthen and spur NLP research and development in SEA languages.

The workshop received 14 submissions of technical papers (12 long, 2 short), of which 10 were accepted (8 long, 2 short), for an acceptance rate of 71%. We thank the Programme Committee members who provided extremely valuable reviews in terms of technical content.

The accepted papers cover a wide range of natural language processing research, including research on languages in the Philippines and Indonesia, as well as languages in South Asia such as Bangla, Hindi, and Indic languages. The papers tackle a variety of tasks in NLP, including named entity recognition, word sense and synset induction, grammatical error correction, machine translation, dialogue systems, sentiment analysis, text generation, large language models alignment, as well as datasets, benchmarks, and language resources construction. In the future, we hope that this workshop will continue to attract submissions of diverse research works on SEA languages.

We look forward to an enriching discussion on research in South East Asian language processing at the hybrid event on November 1, 2023!

November 2023

Derry Wijaya, Alham Fikri Aji, Clara Vania, Genta Indra Winata, Ayu Purwarianti

Organizing Committee

Derry Wijaya, Monash University Indonesia

Alham Fikri Aji, Mohamed bin Zayed University of Artificial Intelligence (MBZUAI)

Clara Vania, Amazon

Genta Indra Winata, Bloomberg

Ayu Purwarianti, Bandung Institute of Technology (ITB)

Program Committee

Peerat Limkonchotiwat, Vidyasirimedhi Institute of Science and Technology (VISTEC)

Jan Christian Blaise Cruz, Samsung R&D Institute Philippines

Garry Kuwanto, Boston University

Phu Mon Htut, Amazon Web Services AI Labs (AWS AI Labs)

Samuel Cahyawijaya, Hong Kong University of Science and Technology (HKUST)

David Moeljadi, Kanda University of International Studies

Haryo Akbarianto Wibowo, Mohamed bin Zayed University of Artificial Intelligence (MBZUAI)

Radityo Eko Prasojo, Pitik.id

Andros Tjandra, Facebook AI Research (FAIR, Meta)

Rahmad Mahendra, RMIT University

Zilu Tang, Boston University

Holy Lovenia, AI Singapore, National University of Singapore

Samuel Louvan, Amazon

Table of Contents

Towards Automatic Construction of Filipino WordNet: Word Sense Induction and Synset Induction Using Sentence Embeddings
Dan John Velasco, Axel Alba, Trisha Gail Pelagio, Bryce Anthony Ramirez, Jan Christian Blaise Cruz, Unisse Chua, Briane Paul Samson and Charibeth Cheng 1

Developing a Named Entity Recognition Dataset for Tagalog
Lester James Miranda 13

Balarila: Deep Learning for Semantic Grammar Error Correction in Low-Resource Settings
Andre Dominic H. Ponce, Joshue Salvador A. Jadie, Paolo Edni Andryn Espiritu and Charibeth Cheng 21

Utilizing Weak Supervision to Generate Indonesian Conservation Datasets
Mega Fransiska, Diah Pitaloka, Saripudin Saripudin, Satrio Putra and Lintang Sutawika* 30

InstructAlign: High-and-Low Resource Language Alignment via Continual Crosslingual Instruction Tuning
Samuel Cahyawijaya, Holy Lovenia, Tiezheng Yu, Willy Chung and Pascale Fung 55

SentMix-3L: A Novel Code-Mixed Test Dataset in Bangla-English-Hindi for Sentiment Analysis
Md Nishat Raihan, Dhiman Goswami, Antara Mahmud, Antonios Anastasopoulos and Marcos Zampieri 79

IndoToD: A Multi-Domain Indonesian Benchmark For End-to-End Task-Oriented Dialogue Systems
Muhammad Kautsar, Rahmah Nurdini, Samuel Cahyawijaya, Genta Winata and Ayu Purwarianti 85

Replicable Benchmarking of Neural Machine Translation (NMT) on Low-Resource Local Languages in Indonesia
Lucky Susanto, Ryandito Diandaru, Adila Krisnadhi, Ayu Purwarianti and Derry Tanti Wijaya 100

Conference Program

14:00–14:05 ***Welcome Remarks***

14:05–14:20 *Towards Automatic Construction of Filipino WordNet: Word Sense Induction and Synset Induction Using Sentence Embeddings*
Dan John Velasco, Axel Alba, Trisha Gail Pelagio, Bryce Anthony Ramirez, Jan Christian Blaise Cruz, Unisse Chua, Briane Paul Samson and Charibeth Cheng

14:20–14:35 *Low-Resource Clickbait Spoiling for Indonesian via Question Answering*
Ni Putu Intan Maharani, Ayu Purwarianti and Alham Fikri Aji

14:35–14:50 *Developing a Named Entity Recognition Dataset for Tagalog*
Lester James Miranda

14:50–15:05 *Balarila: Deep Learning for Semantic Grammar Error Correction in Low-Resource Settings*
Andre Dominic H. Ponce, Joshue Salvador A. Jadie, Paolo Edni Andryn Espiritu and Charibeth Cheng

15:05–15:20 *Unsupervised Approach to Evaluate Sentence-Level Fluency: Do We Really Need Reference?*
Gopichand Kanumolu, Lokesh Madasu, Pavan Baswani, Ananya Mukherjee and Manish Shrivastava

15:20–15:50 ***Coffee Break***

15:50–16:05 *Utilizing Weak Supervision to Generate Indonesian Conservation Datasets*
Mega Fransiska, Diah Pitaloka, Saripudin Saripudin, Satrio Putra and Lintang Sutawika*

16:05–16:20 *InstructAlign: High-and-Low Resource Language Alignment via Continual Crosslingual Instruction Tuning*
Samuel Cahyawijaya, Holy Lovenia, Tiezheng Yu, Willy Chung and Pascale Fung

16:20–16:35 *SentMix-3L: A Novel Code-Mixed Test Dataset in Bangla-English-Hindi for Sentiment Analysis*
Md Nishat Raihan, Dhiman Goswami, Antara Mahmud, Antonios Anastasopoulos and Marcos Zampieri

16:35–16:50 *IndoToD: A Multi-Domain Indonesian Benchmark For End-to-End Task-Oriented Dialogue Systems*
Muhammad Kautsar, Rahmah Nurdini, Samuel Cahyawijaya, Genta Winata and Ayu Purwarianti

16:50–17:05 *Replicable Benchmarking of Neural Machine Translation (NMT) on Low-Resource Local Languages in Indonesia*
Lucky Susanto, Ryandito Diandaru, Adila Krisnadhi, Ayu Purwarianti and Derry Tanti Wijaya

No Day Set (continued)

17:05–17:10 ***Best Paper Award Announcement***

17:10–17:20 ***Closing Remarks***

Towards Automatic Construction of Filipino WordNet: Word Sense Induction and Synset Induction Using Sentence Embeddings

Dan John Velasco[*1] **Axel Alba**[1] **Trisha Gail Pelagio**[1] **Bryce Anthony Ramirez**[1]
Unisse Chua[1] **Briane Paul Samson**[1]
Jan Christian Blaise Cruz[†2] **Charibeth Cheng**[1]
[1]De La Salle University, Manila [2]Samsung R&D Institute Philippines

Abstract

Wordnets are indispensable tools for various natural language processing applications. Unfortunately, wordnets get outdated, and producing or updating wordnets can be slow and costly in terms of time and resources. This problem intensifies for low-resource languages. This study proposes a method for word sense induction and synset induction using only two linguistic resources, namely, an unlabeled corpus and a sentence embeddings-based language model. The resulting sense inventory and synonym sets can be used in automatically creating a wordnet. We applied this method on a corpus of Filipino text. The sense inventory and synsets were evaluated by matching them with the sense inventory of the machine translated Princeton WordNet, as well as comparing the synsets to the Filipino WordNet. This study empirically shows that the 30% of the induced word senses are valid and 40% of the induced synsets are valid in which 20% are novel synsets.

1 Introduction

In Natural Language Processing (NLP), a language resource such as the Princeton WordNet or PWN (Miller et al., 1993) has been widely used in several NLP tasks, including sentiment analysis (Kumar et al., 2018), word sense disambiguation (Mizuki and Okazaki, 2023), and machine translation (Ngo et al., 2019). A wordnet contains *word senses* which is a discrete representation of one aspect of the meaning of a word (Jurafsky and Martin, 2023), *synsets* or synonym sets which are sets of near-synonyms, *word definitions*, *example sentences*, *part-of-speech*, and *semantic links* (e.g syn-onyms, hyponyms, and meronyms). Such lexical resource can be useful for language documentation, language preservation, and linguistics research.

For the Filipino language, there is the Filipino WordNet or FilWordNet (Borra et al., 2010) which was manually constructed by translating PWN senses to Filipino and adding unique Filipino words that are not in the PWN. Overall, it consists of 13,539 unique words and 9,519 synsets. Each synset in the FilWordNet includes semantic information such as the word's definition, part-of-speech, word senses, and Suggested Upper Merged Ontology terms (Niles and Pease, 2001).

However, the FilWordNet was not updated since its creation. It does not contain new words and senses that emerged in the Filipino language, most notably the colloquial words used in digital media and platforms. For comparison, the University of the Philippines Diksiyonaryong Filipino, a monolingual Filipino dictionary, contains over 200,000 word senses (Lim, 2010), while FilWordNet only documents 15,929 word senses. One probable reason for FilWordNet not being updated is the expensive cost of manually creating and updating a wordnet in terms of time and resources.

Advancements in NLP can be leveraged to make wordnet construction more efficient. In this study, we propose a method for automatic generation of sense inventory and synset inventory, remedying the inefficiencies in the pure manual process. Our approach only requires an unlabeled corpus and a sentence embeddings-based language model. Human supervision is not required during the generation process. Our technique is language-agnostic, but for this work, we use Filipino as a case study to produce sense inventories and synset inventories, which are among the core components of a wordnet.

2 Related Work

2.1 Automatic Wordnet Construction

According to Vossen (1998), wordnets are typically built using two approaches: (1) the merge ap-

*Corresponding author. Direct all communications to: dan_velasco@dlsu.edu.ph

†Work done while at De La Salle University, Manila.

Proceedings of the First Workshop in South East Asian Language Processing, pages 1–12
November 1, 2023.

proach, where lexicographers manually construct the wordnet, and (2) the expansion approach, which utilizes an existing reference wordnet as a guide in constructing the new wordnet. There is a trade-off between quality and cost with merge approach producing higher quality wordnets at a high cost and with expansion approach producing relatively lower quality but at a significantly lower cost (Bhattacharyya, 2010). Sense inventory and synsets are one of the core components of a wordnet and the focus of this paper. Different approaches to induce these components will be discussed in Sections 2.1.1 and 2.1.2.

2.1.1 Synset Induction

According to the recent survey paper on automatically constructed wordnets by Neale (2018), most works follow the expansion approach which uses a reference wordnet (usually PWN) and a lexical resource such as encyclopedia (Ruiz-Casado et al., 2005), bilingual dictionary or machine translator (Barbu and Mititelu, 2005; Montazery and Faili, 2010; Khodak et al., 2017; Rahit et al., 2018), and parallel corpus (Oliver and Climent, 2014) to construct synsets for their target language and often used in conjunction with word embeddings. These approaches are efficient but have a hard requirement of having a reference wordnet and a lexical resource. Our approach differs from these works by not requiring a reference wordnet or a lexical resource to induce synsets.

2.1.2 Word Sense Induction

Most works on Word Sense Induction (WSI) are not directly motivated in the automatic construction of wordnet but are still related. WSI is an essential component of automatic wordnet construction without a reference wordnet and a lexical resource, which is the goal of this paper. Recent works on WSI use clustering of sense embeddings derived from word embeddings (Song et al., 2016), lexical substitutions derived from language models (Amrami and Goldberg, 2019; Arefyev et al., 2019), word co-occurence graphs (Bekavac and Šnajder, 2016), sparse coding and sentence embeddings (Khodak et al., 2017), and clustering of sentence embeddings (Tallo, 2020). Our work is closely related to Tallo (2020) where we learn sentence embeddings following SBERT (Reimers and Gurevych, 2019) but for Filipino and then induce senses by clustering sentence embeddings. Another difference is that our work used Affinity Propagation[1] which does not require knowing the number of clusters beforehand while Tallo (2020) used K-Means Clustering which requires specifying the number of clusters in advance.

While many automatic wordnet construction approaches rely on a reference wordnet or other lexical resources, our method eliminates the need for these references. This is particularly beneficial for low-resource languages, where such lexical resources are often lacking. Our approach offers greater accessibility to low-resource languages, enabling the induction of culturally and regionally specific concepts unique to each language. Moreover, it avoids the distraction and constraints imposed by reference wordnets in other languages, as it does not depend on words with direct translations. For instance, consider the word 'gigil,' which describes the trembling response to situations overwhelming our self-control, a concept not directly translatable to English. It's likely that this word would not be covered in the English wordnet, as it is unique to the Filipino language.

2.2 Sentence Embeddings

Sentence embeddings maps a sentence to a vector space such that semantically similar sentences are close in proximity. A simple method for creating sentence embeddings is to average token embeddings of a sentence (Arora et al., 2017). However, this approach ignores word interactions within a sentence. This was addressed by Reimers and Gurevych (2019) where they used BERT in a siamese and triplet network setup to generate meaningful sentence embeddings by training on SNLI (Bowman et al., 2015) and MultiNLI (Williams et al., 2018) datasets which achieved state-of-the-art results in Semantic Textual Similarity (STS) tasks at time of publication. In recent years, unsupervised methods for learning sentence embeddings have been proposed such as TSDAE (Wang et al., 2021), SimCSE (Gao et al., 2021). and DiffCSE (Chuang et al., 2022) but for this paper, we only experimented on the approach following Reimers and Gurevych (2019). We apply sentence embeddings for WSI through clustering. Our method assumes that semantically similar sentences exhibit proximity to one another, rendering them suitable for clustering and WSI.

[1] https://scikit-learn.org/stable/modules/generated/sklearn.cluster.AffinityPropagation.html

3 Datasets

3.1 Corpus

Filipino texts were collected from various domains such as news sites, books, social media, online forums, and Wikipedia to build a diverse corpus that represents wide range of writing styles using the Filipino language. Table 1 shows the number of words and the average sentence length for each domain. Personal identifiers, symbols, and entities that are irrelevant to the study, such as emails, emojis, links, hashtags, non-alphanumeric symbols were removed. The documents were splitted into sentences using NLTK sentence tokenizer[2]. The following tokens are treated as sentence delimiters: question marks (?), exclamation points (!), ellipses (...), periods (.), and line breaks. The language of each sentence were identified using fastText (Joulin et al., 2016). For the purpose of this work, we only retained sentences that were identified as Tagalog/Filipino. The resulting corpus contains around 997 million words of which 5.37 million words are unique. All of this unique words should not be assumed to be valid words since it may contain non-natural language such as symbols.

For sources that are small enough and do not update frequently, such as Google Books and Bible[3], they were downloaded manually. For YouTube, the official YouTube Data API[4] was used. We curated a set of YouTube channels of Filipino content creators and collected all the comments of their videos. The curated list of YouTube channels can be found at Appendix A. For Twitter, the official Twitter API with Academic Research access[5] was used. We only collected tweets with 'fil' language tag which is the BCP47 language tag for Filipino. For Reddit, the Pushshift API[6] was used to collect posts and responses in subforums or what they call subreddits. We curated a list of subreddits where Filipinos interact. The curated list of subreddits can be found at Appendix B. For Tagalog Wikipedia, a dump file from Wikimedia[7] were downloaded and preprocessed. For news sites, web scrapers were built for each website using Scrapy[8] for sites with pagination and Selenium[9] for sites with infinite scrolling. For a complete list of sources, refer to Appendix C.

Domain	Total Words	Mean Sentence Length
Books	8,923,001	23
News	94,466,149	20
Online Forums	92,342,868	15
Social Media	792,778,696	12
Wikipedia	9,177,188	32

Table 1: Corpus statistics showing total words and mean sentence length of each domain.

3.2 Filipino WordNet (FilWordNet)

The Filipino WordNet (Borra et al., 2010) was manually constructed by translating the Princeton WordNet (Miller et al., 1993) and then adding unique Filipino words. FilWordNet contains 13,539 unique words and 9,519 synsets. Our approach does not require a reference wordnet and FilWordNet was only used for evaluation purposes. All experiments used the vocabulary of FilWordNet as seed words, with a few exceptions. FilWordNet words that have less than 20 example sentences in our corpus were excluded. FilWordNet words that start with an uppercase letter were excluded to remove proper nouns. FilWordNet words with only 2 letters or less were also excluded. Lastly, FilWordNet words that represent a number were also removed. From the initial 13,539 words of the FilWordNet, only 2,598 remained after filtering and were used as seed words. Unless otherwise stated, all experiments used the filtered seed words from FilWordNet. We restrict this procedure to direct comparisons. In practice, the seed words can originate from the target corpus's vocabulary or its set of distinct words. Nonetheless, based on the specific use case, additional preprocessing may be required, as the corpus vocabulary may include non-natural language tokens, such as emojis or symbols.

4 Methodology

4.1 Language Model Training

The training goes through two phases: (1) Masked Language Modeling (MLM) and (2) Contrastive Learning. In the first phase, we adapt the language

[2]https://www.nltk.org/api/nltk.tokenize.html

[3]https://www.wordproject.org/bibles/tl/index.htm

[4]https://developers.google.com/youtube/v3

[5]https://developer.twitter.com/en/use-cases/do-research/academic-research

[6]https://reddit-api.readthedocs.io/en/latest/

[7]https://dumps.wikimedia.org/tlwiki/latest/

[8]https://scrapy.org/

[9]https://www.selenium.dev/

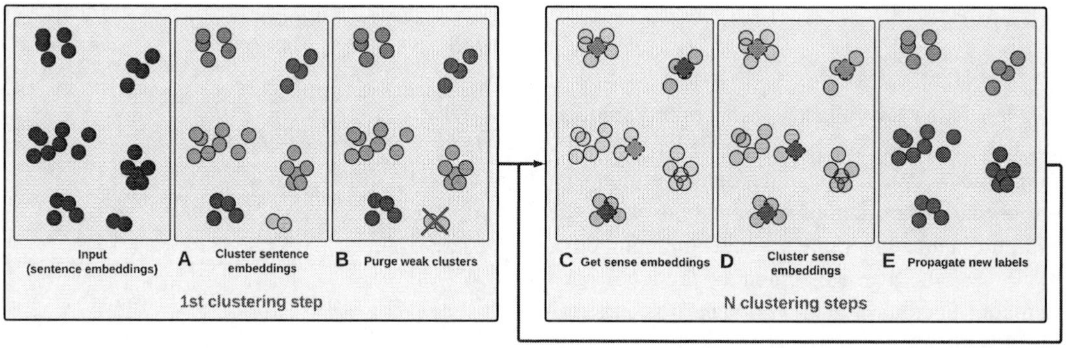

Figure 1: **N-STEP Clustering**. First clustering step (**A** to **B**) clusters sentence embeddings (**A**) and purges weak clusters (**B**). N clustering steps (**C** to **E**) is iterative. (**C**) Computes sense embeddings followed by (**D**) clustering, effectively reducing the points to cluster. (**E**) Propagates the new labels to its cluster members and goes back to (**C**).

model to our corpus by finetuning the pretrained RoBERTa for Filipino (Cruz and Cheng, 2022) on our corpus for 1,176,690 steps (equivalent to 10 epochs) with a maximum learning rate of 5e-5 and then linearly decayed. Doing so can improve representations especially for social media writing styles since our corpus mostly contains social media data and the pretrained RoBERTa was only trained on more formal writing styles such as news data and Wikipedia articles. The AdamW optimizer (Loshchilov and Hutter, 2019) was used with the following hyperparameters: $\beta_1 = 0.9$, $\beta_2 = 0.999$, and ϵ = 1e-6. The pretrained RoBERTa was finetuned on Google Compute servers with TPUv3-8 accelerators.

In the second phase, we finetune the model from the first phase on NewsPH-NLI dataset (Cruz et al., 2021) in a contrastive learning setup following the work of Reimers and Gurevych (2019) but used Multiple Negatives Ranking Loss[10] instead of the Softmax Loss used in the original work. We used mean of contextual token embeddings as pooling method. The positive entailment pairs used in training are 237,679 sentence pairs. The model was optimized with AdamW optimizer using the following hyperparameters: *epochs* = 1, *max learning rate* = 2e-5, *max sequence length* = 128, and *batch size* = 16. The learning rate gradually increases up to max learning rate for the first 10% of training and then linearly decayed. We will refer to this model as *filipino-sentence-RoBERTa*[11]. The model was trained on one NVIDIA GeForce RTX 3060Ti GPU.

4.2 Word Sense Induction using N-STEP Clustering

This method is iterative. For each word in the list of seed words, the Sentence Sampling (Section 4.2.1) and N-STEP Clustering (Section 4.2.2) are repeated.

4.2.1 Sentence Sampling

The first step in WSI is to sample sentences from a corpus. For each word, sentences are sampled from each domain in the corpus (e.g. books, news sites, etc.) for sentences containing the target word through substring matching wrapped with whitespaces (e.g. " hot "). The sample sentences are splitted by whitespace to apply windowing with the target word at the center[12]. For this study, a fixed window size of 4 for both left and right was set through trial and error and was not extensively studied. Due to time and memory constraints, a maximum sample size of 1,000 sentences per source was set. The resulting sample sentences for a target word will be encoded to sentence embeddings using filipino-sentence-RoBERTa.

4.2.2 N-STEP Clustering

Applying clustering once on a large sample of sentences results to hundreds of clusters. Through manual inspection, we observed that many clusters are redundant i.e. multiple clusters pertain to the same sense. To address this, we proposed **N-STEP Clustering** (see Figure 1) approach for WSI which

[10] `https://www.sbert.net/docs/package_reference/losses.html`

[11] `https://huggingface.co/danjohnvelasco/filipino-sentence-roberta-v1`

[12] refer to Undesirable property of sentence embeddings for synset and word sense induction section on why windowing was done

performs clustering multiple times to reduce redundant clusters. The clustering algorithm used is *Affinity Propagation* (AP) which does not require knowing the number of clusters in advance. We propose two (2) ways to implement N-STEP Clustering.

Fixed N-STEP Clustering. The number of clustering steps N is fixed and must be set in advance. It works by clustering the sentence embeddings only at the first clustering step. In the succeeding steps until step N, these clusters are iteratively merged together by clustering the *sense embeddings* or the centroids (see Figure 1). The use of centroids to represent a sense is similar to Hu et al. (2019); Amrami and Goldberg (2019).

Dynamic N-STEP Clustering. The process is similar to Fixed N-STEP Clustering. The only difference is that the number of clustering steps are dynamically set for each target word by maximizing the silhouette score. Silhouette score (Rousseeuw, 1987) is a metric for evaluating the quality of clusters by looking at the closeness of each members within a cluster and the separation among the clusters. The silhouette score ranges from -1 to 1, where higher values indicates higher quality clusters. This allows for different number of clustering steps for each word which highly depends on the distribution of the sample sentences. N-STEP Clustering stops at the highest silhouette score after not improving for two (2) consecutive clustering steps. In the first clustering step, weak clusters were removed. Weak clusters are defined as clusters with less than k members as they are often just noise. The idea of removing weak clusters is similar to Amrami and Goldberg (2019) but instead of merging the weak clusters with strong cluster, we simply remove the weak cluster. For our dataset, we set k=3 but it can be adjusted depending on the dataset.

In this work, we used Fixed 3-STEP Clustering because it outperformed Dynamic N-STEP Clustering (see Appendix D) on our dataset. This may not generalize to other datasets and we suggest using Dynamic N-STEP Clustering as a starting point. For all clustering steps, the damping parameter of the AP algorithm is set to 0.5. The justifications behind this value are explained in Appendix E. Currently, there are no automatic methods to tune these parameters, but Appendix D to F can provide some ideas to help future researchers find the best parameters for their own application.

4.3 Synset Induction

In synset induction, all senses in the sense inventory will be clustered by clustering the sense embeddings. This is in contrast with WSI where clustering happens for each word. For synset induction, it is ideal to cluster only the similar senses without forcing other senses to belong to a synset. To achieve this effect, we used Agglomerative Clustering[13], where the cosine distance threshold can be set. In this paper, the distance threshold has been set to 0.12, meaning only senses with a cosine distance of 0.12 or less will be clustered with other senses. The justification behind this threshold value are explained in Appendix F.

5 Evaluation

5.1 Sense Inventory Evaluation

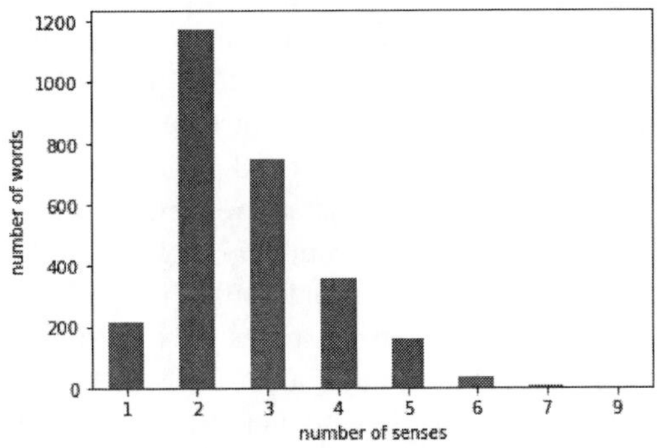

Figure 2: The distribution of the number of senses per word shows that most induced words have 2 senses. Words with higher sense count become less frequent as the number of senses per word increases. This also shows that it can induce single senses.

The induced sense inventory contains 2,598 unique words and 7,177 senses. Most words have 2-3 senses and some words can have up to 9 senses (see Figure 2). We evaluate the sense inventory in a Word Sense Disambiguation (WSD) setup adapted from Hu et al. (2019), where sentences from a reference sense inventory are tagged using our sense inventory. The sense embedding with the highest cosine similarity with the input sentence and is greater than or equal to the threshold is chosen as the sense for that input sentence. The induced senses were classified as valid if it is used as a tag in WSD at least once. In this paper, the average

[13]https://scikit-learn.org/stable/modules/generated/sklearn.cluster.AgglomerativeClustering.html

cosine similarity (0.63) was used as threshold for simplicity and was not extensively studied.

Evaluating in this setup requires a reference sense inventory but since the FilWordNet has no example sentences and there is no other existing lexical resource in Filipino that can be used to evaluate the sense inventory, we resorted to translating sentences from PWN as our evaluation data. For this step, we used the Google Translate API as a translation tool[14] and NLTK[15] to access PWN. The Filipino words were translated to English and were used to retrieve PWN senses. The example sentences of the PWN were translated back to Filipino. However, not all of the translations of the induced senses can be found in the PWN because some Filipino words do not have a direct English translation. In addition, some of the PWN entries were discarded because the English to Filipino backtranslation does not contain the target word in Filipino. As a result, the final evaluation data can only evaluate 23% of the unique words (601 out of 2,598 words) of the generated sense inventory.

The results show that around 30% (552 out of 1,864) of the induced senses were matched with at least one of the senses from the PWN. Upon manual inspection of the remaining 70%, it is observed that most of the induced senses are either: (1) a sense that are not found in the PWN or English language, (2) clusters with multiple senses inside, (3) redundant clusters that represent an already existing sense. Thus, not finding the induced sense in the PWN does not necessarily mean that the induced sense is invalid. Further analysis, such as a human evaluation, is needed to determine whether the unmatched senses are incorrect. We leave this for future work.

5.2 Synset Evaluation

5.2.1 Automatic Synset Evaluation

We evaluate the correctness of the induced synsets by comparing it with FilWordNet synsets using Jaccard Index where a score of 1 means exact match and 0 means exact mismatch. For fair comparison, FilWordNet synsets with only one sense were excluded. While our sense inventory and FilWordNet share the same vocabulary, some words are not found in the corpus used for WSI. Hence, FilWordNet synsets containing words that are not in the vocabulary of our sense inventory were excluded. After filtering, the total number of FilWordNet synsets is down from 9,519 to 639 synsets. This evaluation is comparing 1,109 induced synsets to 639 FilWordNet synsets.

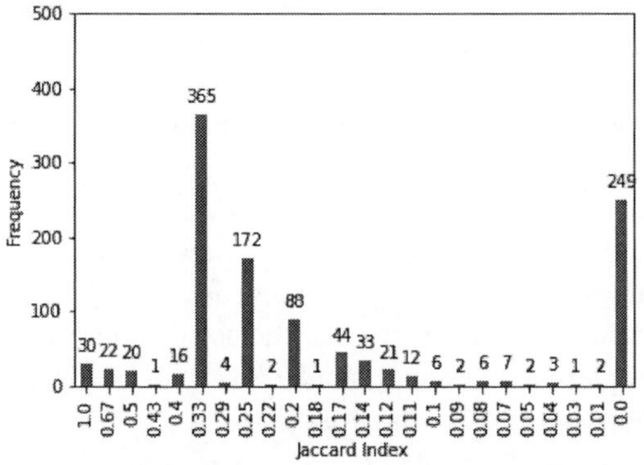

Figure 3: Jaccard Index of the induced synsets and FilWordNet synsets.

Figure 3 shows that 3% (30 synsets) of the induced synsets are exact match in FilWordNet. The Jaccard Index with the highest frequency is 0.33 which comprised of 33% (365 synsets) of the induced synsets. On the other hand, 22% (249 synsets) are exact mismatch. For this experiment, a high Jaccard Index is preferred but getting low scores does not necessarily mean that the induced synsets are of poor quality. There could be several reasons that could lead to a low Jaccard index score such as the discovery of new senses and synsets that are not in FilWordNet. With these results, a human evaluation is needed to better validate the quality of the induced synsets that is independent from FilWordNet synsets.

5.2.2 Manual Synset Evaluation

To give a better assessment of synset quality that is independent from FilWordNet synsets, a human evaluation is needed. This was done by scoring the synsets with the percentage of correct senses in the synset. For example, given A = *{'big', 'large'}*, it would be labeled with a score of 1.0. On the other hand, given B = *{'hard', 'difficult', 'challenging', 'large', 'blue'}*, it would be labeled with a score of 0.60 as three out of the five words (*'hard', 'difficult', 'challenging'*) are synonyms while the other words are irrelevant. To simplify the annotation, synsets with more than 10 senses were labelled as 0 since most FilWordNet synsets only contains 1 to 4 words inside the set. In addition, synsets that contain only 2 senses can only be labeled as 1 or 0.

[14]https://cloud.google.com/translate

[15]https://www.nltk.org/

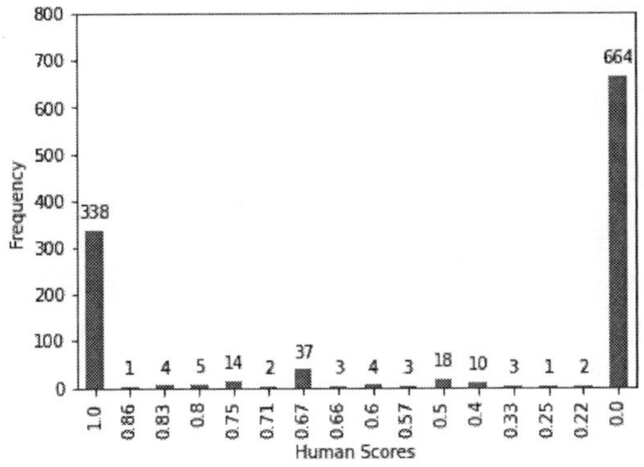

Figure 4: Frequency distribution of human scores from manual synset evaluation.

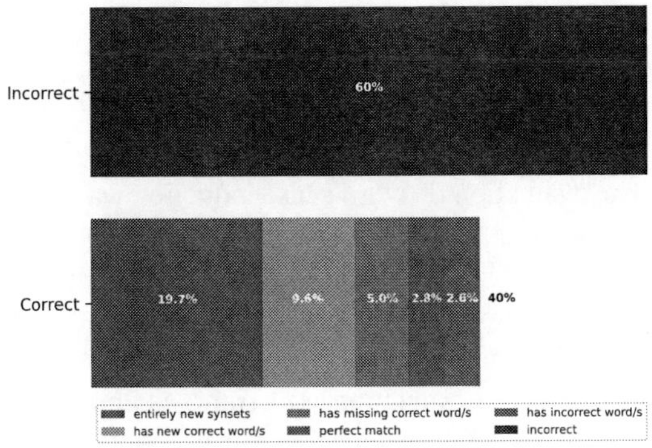

Figure 5: Types of correct synsets. The top two most frequent types shows the potential of our approach in synset discovery.

Figure 4 shows the distribution of scores made by humans. The extreme values of 1.0 and 0.0 obtained the highest number of synsets. Specifically, 30% (338 synsets) of the induced synsets are 100% correct and around 10% (107 synsets) are partially correct. This is a big difference from the automatic results which shows that only 3% of the induced synsets are 100% correct. On the other hand, synsets with a score of 0.0 remained to have the highest number of counts which is 60% (664 synsets) of the induced synsets.

5.2.3 Types of Correct Synsets

To give a better view of what the correct and partially correct synsets are, we manually identified the types of correct synsets (see Figure 5). The top two most frequent type of correct synset is "entirely new synsets" (19.7%) and "has new correct word/s" (9.6%), followed by "has missing correct word/s" (5.0%), "perfect match" (2.8%), and "has incorrect word/s" (2.6%). The top two most frequent type relates to inducing new synsets which indicates the potential of our approach in the discovery of synsets in an unsupervised manner.

Overall, the synset evaluation demonstrates the potential of our approach to synset induction which could greatly remedy the inefficiencies in the pure manual process of constructing a wordnet.

6 Conclusions and Future Work

In this work, we proposed (1) N-STEP clustering of sentence embeddings for word sense induction and (2) clustering of sense embeddings or centroids for synset induction. Both can be used towards automatic construction of a wordnet. The advantage of our method is that the generation is fully unsupervised and has only two requirements: unlabeled corpus and sentence embeddings-based language model, which are both accessible even for low-resource languages.

For word sense induction, the results showed that approximately 30% (552 out of 1,864) of the induced senses are valid. Upon manual inspection of the remaining 70%, it is observed that most of the induced senses are either: (1) sense that is not found in the PWN or English language; (2) clusters with multiple senses inside; (3) redundant clusters that represent an already existing sense. For synset induction, the results showed the potential of our approach to synset induction given that 40% of the induced synsets are correct (30% are perfectly correct and 10% are partially correct). Among the correct synset types, the top two most frequent type pertains to discovering new synsets which demonstrates the potential of our approach in sense and synset discovery in an unsupervised manner.

For future work, an evaluation set for WSI in Filipino similar to SemEval 2010 Task 14 (Manandhar et al., 2010) can be developed to get a better assessment of WSI performance. Future work may also look into the automatic induction of semantic links (e.g synonyms, hyponyms, and meronyms) without a reference wordnet to enable efficient construction of wordnets in low-resource languages. Further improvements to our work may come from the knowledge representation (e.g. better sentence embeddings or directly learning sense embeddings for WSI and synset induction). The use of unsupervised approaches to learning sentence embeddings (Gao et al., 2021; Chuang et al., 2022) can also be explored.

Limitations

Evaluating on machine translated Princeton WordNet

The evaluation on word sense induction was done on machine translated Princeton WordNet due to the lack of language resource in Filipino suitable for evaluation. There are several issues with this setup: (a) machine translation can introduce more errors to the evaluation; (b) some example sentences from Princeton WordNet are too short to disambiguate the word sense which influences the evaluation through word sense disambiguation; (c) some senses in the Filipino language may not appear in the English language (vice versa) which can lead to high false negatives.

Undesirable property of sentence embeddings for synset and word sense induction

While sentence embeddings shows its potential application for automatic wordnet construction, our approach produced a large number of incorrect synsets (60%). The clusterability of the representations largely influences the performance on word sense induction and synset induction. One instance that highlights this problem is the problem of collocating words. When using sentence embeddings for WSI, words that do not necessarily have the same meaning would be closely related in terms of context. For example, the collocated words *angat (raise)* and *bandera (flag)* have different meanings but they were clustered as a synset since they are close in the embeddings space because they often appear together in the same context (e.g. "to raise the flag").

Using sentence embeddings in clustering is not always a robust way to identify senses that are used in very diverse contexts. For example, the word *bank* as in the financial institution, can appear in very different contexts. The assumption of sentence embeddings is that sentences with similar meaning are close together in the vector space. Which means, even if the sample sentences only have one usage of the word *bank* but it appears in very diverse contexts, there is the tendency to produce multiple clusters even though they represent the same meaning. This happens because the representations represents the semantics of the sentence itself rather than the sense usage. This is the intuition on why we implemented windowing before word sense induction. This also explains the high number of redundant clusters in word sense induction.

Acknowledgements

This research was funded by the Philippine Department of Science and Technology - Philippine Council for Industry, Energy and Emerging Technology Research and Development. The authors would also like to acknowledge TensorFlow Research Cloud (TRC) program which made training models on TPUs possible.

References

Asaf Amrami and Yoav Goldberg. 2019. Towards better substitution-based word sense induction.

Nikolay Arefyev, Boris Sheludko, and Alexander Panchenko. 2019. Combining lexical substitutes in neural word sense induction. In *Proceedings of the International Conference on Recent Advances in Natural Language Processing (RANLP 2019)*, pages 62–70, Varna, Bulgaria. INCOMA Ltd.

Sanjeev Arora, Yingyu Liang, and Tengyu Ma. 2017. A simple but tough-to-beat baseline for sentence embeddings. In *ICLR*.

Eduard Barbu and Verginica Barbu Mititelu. 2005. A case study in automatic building of wordnets. In *Proceedings of OntoLex 2005 - Ontologies and Lexical Resources*.

Marko Bekavac and Jan Šnajder. 2016. Graph-based induction of word senses in Croatian. In *Proceedings of the Tenth International Conference on Language Resources and Evaluation (LREC'16)*, pages 3014–3018, Portorož, Slovenia. European Language Resources Association (ELRA).

Pushpak Bhattacharyya. 2010. IndoWordNet. In *Proceedings of the Seventh International Conference on Language Resources and Evaluation (LREC'10)*, Valletta, Malta. European Language Resources Association (ELRA).

Allan Borra, Adam Pease, Rachel Edita O. Roxas, and Shirley Dita. 2010. Introducing filipino wordnet. In *Principles, Construction and Application of Multilingual Wordnets: Proceedings of the 5th Global WordNet Conference*, pages 306–310.

Samuel R. Bowman, Gabor Angeli, Christopher Potts, and Christopher D. Manning. 2015. A large annotated corpus for learning natural language inference. In *Proceedings of the 2015 Conference on Empirical Methods in Natural Language Processing*, pages 632–642, Lisbon, Portugal. Association for Computational Linguistics.

Yung-Sung Chuang, Rumen Dangovski, Hongyin Luo, Yang Zhang, Shiyu Chang, Marin Soljacic, Shang-Wen Li, Scott Yih, Yoon Kim, and James Glass. 2022.

DiffCSE: Difference-based contrastive learning for sentence embeddings. In *Proceedings of the 2022 Conference of the North American Chapter of the Association for Computational Linguistics: Human Language Technologies*, pages 4207–4218, Seattle, United States. Association for Computational Linguistics.

Jan Christian Blaise Cruz and Charibeth Cheng. 2022. Improving large-scale language models and resources for Filipino. In *Proceedings of the Thirteenth Language Resources and Evaluation Conference*, pages 6548–6555, Marseille, France. European Language Resources Association.

Jan Christian Blaise Cruz, Jose Kristian Resabal, James Lin, Dan John Velasco, and Charibeth Cheng. 2021. Exploiting news article structure for automatic corpus generation of entailment datasets. In *PRICAI 2021: Trends in Artificial Intelligence*, pages 86–99, Cham. Springer International Publishing.

Tianyu Gao, Xingcheng Yao, and Danqi Chen. 2021. SimCSE: Simple contrastive learning of sentence embeddings. In *Proceedings of the 2021 Conference on Empirical Methods in Natural Language Processing*, pages 6894–6910, Online and Punta Cana, Dominican Republic. Association for Computational Linguistics.

Renfen Hu, Shen Li, and Shichen Liang. 2019. Diachronic sense modeling with deep contextualized word embeddings: An ecological view. In *Proceedings of the 57th Annual Meeting of the Association for Computational Linguistics*, pages 3899–3908, Florence, Italy. Association for Computational Linguistics.

Armand Joulin, Edouard Grave, Piotr Bojanowski, and Tomas Mikolov. 2016. Bag of tricks for efficient text classification. *arXiv preprint arXiv:1607.01759*.

Dan Jurafsky and James Martin. 2023. Speech and language processing (3rd ed. draft).

Mikhail Khodak, Andrej Risteski, Christiane Fellbaum, and Sanjeev Arora. 2017. Automated WordNet construction using word embeddings. In *Proceedings of the 1st Workshop on Sense, Concept and Entity Representations and their Applications*, pages 12–23, Valencia, Spain. Association for Computational Linguistics.

Abhishek Kumar, Daisuke Kawahara, and Sadao Kurohashi. 2018. Knowledge-enriched two-layered attention network for sentiment analysis. In *Proceedings of the 2018 Conference of the North American Chapter of the Association for Computational Linguistics: Human Language Technologies, Volume 2 (Short Papers)*, pages 253–258, New Orleans, Louisiana. Association for Computational Linguistics.

Ronald Lim. 2010. One tongue.

Ilya Loshchilov and Frank Hutter. 2019. Decoupled weight decay regularization.

Suresh Manandhar, Ioannis Klapaftis, Dmitriy Dligach, and Sameer Pradhan. 2010. SemEval-2010 task 14: Word sense induction &disambiguation. In *Proceedings of the 5th International Workshop on Semantic Evaluation*, pages 63–68, Uppsala, Sweden. Association for Computational Linguistics.

George Miller, Richard Beckwith, Christiane Fellbaum, Derek Gross, and Katherine Miller. 1993. Introduction to wordnet: An on-line lexical database*. 3:235–0244.

Sakae Mizuki and Naoaki Okazaki. 2023. Semantic specialization for knowledge-based word sense disambiguation. In *Proceedings of the 17th Conference of the European Chapter of the Association for Computational Linguistics*, pages 3457–3470, Dubrovnik, Croatia. Association for Computational Linguistics.

Mortaza Montazery and Heshaam Faili. 2010. Automatic Persian WordNet construction. In *Coling 2010: Posters*, pages 846–850, Beijing, China. Coling 2010 Organizing Committee.

Steven Neale. 2018. A survey on automatically-constructed WordNets and their evaluation: Lexical and word embedding-based approaches. In *Proceedings of the Eleventh International Conference on Language Resources and Evaluation (LREC 2018)*, Miyazaki, Japan. European Language Resources Association (ELRA).

Thi-Vinh Ngo, Thanh-Le Ha, Phuong-Thai Nguyen, and Le-Minh Nguyen. 2019. Overcoming the rare word problem for low-resource language pairs in neural machine translation. In *Proceedings of the 6th Workshop on Asian Translation*, pages 207–214, Hong Kong, China. Association for Computational Linguistics.

Ian Niles and Adam Pease. 2001. Towards a standard upper ontology. In *Proceedings of the International Conference on Formal Ontology in Information Systems - Volume 2001*, FOIS '01, page 2–9, New York, NY, USA. Association for Computing Machinery.

Antoni Oliver and Salvador Climent. 2014. Automatic creation of WordNets from parallel corpora. In *Proceedings of the Ninth International Conference on Language Resources and Evaluation (LREC'14)*, pages 1112–1116, Reykjavik, Iceland. European Language Resources Association (ELRA).

K.M. Tahsin Hassan Rahit, Khandaker Tabin Hasan, Md. Al Amin, and Zahiduddin Ahmed. 2018. BanglaNet: Towards a WordNet for Bengali language. In *Proceedings of the 9th Global Wordnet Conference*, pages 1–9, Nanyang Technological University (NTU), Singapore. Global Wordnet Association.

Nils Reimers and Iryna Gurevych. 2019. Sentence-BERT: Sentence embeddings using Siamese BERT-networks. In *Proceedings of the 2019 Conference on Empirical Methods in Natural Language Processing and the 9th International Joint Conference on Natural Language Processing (EMNLP-IJCNLP)*, pages

3982–3992, Hong Kong, China. Association for Computational Linguistics.

Peter J. Rousseeuw. 1987. Silhouettes: A graphical aid to the interpretation and validation of cluster analysis. *Journal of Computational and Applied Mathematics*, 20:53–65.

Maria Ruiz-Casado, Enrique Alfonseca, and Pablo Castells. 2005. Automatic extraction of semantic relationships for wordnet by means of pattern learning from wikipedia. In *Natural Language Processing and Information Systems*, pages 67–79, Berlin, Heidelberg. Springer Berlin Heidelberg.

Linfeng Song, Zhiguo Wang, Haitao Mi, and Daniel Gildea. 2016. Sense embedding learning for word sense induction. In *Proceedings of the Fifth Joint Conference on Lexical and Computational Semantics*, pages 85–90, Berlin, Germany. Association for Computational Linguistics.

Philip Tallo. 2020. Using sentence embeddings for word sense induction. Master's thesis, University of Cincinnati.

Piek Vossen. 1998. Introduction to eurowordnet. *Computers and the Humanities*, 32(2/3):73–89.

Kexin Wang, Nils Reimers, and Iryna Gurevych. 2021. TSDAE: using transformer-based sequential denoising auto-encoder for unsupervised sentence embedding learning. *CoRR*, abs/2104.06979.

Adina Williams, Nikita Nangia, and Samuel Bowman. 2018. A broad-coverage challenge corpus for sentence understanding through inference. In *Proceedings of the 2018 Conference of the North American Chapter of the Association for Computational Linguistics: Human Language Technologies, Volume 1 (Long Papers)*, pages 1112–1122, New Orleans, Louisiana. Association for Computational Linguistics.

A YouTube Channels

The list of YouTube channels were manually curated. The criteria for YouTube channel selection is that the channel owners are Filipino, preferably, speaking in Filipino in their videos to increase the likelihood that the comments are in Filipino or mostly written by Filipinos. The following is the complete list of YouTube channels we collected data from: cong tv, slater young, kryzzzie, alodia gosiengfiao, rei germar, ry velasco, anna cay, anne clutz, anneclutzvlogs, itsclaudineco, abs cbn news, abs cbn entertainment, alliana dolina, donnalyn bartolome, akosi dogie, carlo ople, oliver austria, kenny manalad, doc willie ong, rendon labador, kiko matos, mika salamanca, presello, alex gonzaga official, h2wo, shinejonzoief2p, junnie boy, benedict cua, toni gonzaga studio, tryke gutierrez, reccreate, bermor, rj jacinto, xtian c, fliptopbattles, panlasang pinoy, bea alonzo, karl jolice tv, dubstep, front seat foodies, nisky, ninong ry, gma public affairs, raffy tulfo in action, bonoy pinty gonzaga, leti sha, wish 1075, homesearch philippines, kiyo, ben&ben, vice ganda, jah de dios, araw na itim tagalog animated horror, paolul, mavs phenomenal basketball, jonahrenz jacob, sb19 official, karla cayabyab, mocha uson official, leni robredo, jinkee pacquiao, team pacquiao, bongbong marcos, karen davila, rappler, isko moreno domagoso, kuya kim atienza, euphoniaco tv, kathryn bernardo, viva records, dr. vicki belo, schizo pelma tv, joyce pring, nicole alba, juancho trivino, yow, latest scoop, mimiyuuuh, marjorie barretto, tiktok pinas, tiktok philippines, erwin tulfo, luis azcona sharlene menu, pinoy knows tech, eat bulaga, kusina ni lola, beebuyog, alvin tries tech, unbox ph, sulit tech reviews, choox tv, pepesan tv, olip tv, khent bernardo, the juans, clr, richard gomez, pinoy mystery channel, tinagalog, historya channel, hazel quing, ivana alawa, niana guerrero, zeinab harake, jelai andres, ramon bautista, empoy official, kuya jobert tv, gretchen ho, tv5 philippines, luis manzano, ogie diaz, love marie escudero, master long mejia, viy cortez, mentot, kevin hermosada, datwo, boss keng, vien, pat velasquez, beks battalion, youlol, jamill, chad kinis, riva quenery, wilbert tolentino, rana harake, daisy lopez, tita krissy achino, jamichtv, lloyd cafe cadena, limuel huet, mary bautista, michelle dy, kathsepaganvlogs, mikhaela cruz, peachytwice, john ryan santos, i can see your voice ph, the boy abunda talk channel, pinoy big brother, unbox diaries, the voice of the philippines.

B Subreddits

The list of subreddits were manually curated. The criteria for subreddit selection is that most of the posters or members under that subreddit should be Filipinos. We determine this by looking for subreddits with the "PH" prefix or suffix in the subreddit name. We also included subreddits whose name represents a concept that only makes sense in the Philippine context (e.g. dlsu, ADMU, Tomasino, peyups subreddits refer to the Philippine universities). The following is a complete list of subreddits that we collected data from: phinvest, Philippines, NintendoPH, peyups, ADMU, dlsu, Tomasino, filipinofood, OldSchoolPH, Pam-

pamilyangPaoLUL, 3DSPH, beautytalkph, Bicol , BPOinPH, cagayandeoro, Cebu, davao, FilipinoFreethinkers, FilmClubPH, Iloilo, ilustrado, indiemusicph, KakaiBalita, Kwaderno, LoLPHSubreddit, mnl, opm, palawan, PBA, PHBookClub, phclassifieds, PHGamers, PHikingAndBackpacking, phlgbt, phr4r, Pilipinas, pinoyent, RedditPHCyclingClub, Tagalog, Tiangge, Gulong, dostscholars, AkoBaYungGago, Coronavirus_PH, exIglesiaNiCristo, studentsph, medschoolph, lawstudentsph, DotA2, artph, FilipinoHistory, phclassifieds, Filipinology, CasualPH

C Data Sources

The complete list of data sources are listed at Table 2.

Domain	Source	URL
News	Abante	abante.com.ph
	ABS-CBN	news.abs-cbn.com
	Bandera	bandera. inquirer.net
	GMA	gmanetwork.com
	Manila Bulletin	mb.com.ph
	Philippine Star	philstar.com
	Radyo Inquirer	radyo.inquirer.net
Social Media	X/Twitter	twitter.com
	YouTube	youtube.com
Encyclopedia	Wikipedia	dumps.wikimedia .org/tlwiki/ latest
Online Forums	Reddit	reddit.com
Books	Project Gutenberg	gutenberg.org
	Google Books	books.google.com
	Bible	wordproject.org

Table 2: List of sources per domain and its corresponding URLs.

D Dynamic N-STEP vs Fixed N-STEP Clustering

While Dynamic N-STEP Clustering allows for different number of clustering steps for each word, we want to know how it compares to its fixed counterpart. In this experiment, we compare Dynamic N-STEP and Fixed N-STEP clustering approach. We set N to 3, which means there will be a fixed 3 clustering steps for each word, which we will refer to as 3-STEP Clustering from hereon.

To compare both approaches, two independent wordnets were generated using the Dynamic N-STEP and 3-STEP clustering. The goal of this experiment is to see which approach can induce more synsets that matches with FilWordNet measured by Jaccard Index. The synset match counts were grouped into two groups, $>= 0.6$ and $>= 1.0$ (see Figure 6). For both approaches, the same parameters was used as described in Section 4.2.

The results shows that the 3-STEP Clustering induced more correct synsets than Dynamic N-STEP Clustering. One possible explanation is that the larger sense count of 3-STEP Clustering (7,177 senses) compared to Dynamic N-STEP Clustering (5,452 senses) contributed to more correct and partially correct synsets, leading to higher coverage. The results suggests that, for our dataset, the 3-STEP clustering is much more effective than Dynamic N-STEP Clustering. However, this may not generalize to other datasets and we suggest using Dynamic N-STEP Clustering as a starting point for any datasets.

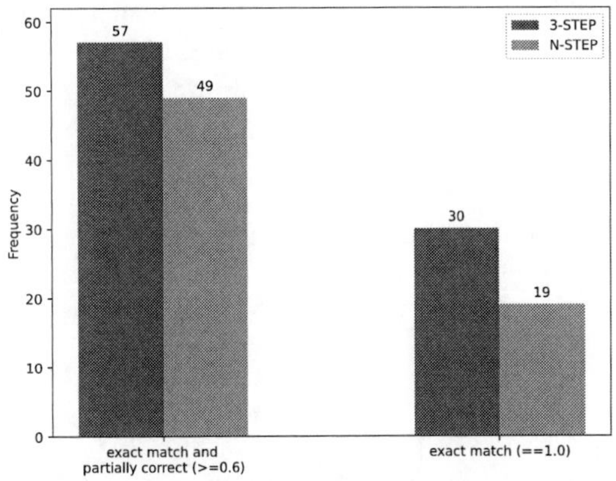

Figure 6: The 3-STEP algorithm consistently outperforms Dynamic N-STEP algorithm in terms of the number of synsets perfectly matched and the number of synsets that are at least 60% correct.

E Setting the Damping Parameter

The range of possible values for the damping parameter is 0.5 to 1, exclusive. Generally, the higher the damping, the lower the number of clusters. For

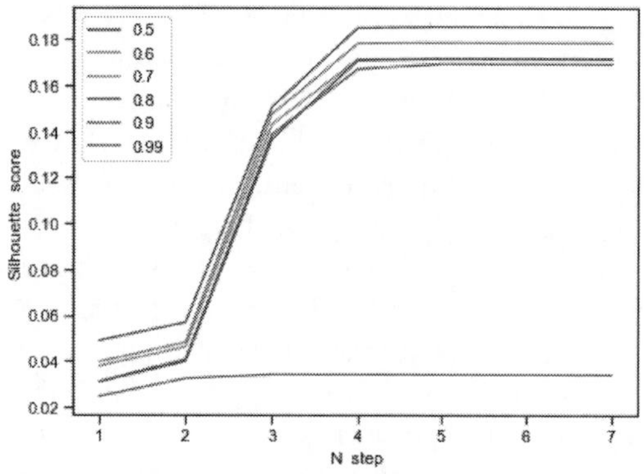

Figure 7: The damping parameter of 0.5 shows consistently higher average silhouette scores throughout all clustering steps compared to other damping values. This shows that the ideal damping value is 0.5.

example, setting the damping to 0.999 will result to just 1 cluster. To find the value for damping that maximizes the average silhouette score, different values were tested including 0.5, 0.6, 0.7, 0.8, 0.9, and 0.99. The clustering were tested on a fixed clustering steps for each word (7-STEP clustering) to observe the behavior of the silhouette score as the number of clustering steps increases.

Figure 7 shows that damping = 0.5 consistently gives higher average silhouette scores for all clustering steps compared to other values. For damping = 0.99, it stopped improving the silhouette score at the second clustering step while all other values keeps improving until the fourth clustering step. With these results, we set the final damping parameter to 0.5.

F Setting the Distance Threshold

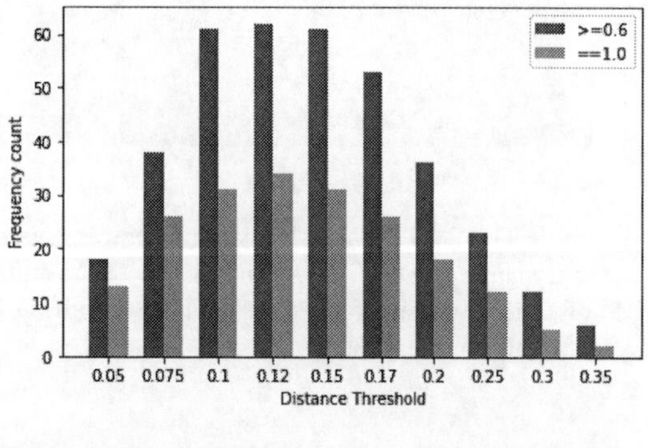

Figure 8: The distribution of Jaccard Index per distance threshold shows that distance threshold of 0.12 obtains the most partial and exact matches.

One of the most important parameter of the Agglomerative Clustering algorithm is the distance threshold which decides whether to cluster or not. For synset induction, the ideal distance threshold is the one that maximizes the Jaccard Index of the induced synsets and FilWordNet synsets. To find that ideal threshold, different threshold values were tested (See Figure 8).

All of the synset entries that obtained a Jaccard Index of 0.6 or higher were counted. A Jaccard Index of 0.6 has been considered to give credit to partial correctness. Aside from this, Jaccard Index of 1 were also counted for comparison. The distance threshold of 0.12 achieved the highest frequency in terms of exact and partial matches of FilWordNet synsets for this particular dataset (see Figure 8). With these results, we set final cosine distance threshold parameter to 0.12.

Developing a Named Entity Recognition Dataset for Tagalog

Lester James V. Miranda
ljvmiranda@gmail.com

Abstract

We present the development of a Named Entity Recognition (NER) dataset for Tagalog. This corpus helps fill the resource gap present in Philippine languages today, where NER resources are scarce. The texts were obtained from a pretraining corpora containing news reports, and were labeled by native speakers in an iterative fashion. The resulting dataset contains ~7.8k documents across three entity types: Person, Organization, and Location. The inter-annotator agreement, as measured by Cohen's κ, is 0.81. We also conducted extensive empirical evaluation of state-of-the-art methods across supervised and transfer learning settings. Finally, we released the data and processing code publicly to inspire future work on Tagalog NLP.

1 Introduction

Tagalog (`tl`) is one of the major languages in the Philippines with over 28 million speakers in the country (Lewis, 2009). It constitutes the bulk of Filipino, the country's official language, by sharing its lexical items and grammatical structure. Despite this fact, there are little to no resources for Tagalog (Cruz and Cheng, 2022), hampering the development of reliable language technologies.

In this paper, we present TLUNIFIED-NER,[1] a Tagalog dataset for Named Entity Recognition (NER). The texts were obtained from TLUnified (Cruz and Cheng, 2022), a pretraining corpora containing news reports and other types of text. We focused on NER because of its foundational role in several NLP tasks (Tjong Kim Sang and De Meulder, 2003; Lample et al., 2016), especially in problems that require the extraction of structured information. TLUNIFIED-NER consists of ~7.8k documents across three entity types (*Person*, *Organization*, *Location*), modeled closely to the CoNLL Shared Tasks (Tjong Kim Sang, 2002; Tjong Kim Sang and De Meulder, 2003). Three native speakers conducted the annotation process, resulting to an inter-annotator agreement (IAA) score of 0.81.

We hope that TLUNIFIED-NER will allow researchers to build better NER classifiers for Tagalog, and thereby inspire future research on Tagalog NLP through the following contributions:

1. We curated and annotated texts from a large pretraining corpora to represent the modern usage of Tagalog in the news domain.
2. We provided performance baselines across a variety of supervised and transfer learning settings.

2 Related Work

Tagalog language Tagalog is an agglutinative language within the Austronesian family (Kroeger, 1992). It uses the Latin script for its writing system with 28 letters in its alphabet. Twenty-six letters are the same as in English, with the addition of Ñ/ñ and Ng/ng. Tagalog typically follows the VSO word order, but VOS and SVO are also accepted (Schachter and Otanes, 1973). Although Filipino is the country's official language, it has little to no linguistic differences with Tagalog.

Tagalog NER datasets Unfortunately, resources for Tagalog NER are meager. One major resource is WikiANN (Pan et al., 2017), a silver-standard corpora based on a framework designed for 282 other languages. However, the Tagalog portion of WikiANN is full of annotation errors, often misconstruing one entity type as another. Another NER dataset is the Filipino Storytelling corpora (Costiniano et al., 2022). Although gold-standard, its entity labels (e.g., *Humans & Body*, *Natural Environment*, etc.) are too domain-specific for general use. Finally, the LORELEI project also provides

[1]The dataset is accessible at `https://huggingface.co/datasets/ljvmiranda921/tlunified-ner`

Proceedings of the First Workshop in South East Asian Language Processing, pages 13–20
November 1, 2023. ©2023 Association for Computational Linguistics

Entity	Short Description	Examples
Person (PER)	Person entities limited to humans. It may be a single individual or group.	Juan de la Cruz, Jose Rizal, Quijano de Manila
Organization (ORG)	Organization entities limited to corporations, agencies, and other groups of people defined by an organizational structure.	Meralco, DPWH, United Nations
Location (LOC)	Location entities are geographical regions, areas, and landmasses. Geo-political entities are also included within this group.	Pilipinas, Manila, CALABARZON, Ilog Pasig

Table 1: Entity types used for annotating TLUNIFIED-NER (derived from the TLUnified pretraining corpus of Cruz and Cheng, 2022).

language packs for Tagalog (Strassel and Tracey, 2016), but they're not publicly-accessible.

TLUNIFIED-NER aims to fill this resource gap by providing a publicly-assessible gold standard resource for Tagalog NER.

3 Dataset Collection

The texts were obtained from Cruz and Cheng (2022)'s TLUnified pretraining corpora. It combines news reports (Cruz et al., 2020), a preprocessed version of CommonCrawl (Suarez et al., 2019), and several other datasets. We manually filtered this dataset to contain news reports so as to resemble the CoNLL Shared Tasks (Tjong Kim Sang, 2002; Tjong Kim Sang and De Meulder, 2003).

The texts are diverse. It contains articles from different news sites online that ran a published print media or news channel in Metro Manila from 2009 to early 2020. The topics range from politics, weather, and popular science among others.

4 Annotation Setup

We used Prodigy as our annotation tool.[2] We set up a web server on the Google Cloud Platform and routed the examples through Prodigy's built-in task router. Figure 1 shows the labeling interface as seen by the annotator. Finally, we used the `ner.manual` recipe to highlight spans during the annotation process. We used three entity labels for TLUNIFIED-NER as shown in Table 1. Unlike CoNLL, we decided to exclude the *Miscellaneous (MISC)* tag to reduce confusion.

Annotation Process The annotation process was done iteratively with three annotators (including the author) who are native Tagalog speakers. Given a set annotation budget, we paid the annotators above the country's minimum daily wage. Each annotation round spans for two to three weeks, for a total of six rounds (18 weeks). The annotators labeled the same batch of examples to ensure high overlap.

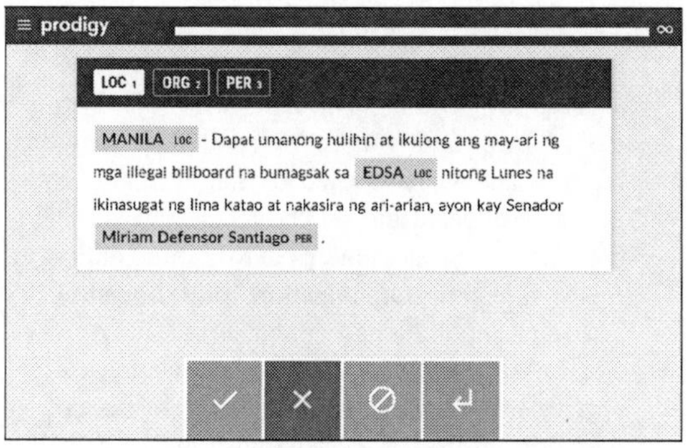

Figure 1: Prodigy's annotation interface for a given text. (Translation: *MANILA - The owner of the illegal billboards that fell on EDSA this Monday, injuring five people and damaging property, should be caught and imprisoned according to Senator Miriam Defensor Santiago.*)

After each round, the annotators hold a retrospective meeting and discussed examples they found confusing, inconsistent with the annotation guidelines, and noteworthy. This process continued until we reached ∼10k examples or if we exhausted our annotation budget. In addition, we also tracked the training curve to determine the quality of the collected annotations. If the F1-score improved within the last 25% of the training data, then it is a good sign that obtaining more labels will result to better accuracy.

Annotation Guidelines We developed the annotation guidelines in an iterative fashion.

[2]https://prodigy.ai

Dataset	Examples	Tokens	PER	ORG	LOC	Length	SD	BD
Training	6252	198579	6418	3121	3296	1.49	2.66	1.26
Development	782	25069	793	392	409	1.51	2.77	1.37
Test	782	25100	818	423	438	1.48	2.77	1.34

Table 2: Dataset statistics for TLUNIFIED-NER. It shows the number of examples, number of tokens, and span-level statistics. SD stands for span distinctiveness whereas BD is boundary distinctiveness (Papay et al., 2020).

Metric	IAA
Cohen's κ on all tokens	0.81
Cohen's κ on annotated tokens only	0.65
F1 score	0.91

Table 3: Inter-annotator agreement (IAA) measurements. We obtained these values by computing for the pairwise comparisons on all annotator-pairs and averaging the results.

The Automatic Content Extraction (ACE 2004/05) annotation document (Doddington et al., 2004) heavily inspired our initial draft. We co-developed the guidelines after each annotation round to improve clarity and reduce disagreements. These guidelines are accessible on GitHub: `https://github.com/ljvmiranda921/calamanCy/tree/master/datasets/tl_calamancy_gold_corpus/guidelines`

5 Corpus Statistics and Evaluation

Table 2 shows the final dataset statistics for TLUNIFIED-NER. We also included span- (SD) and boundary-distinctiveness (BD) metrics (Papay et al., 2020). They measure the KL-divergence of the unigram word distributions between the span (or its boundaries) and the rest of the corpora. These metrics can be used to gauge the difficulty of the span labeling task, (e.g., more distinct spans means it's "easier" to detect them in the text).

5.1 Inter-annotator Agreement (IAA)

Similar to Brandsen et al. (2020), we measured two types of Cohen's κ. The first metric calculates κ for tokens where at least one annotator has made an annotation. The second metric computes for all tokens while ignoring the 'O' label. In addition, we had a third measure: the F1-score using one set of annotations as reference (Deleger et al., 2012). We did these computations for each annotator-pair and averaged the results as shown in Table 3.

Finally, Figure 2 shows the growth of IAA for each annotation round. Because of our annotation process, we were able to label the same batch of documents and track the agreement every round.

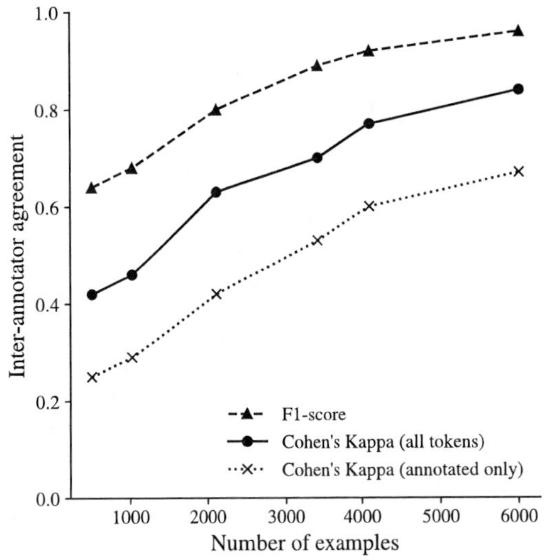

Figure 2: Growth of IAA for each annotation round.

5.2 Benchmark results

We trained several NER models using spaCy's transition-based parser (Honnibal et al., 2020). The state transitions are based on the BILUO sequence encoding scheme and the actions are decided by a convolutional neural network with a maxout (Goodfellow et al., 2013) activation function.

While keeping the NER classifier constant, we experimented with various word embeddings that led to the following configurations:

- **Baseline:** we trained the transition-based parser "from scratch" without additional information from static or context-sensitive vectors.

- **Static vectors:** we used Tagalog fastText vectors (Bojanowski et al., 2017) and included a simple pretraining process to initialize the

Word Embeddings	Person	Organization	Location	Overall
Baseline (no additional embeddings)	87.85±0.01	74.80±0.02	81.03±0.01	84.57±0.02
fastText (Bojanowski et al., 2017)	91.20±0.02	85.39±0.03	88.38±0.01	88.90±0.01
RoBERTa Tagalog (Cruz and Cheng, 2022)	92.18±0.01	87.30±0.00	90.01±0.02	90.34±0.02
XLM-RoBERTa (Conneau et al., 2020)	91.95±0.04	84.84±0.02	88.92±0.01	88.03±0.03
Multilingual BERT (Devlin et al., 2019)	90.78±0.03	85.08±0.01	88.45±0.03	87.40±0.02

Table 4: Benchmark results on TLUNIFIED-NER across different word embeddings using spaCy's transition-based parser (Honnibal et al., 2020). Reported results are F1-scores on the test set across three trials.

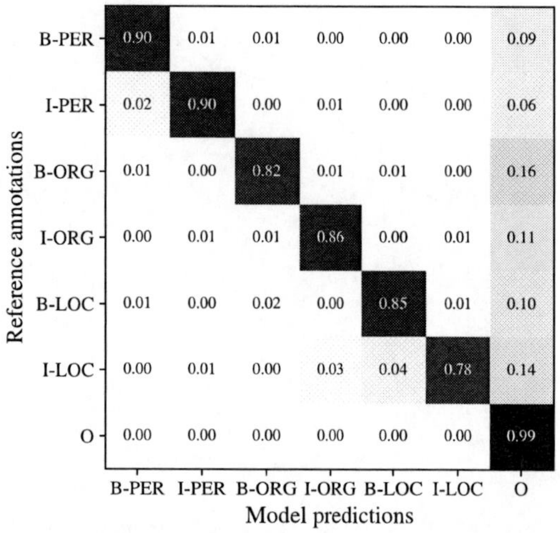

Figure 3: Development set confusion matrix of the Baseline model predictions in the IOB format.

weights of the model. The pretraining objective asks the model to predict some number of leading and trailing UTF-8 bytes for the words—a variant of the cloze task.

- **Transformer-based vectors (monolingual):** we used RoBERTa Tagalog (Cruz and Cheng, 2022), the only pretrained language model for Tagalog, and finetuned it with our annotations.
- **Transformer-based vectors (multilingual):** we tested on XLM-RoBERTa (Conneau et al., 2020) and multilingual BERT (Devlin et al., 2019) for transfer learning. These models include Tagalog in their training pool albeit underrepresented.

This experimental setup allows us to see the expected performance when training Tagalog NER classifiers using standard techniques. Table 4 reports the F1-score on the test set across three trials.

	Rel. error reduction	
Embeddings set-up	ORG	LOC
Shared	+5%	+3%
Context-sensitive	+12%	+18%

Table 5: Relative error reduction (with respect to the Baseline) for classifying ORG and LOC entities. Reported results are F1-scores on the development set.

5.3 Error analysis

From our benchmark results, we noticed that most models are having trouble predicting the *Location* or *Organization* tags. Figure 3 shows the confusion matrix of the Baseline model on the development set in the IOB format.

Most of the mistakes came from incorrectly tagging a token with the outside 'O' label. However, we also noticed instances where the model confuses between the lexical and semantic tag of an entity. For example, in the span, "*...panukala ng Ombudsman...*" ("...proposed by the Ombudsman..."), the token `Ombudsman` might be a Person or Organization depending on the context. We hypothesize that including context-sensitive training, which the baseline model lacks, can help mitigate this issue.

To test this hypothesis, we experimented on two training configurations. First, we trained a POS tagger together with our transition-based NER with shared weights. This process may help provide extra information to the transition-based parser so it can disambiguate between entities. Second, we finetuned context-sensitive vectors from RoBERTa Tagalog (Cruz and Cheng, 2022) for NER. Table 5 shows the relative error reduction between LOC and ORG entities. Given these results, we encourage researchers to utilize context-sensitive vectors such as RoBERTa Tagalog (or other BERT variants) when training models from this corpora.

Model	Training dataset	
	WikiANN	TLUNIFIED-NER
Baseline (no additional embeddings)	19.92±0.03	**30.24±0.02**
fastText (Bojanowski et al., 2017)	24.41±0.01	**45.09±0.02**
RoBERTa Tagalog (Cruz and Cheng, 2022)	23.38±0.02	**58.90±0.03**
XLM-RoBERTa (Conneau et al., 2020)	31.28±0.01	**57.67±0.01**
Multilingual BERT (Devlin et al., 2019)	29.20±0.03	**59.26±0.03**

Table 6: Cross-dataset comparison between WikiANN (Pan et al., 2017) and TLUNIFIED-NER. We trained a model from WikiANN then applied it to TLUNIFIED-NER (and vice-versa). Reported results are F1-scores on the test set across three trials.

Entity label	F1-score
Person (PER)	67.95
Organization (ORG)	00.59
Location (LOC)	35.17

Table 7: Comparing the overlap between the original (silver-standard) WikiANN annotations against our reannotated version.

5.4 Comparison to WikiANN

The WikiANN dataset (Pan et al., 2017) is another resource for Tagalog NER. However, we found many annotation errors in the dataset, from misclassifications to fragmented sentences. We investigated how TLUNIFIED-NER fares against WikiANN's silver-standard annotations.

We finetuned several models similar to Section 5.2 on the Tagalog portion of WikiANN's training set and tested it on TLUNIFIED-NER's test set (and vice-versa). In order to properly evaluate on WikiANN, we reannotated the test dataset using the same annotation guidelines described in Section 4.

Our results in Table 6 suggest that models built from the TLUNIFIED-NER corpus are more performant than with WikiANN. Additionally, the gap between WikiANN's silver-standard annotations and our corrections is large, as shown in Table 7. We then posit that the gold-standard nature of TLUNIFIED-NER led to better performance than WikiANN, which predominantly consists of text fragments and low-quality annotations.

5.5 Experiments on large language models

Large language models (LLMs) have been shown to exhibit multilingual capabilities—incidental or not (Briakou et al., 2023). We investigated this property by performing a zero-shot prompting approach on TLUNIFIED-NER's test set across a variety of commercial and open-source LLMs. Table 8 reports the F1-score across three trials.

Model	F1-score
GPT-4 (OpenAI, 2023)	65.89±0.44
GPT-3.5-turbo	53.05±0.42
Claude v1 (Anthropic, 2023)	58.88±0.03
Command (Cohere, 2023)	25.48±0.11
Dolly v2* (Conover et al., 2023)	13.07±0.14
Falcon* (Almazrouei et al., 2023)	8.65±0.04
StableLM v2* (Stability-AI, 2023)	0.25±0.03
OpenLLaMa* (Geng and Liu, 2023)	15.09±0.48

Table 8: Benchmark results on TLUNIFIED-NER across a variety of open-source and commercial LLMs. We used the 7B-parameter variants for models denoted with an asterisk ($*$) due to budget constraints.

Our results suggest that supervised learning reliably outperforms zero-shot prompting for TLUNIFIED-NER given our prompt (see Appendix A.1). However, we acknowledge that these results are not a definitive comparison between two methods as prompt engineering is unstable with high variance (Webson and Pavlick, 2022; Zhao et al., 2021). In the future, we plan to explore different prompting techniques such as PromptNER (Ashok and Lipton, 2023) and chain-of-thought (Wei et al., 2023) to uncover the language models' full capabilities.

6 Conclusion

In this paper, we introduced TLUNIFIED-NER, a Named Entity Recognition dataset for Tagalog. Unlike other Tagalog NER datasets, TLUNIFIED-NER is publicly-accessible and gold standard. Our iterative annotation process, together with our inter-annotator agreement, shows that the corpus is of high quality. In addition, our benchmarking results suggest that the task is learnable even with a simple baseline method. We hope that TLUNIFIED-NER fills the resource gap present in Tagalog NLP today. In the future, we plan to create a more fine-grained (and perhaps, overlapping) NER tag set similar to the ACE project and expand on other major Philippine languages. Finally, the dataset is available online (`https://huggingface.co/datasets/ljvmiranda921/tlunified-ner`) and we encourage researchers to improve upon our benchmark results.

Limitations

The TLUNIFIED-NER corpora is comprised mostly by news reports. Although the texts demonstrate the standard usage of Tagalog, its domain is limited. In addition, we only trained a transition-based parser model for our NER classifier. In the future, we plan to extend these benchmarks and include CRFs or other tools such as Stanford Stanza.

Acknowledgements

We would like to express our gratitute to all those who contributed to the completion of this resource. We extend our appreciation to the anonymous reviewers for their constructive comments, which greatly improved the quality of this paper.

References

Ebtesam Almazrouei, Hamza Alobeidli, Abdulaziz Alshamsi, Alessandro Cappelli, Ruxandra Cojocaru, Merouane Debbah, Etienne Goffinet, Daniel Heslow, Julien Launay, Quentin Malartic, Badreddine Noune, Baptiste Pannier, and Guilherme Penedo. 2023. Falcon-40B: an open large language model with state-of-the-art performance.

Anthropic. 2023. Model card and evaluations for claude models.

Dhananjay Ashok and Zachary C. Lipton. 2023. Promptner: Prompting for named entity recognition.

Piotr Bojanowski, Edouard Grave, Armand Joulin, and Tomas Mikolov. 2017. Enriching Word Vectors with Subword Information. *Transactions of the Association for Computational Linguistics*, 5:135–146.

Alex Brandsen, Suzan Verberne, Milco Wansleeben, and Karsten Lambers. 2020. Creating a Dataset for Named Entity Recognition in the Archaeology Domain. In *Proceedings of the Twelfth Language Resources and Evaluation Conference*, pages 4573–4577, Marseille, France. European Language Resources Association.

Eleftheria Briakou, Colin Cherry, and George Foster. 2023. Searching for needles in a haystack: On the role of incidental bilingualism in PaLM's translation capability. In *Proceedings of the 61st Annual Meeting of the Association for Computational Linguistics (Volume 1: Long Papers)*, pages 9432–9452, Toronto, Canada. Association for Computational Linguistics.

Cohere. 2023. Command Model: The AI-Powered Solution for the Enterprise.

Alexis Conneau, Kartikay Khandelwal, Naman Goyal, Vishrav Chaudhary, Guillaume Wenzek, Francisco Guzmán, Edouard Grave, Myle Ott, Luke Zettlemoyer, and Veselin Stoyanov. 2020. Unsupervised Cross-lingual Representation Learning at Scale. In *Proceedings of the 58th Annual Meeting of the Association for Computational Linguistics*, pages 8440–8451, Online. Association for Computational Linguistics.

Mike Conover, Matt Hayes, Ankit Mathur, Jianwei Xie, Jun Wan, Sam Shah, Ali Ghodsi, Patrick Wendell, Matei Zaharia, and Reynold Xin. 2023. Free dolly: Introducing the world's first truly open instruction-tuned llm.

Sherwyne Costiniano, Rose Ann Mae Santos, Julius Simon Mendoza, and Allen Jay Gale. 2022. Custom Coarse Grained Named Entity Recognition for Filipino Storytelling Data Using Uncased Transformer Models. *SSRN Electronic Journal*.

Jan Christian Blaise Cruz and Charibeth Cheng. 2022. Improving Large-scale Language Models and Resources for Filipino. In *Proceedings of the Thirteenth Language Resources and Evaluation Conference*, pages 6548–6555, Marseille, France. European Language Resources Association.

Jan Christian Blaise Cruz, Jose Kristian Resabal, James Lin, Dan John Velasco, and Charibeth Ko Cheng. 2020. Exploiting News Article Structure for Automatic Corpus Generation of Entailment Datasets. In *Pacific Rim International Conference on Artificial Intelligence*.

Louise Deleger, Qi Li, Todd Lingren, Megan Kaiser, Katalin Molnar, Laura Stoutenborough, Michal Kouril, Keith Marsolo, and Imre Solti. 2012. Building gold standard corpora for medical natural language processing tasks. In *AMIA Annual Symposium Proceedings*, pages 144–53.

Jacob Devlin, Ming-Wei Chang, Kenton Lee, and Kristina Toutanova. 2019. BERT: Pre-training of deep bidirectional transformers for language understanding. In *Proceedings of the 2019 Conference of the North American Chapter of the Association for Computational Linguistics: Human Language*

Technologies, Volume 1 (Long and Short Papers), pages 4171–4186, Minneapolis, Minnesota. Association for Computational Linguistics.

George Doddington, Alexis Mitchell, Mark Przybocki, Lance Ramshaw, Stephanie Strassel, and Ralph Weischedel. 2004. The automatic content extraction (ACE) program – tasks, data, and evaluation. In *Proceedings of the Fourth International Conference on Language Resources and Evaluation (LREC'04)*, Lisbon, Portugal. European Language Resources Association (ELRA).

Xinyang Geng and Hao Liu. 2023. OpenLLaMA: An Open Reproduction of LLaMA.

Ian Goodfellow, David Warde-Farley, Mehdi Mirza, Aaron Courville, and Yoshua Bengio. 2013. Maxout networks. In *Proceedings of the 30th International Conference on Machine Learning*, volume 28 of *Proceedings of Machine Learning Research*, pages 1319–1327, Atlanta, Georgia, USA. PMLR.

Matthew Honnibal, Ines Montani, Sofie Van Landeghem, and Adriane Boyd. 2020. spaCy: Industrial-strength Natural Language Processing in Python.

Paul R. Kroeger. 1992. Phrase Structure and Grammatical Relations in Tagalog.

Guillaume Lample, Miguel Ballesteros, Sandeep Subramanian, Kazuya Kawakami, and Chris Dyer. 2016. Neural architectures for named entity recognition. In *Proceedings of the 2016 Conference of the North American Chapter of the Association for Computational Linguistics: Human Language Technologies*, pages 260–270, San Diego, California. Association for Computational Linguistics.

Paul M. A. Lewis. 2009. Ethnologue: languages of the world. `https://ethnologue.com/language/tgl`. Accessed: June 2023.

OpenAI. 2023. GPT-4 Technical Report.

Xiaoman Pan, Boliang Zhang, Jonathan May, Joel Nothman, Kevin Knight, and Heng Ji. 2017. Cross-lingual name tagging and linking for 282 languages. In *Proceedings of the 55th Annual Meeting of the Association for Computational Linguistics (Volume 1: Long Papers)*, pages 1946–1958, Vancouver, Canada. Association for Computational Linguistics.

Sean Papay, Roman Klinger, and Sebastian Padó. 2020. Dissecting span identification tasks with performance prediction. In *Proceedings of the 2020 Conference on Empirical Methods in Natural Language Processing (EMNLP)*, pages 4881–4895, Online. Association for Computational Linguistics.

Paul Schachter and Fe T. Otanes. 1973. Tagalog reference grammar. *The Journal of Asian Studies*, 32:760 – 761.

Stability-AI. 2023. StableLM-Alpha v2.

Stephanie Strassel and Jennifer Tracey. 2016. LORELEI language packs: Data, tools, and resources for technology development in low resource languages. In *Proceedings of the Tenth International Conference on Language Resources and Evaluation (LREC'16)*, pages 3273–3280, Portorož, Slovenia. European Language Resources Association (ELRA).

Pedro Ortiz Suarez, Benoît Sagot, and Laurent Romary. 2019. Asynchronous Pipeline for Processing Huge Corpora on Medium to Low Resource Infrastructures. In *7th Workshop on the Challenges in the Management of Large Corpora*.

Erik F. Tjong Kim Sang. 2002. Introduction to the CoNLL-2002 shared task: Language-independent named entity recognition. In *COLING-02: The 6th Conference on Natural Language Learning 2002 (CoNLL-2002)*.

Erik F. Tjong Kim Sang and Fien De Meulder. 2003. Introduction to the CoNLL-2003 shared task: Language-independent named entity recognition. In *Proceedings of the Seventh Conference on Natural Language Learning at HLT-NAACL 2003*, pages 142–147.

Albert Webson and Ellie Pavlick. 2022. Do prompt-based models really understand the meaning of their prompts? In *Proceedings of the 2022 Conference of the North American Chapter of the Association for Computational Linguistics: Human Language Technologies*, pages 2300–2344, Seattle, United States. Association for Computational Linguistics.

Jason Wei, Xuezhi Wang, Dale Schuurmans, Maarten Bosma, Brian Ichter, Fei Xia, Ed Chi, Quoc Le, and Denny Zhou. 2023. Chain-of-thought prompting elicits reasoning in large language models.

Zihao Zhao, Eric Wallace, Shi Feng, Dan Klein, and Sameer Singh. 2021. Calibrate before use: Improving few-shot performance of language models. In *Proceedings of the 38th International Conference on Machine Learning*, volume 139 of *Proceedings of Machine Learning Research*, pages 12697–12706. PMLR.

A Appendix

A.1 Zero-shot prompt template

You are an expert Named Entity Recognition (NER) system. Your task is to accept Text as input and extract named entities for the set of predefined entity labels. From the Text input provided, extract named entities for each label in the following format:

- *PER: <comma delimited list of strings>*
- *ORG: <comma delimited list of strings>*
- *LOC: <comma delimited list of strings>*

Below are definitions of each label to help aid you in what kinds of named entities to extract for each label. Assume these definitions are written by an expert and follow them closely.

- *PER: PERSON*
- *ORG: ORGANIZATION*
- *LOC: LOCATION OR GEOPOLITICAL ENTITY*

Text: {{ text }}

A.2 Reproducibility

All the experiments and models in this paper are available publicly. Readers can head over to `https://github.com/ljvmiranda921/calamanCy/reports/aacl` for all related code and assets. Note that the XLM-RoBERTa and multilingual BERT experiments may at least require a T4 or V100 GPU.

Balarila: Deep Learning for Semantic Grammar Error Correction in Low-Resource Settings

Paolo Espiritu, Joshue Jadie, Andre Ponce, and Charibeth Cheng
College of Computer Studies
De La Salle University, Manila
{paolo_edni_v_espiritu, joshue_jadie, andre_ponce, charibeth.cheng}@dlsu.edu.ph

Abstract

While there are many grammar checkers available for various languages, especially the English language, those that exist for the low-resource Filipino language can only effectively correct lexical errors. There is yet to be a publicly available Filipino grammar checker that can also address semantic errors, which are more complex. As such, this study found an opportunity to introduce *Balarila*, a deep learning-based Filipino GEC model inspired by the GECToR approach. To address the absence of a training and test dataset, an automated error generation pipeline was devised, creating synthetic datasets of error-free and error-filled Filipino sentences sourced from various online news sources. Tagalog BERT and RoBERTa models were fine-tuned in two stages using this generated corpus. Evaluation metrics included precision, recall, and $F_{0.5}$ scores for GEC, and a multi-class confusion matrix for GED. The top-performing model, RoBERTa Tagalog Large, achieved an $F_{0.5}$ score of 70.75, while the RoBERTa Tagalog Base, with a $F_{0.5}$ score of 69.00, demonstrated cost-effectiveness in training. The created datasets can also be used as a benchmark for Filipino grammar checker models.

1 Introduction

Writing sentences in a certain language requires skills that are only developed through a lot of practice. A sufficient understanding of the rules and syntax of a language is necessary to avoid breakdowns in communication. The Filipino language is not exempted from such a necessity.

Grammar checkers such as Grammarly are said to be beneficial in aiding individuals hone the different aspects of their writing skills such as sentence construction, vocabulary usage, proper grammar, and language mechanics (Ghufron and Rosyida, 2018; Jayavalan and Razali, 2018). Using such tools is one of the many ways one can develop better writing skills.

There already exists a Filipino grammar checker called *Gramatika* – which utilizes rule-based methods combined with statistical machine translation (SMT) (Go et al., 2017). However, it is limited by the availability of expert-annotated corpora and by other limitations that come with SMT-based implementations (Solyman et al., 2021; Chollampatt and Ng, 2018). Furthermore, as Gramatika was released in 2017, there is yet to be a Filipino grammar checker that adopts state-of-the-art approaches such as transformer-based models.

In a recent study, a sequence tagging approach was introduced to simplify the task of sequence generation. The proposed model only utilized a transformer encoder and some basic linear layers. The results showed that the inference speed of the model improved 10 times compared to transformer-based seq2seq systems (Omelianchuk et al., 2020).

However, these models require large amounts of data for training. This poses a problem for low-resource languages such as Filipino. Workarounds were created to address this such as synthetic dataset creation (Grundkiewicz et al., 2019) and large-scale corpus creation (Cruz and Cheng, 2021).

In this paper, an opportunity has been found to develop a transformer encoder-based model that will effectively detect and correct grammatical errors in the Filipino language. Furthermore, a demonstration of how a synthetic error-free and error-filled Filipino text dataset can be used as a benchmark for grammar error detection and correction is also provided.

2 Related Literature

GECToR (Omelianchuk et al., 2020) is a transformer encoder-based modelthat approaches GEC as an iterative sequence tagging task instead of sequence generation. The approach essentially reduces the task into a language-understanding problem, which only needs a transformer encoder

Proceedings of the First Workshop in South East Asian Language Processing, pages 21–29
November 1, 2023.

stacked with linear layers. Given a target sentence, the sequence tagger model predicts the tag-encoded transformations for each token. The predicted tags are then applied to the target sentence through post-processing to get the modified sentence. Since some corrections in a sentence may depend on previous corrections, the same process is executed to the modified sentence to correct it further. This is repeated until the sentence is fully corrected.

The model predicts two types of token-level transformations: basic transformations and *g*-transformations (Omelianchuk et al., 2020). Basic transformations are common token-level edit operations such as keeping the token unchanged, deleting the token, and replacing the token with a new token. Meanwhile, *g*-transformations are custom-designed transformations that perform task-specific operations such as changing the case of the current token and splitting the token into two new tokens.

The model training is performed through three stages: (1) pre-train the model on synthetic data, (2) fine-tune the model on a corpus full of grammatically incorrect sentences, and (3) fine-tune the model on a corpus of mixed grammatically correct and incorrect sentences. With pre-trained transformer encoders such as BERT (Devlin et al., 2018), only training stages 2 and 3 are used. Model optimization was done using the Adam optimizer (Kingma and Ba, 2015) with default hyperparameters (Omelianchuk et al., 2020).

3 Methodology

3.1 Covered Grammatical Errors

Two categories of grammatical errors were covered by this study: (1) grammar errors and (2) spelling errors. These were derived from a book and previous studies that tackle Filipino grammatical errors (Komisyon sa Wikang Filipino, 2013; Go and Borra, 2016; Octaviano et al., 2016).

3.1.1 Grammar Errors

- *Morphological Errors.* These are grammatical errors that may be caused by words that went through morphological changes (Octaviano et al., 2016). Due to various morphological processes, certain Filipino words alter their spelling. For example, when the prefix /pang-/ is attached to the word *bili* 'buy', it yields the word *pambili* 'a resource used to by something' since the original word begins with /p/, /b/, or /m/.
- *Wrong use of nang vs. ng.* These are grammatical errors that may be caused by the improper use of the words *nang* and *ng*. These words are commonly interchanged mainly due to their similar pronunciations.

3.1.2 Spelling Errors

- *Duplicate Words.* These are spelling errors caused by mistakenly repeating a word that should not be repeated. Words such as *ang* 'the', *ng* 'of', and *mga* (denotes the plural form of a word) are some of the commonly duplicated words (Octaviano et al., 2016).
- *Missing Spaces.* These are spelling errors caused by improper merging of Filipino words due to a missing space. For example, *pa rin* meaning 'still' is commonly written as *parin* similar to how 'going to' is sometimes written as 'gonna'.
- *Extra Spaces.* These are spelling errors caused by not properly merging Filipino words together. For example, *pinakamalaki* 'biggest' is erroneously spelled as *pinaka malaki.*
- *Wrong Use of Hyphens.* These are spelling errors caused by the wrong use of hyphens - which may be used to separate prefixes from the base word. Hyphens are used when the base word is a proper noun, loan word, or starts with a vowel (Octaviano et al., 2016). For example, *nag-usap* is erroneously written as *nagusap*.
- *Wrong Use of Enclitics.* These are spelling errors caused by confusion on the rules of enclitics starting with /d/ and /r/. For example, the words *din* and *rin* both mean 'also'. However, *rin* is used when the previous words ends with a vowel or semi-vowel, otherwise *din* is used.

3.2 Balarila

The model adopted the approach of the GECToR model (Omelianchuk et al., 2020). It performs the GEC task through iterative sequence tagging instead of sequence generation. The approach consisted of two (2) phases: fine-tuning and inference.

3.2.1 Fine-tuning

As shown in Figure 1, a pre-trained transformer encoder such as BERT was fine-tuned for the GEC

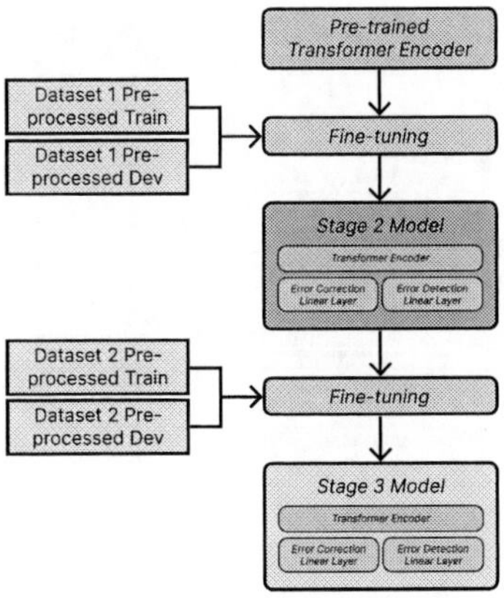

Figure 1: Fine-tuning Pipeline

task. In the second training stage, two (2) linear layers were added on top of the model first which are the error detection and error correction linear layers. This was done to produce the task outputs. Afterwards, the model was fine-tuned with error-filled Filipino sentences (Dataset 1). In the third training stage, the model was fine-tuned with both error-filled and error-free Filipino sentences (Dataset 2). These training stages were performed in sequence as crucial to the model's performance (Omelianchuk et al., 2020). Fine-tuning the model first on error-filled sentences allowed the model to effectively learn the different types of Filipino errors covered, the contexts of the errors, and the patterns of correct Filipino grammar. For model optimization, the Adam optimizer (Kingma and Ba, 2015) with default hyperparameters was utilized.

3.2.2 Inference

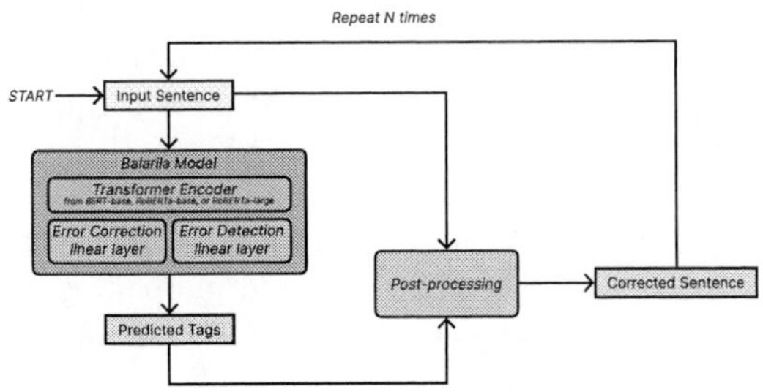

Figure 2: Inference Sequence Tagging Pipeline

Figure 2 shows Balarila's inference pipeline as adopted from GECToR (Omelianchuk et al., 2020). To correct the grammatical errors in an input sentence, the input sentence is first passed into the fine-tuned transformer encoder model to be converted into a context vector. The context vector is then passed to the error detection and correction linear layers, with Softmax layers on the top to predict the transformation tags per token. Based on the predicted tags, transformations are applied to each token through post-processing afterwards to produce the output sentence.

As the technique is iterative, the output sentence may not be fully corrected yet in the first iteration. The process is then repeated to the output sentence to correct it further. Table 1 shows an example of how the iterative sequence tagging technique is used to correct an input sentence.

# of Iterations	Sentence
0	*Punta niya sa mall kahapon*
1	*Punta niya sa mall kahapon*
2	*Punta siya sa mall kahapon.*
3	*Pumunta siya sa mall kahapon.*

Table 1: Iterative sequence tagging example

In three (3) iterations, the sentence was fully corrected by adding a period in the end, replacing *niya* with *siya*, and changing *punta* to *pumunta*. This implied that the higher the number of iterations, the better the result will be. However, it is to be taken into account that the higher the number of iterations, the lower the inference speed of the model. The number of iterations should be configured properly to produce an accurate and fast model (Omelianchuk et al., 2020). For Balarila, the default number of iterations set by GECToR was used, which is five (5). The model corrects one error per iteration. With this approach, errors that can only be corrected based on previous corrections are corrected on the succeeding iterations.

3.2.3 Transformation Tags

Table 2 shows the transformation tags used by the model to correct each covered grammatical error. Most of the tags were adopted from the GECToR (Omelianchuk et al., 2020) model, and a new set of tags was also introduced. These new tags were used for other errors that were not covered by the default set of tags such as Filipino morphological errors and punctuation errors.

The tags used in morphological errors represent Tagalog verb form transformations. Tagalog verb forms are created using four (4) aspects which are completed, incompleted, contemplated, and recently completed. The focus of the verb is also included thus the verb and its aspect can either be in actor-focus or object-focus form. See Table 3 for some examples under each.

Error Types	Tags
Wrong Use of *nang vs. ng*	$REPLACE_*nang*, $REPLACE_*ng*
Wrong Use of Enclitics	$REPLACE_*daw*, $REPLACE_*din*, $REPLACE_*dito*, $REPLACE_*diyan*, $REPLACE_*doon*, $REPLACE_*raw*, $REPLACE_*rin*, $REPLACE_*roon*, $REPLACE_*rito*, $REPLACE_*riyan*
Wrong Use of Hyphens	$MERGE_HYPHEN, $TRANSFORM_INSERT_HYPHEN, $TRANSFORM_SPLIT_HYPHEN
Wrong Use of Spaces	$MERGE_SPACE, $TRANSFORM_SPLIT_SPACE
Duplicate Words	$DELETE
Morphological Errors	$TRANSFORM_VERB_BASE, $TRANSFORM_VERB_COMPACT, $TRANSFORM_VERB_COMPOBJ, $TRANSFORM_VERB_CONTACT, $TRANSFORM_VERB_CONTOBJ, $TRANSFORM_VERB_INCACT, $TRANSFORM_VERB_INCOBJ, $TRANSFORM_VERB_RECCOMP
Wrong Use of Punctuation Marks	$ADD_PUNC_EMARK, $ADD_PUNC_PERIOD, $ADD_PUNC_QMARK, $CHANGE_PUNC_EMARK, $CHANGE_PUNC_PERIOD, $CHANGE_PUNC_QMARK
Improper Word Casing	$TRANSFORM_CASE_CAPITAL, $TRANSFORM_CASE_LOWER
Missing Words	$APPEND_$t_1$
Wrong Use of Ang and Ng Pronouns	$REPLACE_*nila*, $REPLACE_*niya* $REPLACE_*sila*, $REPLACE_*siya*

Table 2: Error Types and Transformation Tags

Tag	Verb Form	Examples
BASE	Base	luto, sagot, sukat
COMPACT	Completed Aspect + Actor Focus	nagluto, sumagot, nagsukat
INCACT	Incompleted Aspect + Actor Focus	nagluluto, sumasagot, nagsusukat
CONTACT	Contemplated Aspect + Actor Focus	magluluto, sasagot, magsusukat
IMPACT	Imperative Aspect + Actor Focus	magluto, magsagot, magsukat
COMPOBJ	Completed Aspect + Actor Focus	niluto, sinagot, sinukat
INCOBJ	Incompleted Aspect + Object Focus	niluluto, sinasagot, sinusukat
CONTOBJ	Contemplated Aspect + Object Focus	lulutuin, sasagutin, susukatin
IMPOBJ	Imperative Aspect + Object Focus	lutuin, sagutin, sukatin
RECCOMP	Recently Completed Aspect	kaluluto, kasasagot, kasusukat

Table 3: Tagalog Verb Form Transformation Tags

3.3 Data Collection

The datasets used for this study are composed of sentences scraped from various publicly available mainstream Filipino news websites - specifically *Abante*, *Bandera*, *GMA*, and *Pilipino Star Ngayon*. In total, 58,464 news articles were scraped, and these articles contained a total of 510,411 raw sentences. It is worth noting that some of these articles are written in *Taglish* - which is a combination of English and Tagalog words. Furthermore, in order to prevent re-introducing the Filipino RoBERTa models (Cruz and Cheng, 2021) to the same news articles they were trained on, only news articles dated January 2021 and onward were included in scraping. The cutoff for the scraped data was May 2023, since this was when the scraping was last performed before the models were finalized.

3.4 Data Cleaning

Some cleaning were performed on the collected raw sentences:

- *Incorrect Enclitics.* Some sentence entries incorrectly use entries (i.e., raw vs. daw, roon vs. doon) prior to scraping. These were corrected using a rule-based enclitic-correcting algorithm.
- *Multiple Sentences.* Some sentence entries contained multiple sentences within themselves separated by periods. These sentences were further split based on the period character's location.
- *Invalid Characters.* Some sentence entries contained invalid characters such as emojis. As such, these sentences were dropped.
- *English-dominant Sentences.* Some sentence entries were dominated by English words. With this, sentences that are composed of at least 50% Filipino words were retained, while the rest were dropped. The 50% threshold was set because using Filipino sometimes still requires borrowed English words.

3.5 Error Automation

In corrupting the cleaned sentences, a variety of approaches were used depending on the grammatical error to be reproduced. It is also worth noting that this pipeline was designed with the assumption that only one error was to be introduced per corrupted sentence.

- *Word Replacement.* Replace a target word with another. Applicable to morphological errors, wrong use of *nang* vs. *ng*, and wrong use of enclitics.
- *Character Replacement.* Replace a single character with another. Applicable to wrong use of hyphens, wrong use of punctuation marks, and improper word casing.
- *Punctuation Removal.* Remove the punctuation mark at the end of the sentence. Applicable to the wrong use of punctuation marks.

- *Word Duplication.* Duplicate a target word within the sentence. Applicable to duplicate word errors.
- *Word Deletion.* Delete a target word within the sentence. Applicable to missing word errors.
- *Word Stitching.* Stitch two words together by removing the space or hyphen in-between them. Applicable to missing spaces and wrong use of hyphens errors.
- *Word Splitting.* Insert a single space in-between a pair of syllables in a target word. Applicable to extra spaces errors.
- *Multiple Sentences.* Given a multi-sentence input, a single sentence is randomly chosen and is corrupted using either the character replacement or punctuation removal approach.

3.6 Datasets

A total of two (2) datasets were needed with respect to the second and third fine-tuning stages in the GECToR model's approach (Omelianchuk et al., 2020). A dataset creation algorithm was used to create the needed datasets using the corrupted sentences produced by the error automation algorithm.

The first dataset is intended for fine-tuning on error-filled sentences alone. The second dataset is intended for fine-tuning on both error-free and error-filled sentences. Each sentence in these datasets had its corrected counterpart as its label – even the error-free ones.

For each transformation tag, it was ensured that each tag was equally represented within the datasets. A 30,000 upper limit on the number of sentences under each transformation tag. However, there were certain tags that contained less than 30,000 sentences, since there was a lack of sentences needed in corrupting for those tags. This was a limitation with the data scraped. An example of this is the $REPLACE_*riyan* tag – which only had a total of 472 corrupted sentences. This is because the word *riyan* was not being used that much in the scraped news articles.

Furthermore, a 17:83 ratio was maintained between error-free and error-filled sentences for each transformation tag. This implies that, if applicable, a given transformation tag contains approximately 5,000 error-free and 25,000 error-filled sentences.

Dataset	Error-free Sentences	Error-filled Sentences	TOTAL
1	0	601,256	601,256
2	155,419	150,283	305,702
TOTAL	155,419	751,539	**906,958**

Table 4: Balarila dataset error-free and error-filled sentences composition

As for the two datasets, a 0:100 error-free and 80:20 error-filled ratio was established between the two. This results in an approximately equal number of error-free and error-filled sentences in Dataset 2. The actual number of sentences per dataset can be seen in Table 4. The whole Balarila dataset contains a total of 906,958 sentences.

The datasets were then split into three (3) subsets each: train, dev, and test with a 70:15:15 ratio of sentence distribution. As for the test sets, its sentences were further grouped according to: (1) its transformation tag and (2) whether it is grammatically correct or not. This is for the easier evaluation of the models under each tag.

Finally, for the distribution of errors, aside from the imposition of a 30,000-sentence cap, the dataset creation algorithm also goes through the sentences under each transformation tag and distributes the error-free and error-filled sentences onto the train, dev, and test subsets with respect to the aforementioned 0:100, 80:20, and 70:15:15 ratios. Since this splitting was performed for each transformation tag, this also ensures that each tag was split in the same manner. Thus, this also ensures better equality and representation for each tag.

3.7 Data Pre-processing

Before feeding the datasets into the models, each source-target pair of sentences were pre-processed first with respect to the pre-processing algorithm used in the GECToR (Omelianchuk et al., 2020) model. This is done to efficiently determine and attach the transformation tags needed to convert the source tokens into their corresponding target tokens.

3.8 Experiment Setup

To achieve the best-performing model, an experimental setup involving the three (3) transformer encoder models was prepared. Specifically, the BERT Tagalog Base (BERT-Base) (Cruz and Cheng, 2019), RoBERTa Tagalog Base (RoBERTa-Base) (Cruz and Cheng, 2021), and RoBERTa Tagalog Large (RoBERTa-Large) (Cruz and Cheng, 2021) models were fine-tuned and tested using the dataset discussed in Subsection 3.6. Furthermore, all of the models were fine-tuned and tested on an NVIDIA RTX A6000 GPU using the GECToR model's default fine-tuning and predicting hyperparameters.

3.9 Evaluation

To evaluate the GEC performance of the models, the precision, recall, and $F_{0.5}$ score metrics from the CoNLL-2014 Shared Task (Ng et al., 2014) were adopted.

For the models' GED performance, a multi-class confusion matrix was used and visualized with a heatmap. With the 39 pre-defined unique tags enumerated in Table 2, the task of the model was to classify the erroneous token in a sentence to its corresponding transformation tag. The lighter the color of the tile in the confusion matrix, the better the performance of the model in detecting errors.

The GED performance was tested on error-free and error-filled datasets separately. To determine the accuracy of the model on error-free sentences, the prediction should correspond with *'NO CHANGES'* since it is expected that the model should not make any corrections on these sentences. When the models are tested on the incorrect sentences, the accuracy is ascertained when the predicted tag matches the target tag.

4 Results & Analysis

The GEC performance results of the three (3) models are shown in Figure 3. In terms of precision, RoBERTa-Large obtained the highest score of 67.94 as illustrated in Figure 3a. On the other hand, Figure 3b shows the performances of the models in regard to recall where RoBERTa-Base and RoBERTa-Large achieved similar scores of 84.69 and 84.76 respectively. For the $F_{0.5}$ scores as displayed in Figure 3c, RoBERTa-Large also obtained the highest score of 70.75 in comparison to RoBERTa-Base's score of 69.00. Moreover, BERT-Base had the poorest performance in every GEC score among the three (3) models.

As for the GED performance of the three (3) models, Table 6 shows the summary of the results from the confusion matrices. These are the grouped average scores of the transformation tags per error type on both error-free and error-filled datasets.

As observed in Table 6a, all three (3) models faced difficulties in identifying errors associated with duplicate words, morphological errors, wrong use of punctuation marks, and missing words.

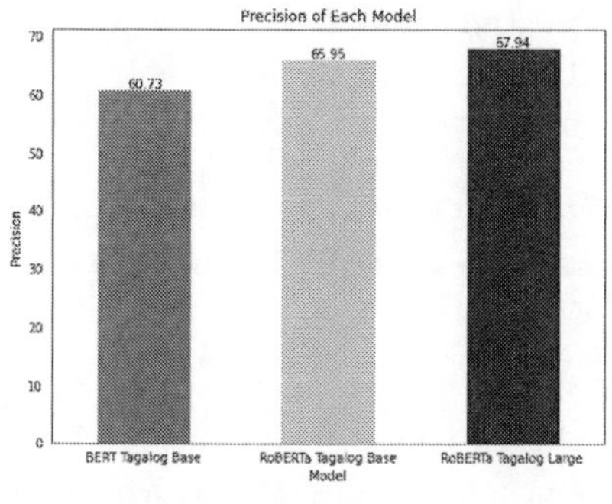

(a) Precision

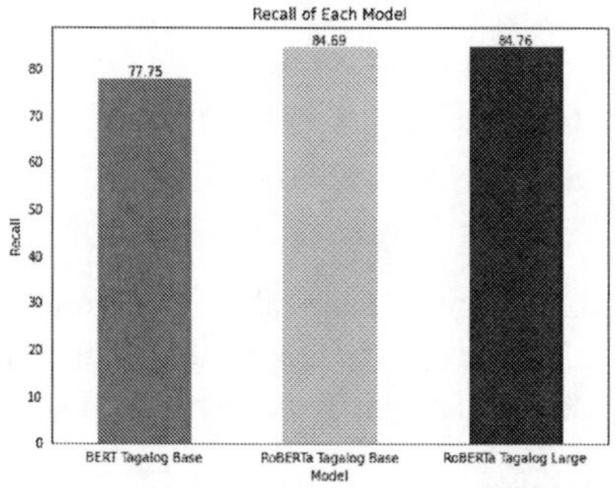

(b) Recall

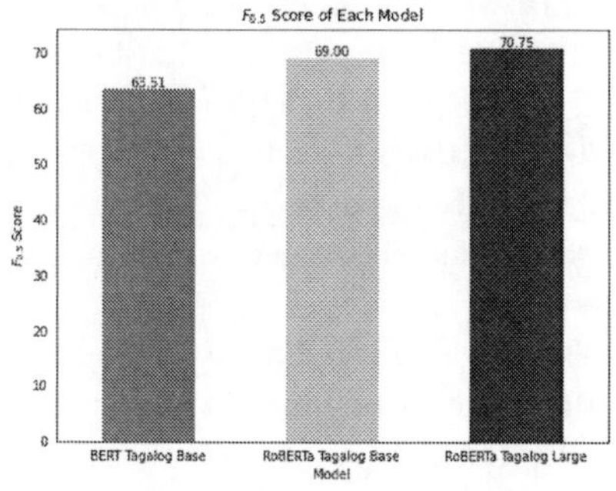

(c) $F_{0.5}$ Score

Figure 3: GEC Performance of the Three Models

The difficulty in detecting duplicate words may be attributed to the error automation algorithm used which is Word Duplication. The problem that may arise from this algorithm is the vagueness of the duplicated word in a sentence since there are no restrictions on when to duplicate a word. This may have resulted in a poor performance towards correcting errors related to Duplicate Words since the models would find it difficult to determine when to delete a word in a sentence given all the unique Filipino words it was introduced to.

For the morphological errors, its error automation randomly replaces a verb by either changing its aspect, focus, or both. With six (6) possible morphological transformations for a single Tagalog

Covered Errors	BERT-Base	RoBERTa-Base	RoBERTa-Large
Wrong Use of *nang* vs. *ng*	96.21%	96.86%	96.73%
Wrong Use of Enclitics	97.48%	87.43%	84.85%
Wrong Use of Hyphens	98.39%	98.61%	98.82%
Wrong Use of Spaces	98.82%	99.28%	99.35%
Duplicate Words	99.48%	98.95%	98.82%
Morphological Errors	91.59%	92.87%	91.61%
Additional Errors			
Wrong Use of Punctuation Marks	95.77%	94.78%	93.58%
Improper Word Casing	98.45%	98.32%	98.49%
Missing Words	98.04%	96.47%	96.99%
Wrong Use of *Ang* and *Ng* Pronouns	89.89%	96.91%	97.41%

(a) Error-Free Dataset

Covered Errors	BERT-Base	RoBERTa-Base	RoBERTa-Large
Wrong Use of *nang* vs. *ng*	94.31%	95.72%	96.45%
Wrong Use of Enclitics	97.24%	98.06%	95.66%
Wrong Use of Hyphens	89.83%	94.65%	93.84%
Wrong Use of Spaces	82.46%	88.42%	88.55%
Duplicate Words	61.31%	80.99%	79.12%
Morphological Errors	56.43%	71.87%	73.13%
Additional Errors			
Wrong Use of Punctuation Marks	67.51%	79.98%	80.76%
Improper Word Casing	93.52%	96.35%	96.31%
Missing Words	27.18%	48.73%	49.40%
Wrong Use of *Ang* and *Ng* Pronouns	95.53%	97.96%	97.78%

(a) Error-Filled Dataset

Table 6: Grouped GED Performance Results of the Three Models

verb, there are occurrences wherein the corrupted sentence may still be grammatically sound which can confuse the models. An example of this would be *'Tira nila ng bola kahapon.'* wherein it was expected that the words *Tira* and *ng* were replaced with *Tinira* and *ang* respectively. Instead, the models replaced *Tira* with *Tumira* and *nila* with *sila*, resulting in *'Tumira sila ng bola kahapon.'* which is still grammatically correct. This may have been the cause regarding the models' performances in this error type for both error-free and error-filled sentences.

Moreover, the models struggled in identifying the wrong use of punctuation marks specifically for EMARK transformation tags as there are no common indicators when a Filipino sentence should be ended with an exclamation mark. Although, the models performed well for the PERIOD and QMARK tags since the PERIOD tags are often used to end a sentence, and the QMARK tags are hinted by many words such as *sino*, *saan*, *ano*, *bakit*, and *ba*, which EMARK does not have. An example of this would be *'Ang galing naman niya.'* wherein it was expected for the models to replace the period with an exclamation mark. However, the models did not perform the correction and treated the sentence as non-erroneous, which is still correct.

For the missing words error, the error automation algorithm used for this error type is Word Deletion which had similar issues with Word Duplication. With all the unique Filipino words it learned to add to the sentence, the models also struggled with adding the appropriate Filipino word given the context of the sentence. This also caused the models to obtain a lower score in this error type.

It was also discovered that some scraped sentences were already erroneous before even going through the error automation pipeline. An example of this are sentences that incorrectly used enclitics - which were fixed in the data cleaning pipeline. However, for the other unaddressed errors, it went through the error automation pipeline with the assumption that it was grammatically correct. As such, there may be some corrupted sentences within the dataset that contain more than one (1) errors. This could have potentially affected the results of the study in a variety of ways such as:

- **A model being able to correct the unexpected error.** Though this may be more practical in real-world uses, this would result in lower performance scores for the model in the context of this study. This is because the gold standard edits assumed that the only errors that the corrupted sentences had were the ones introduced by the error automation pipeline.

- **A model being mistakenly taught that the erroneous sentence is correct.** This could potentially lead to more confusion for the models - mainly due to the inconsistencies with how correct and incorrect sentences are being presented to it. Though this would result in better performance scores in the context of this study, this is not practical when it comes to real-world usage.

There was also an inconsistency towards correcting the same erroneous sentence when more errors were added. An example of this is when given the erroneous sentence *'Ang ado bo ay kinain niya kahapon.'*, wherein the words *ado* and *bo* must be merged together, this will not be corrected by the models anymore when the period ('.') is removed from the erroneous sentence. The inconsistency might have been caused by the dataset's lack of instances to represent the same error in a different setting. In the case of the example sentence, the dataset did not have enough instances to represent the error in sentences without a period at the end. Solving this issue is challenging with the current error automation since only one error was introduced per corrupted sentence.

Overall, RoBERTa-Large was the best model for the Filipino GEC task. Even though BERT-Base and RoBERTa-Base outperformed RoBERTa-Large in some error types as observed in the GED results, RoBERTa-Large generally performed better than them in terms of the GEC scores. This means that when it comes to producing corrections, RoBERTa-Large's outputs were the closest to the gold-standard sentences in the dataset compared to BERT-Base and RoBERTa-Base's outputs.

However, RoBERTa-Large often encountered memory issues during training which caused some modifications to the model's training parameters. The parameter adjustments were necessary due to the lack of available GPU Memory (VRAM) which caused the model's fine-tuning to abruptly terminate intermittently. Such problems were less recurring for BERT-Base and RoBERTa-Base since these two models are smaller in size. With this, RoBERTa-Base was the most cost-effective model since it only had a 1.75% $F_{0.5}$ score difference in comparison to RoBERTa-Large despite utilizing fewer resources during training.

5 Conclusion & Recommendations

In this study, a proof-of-concept deep learning-based model named Balarila was built to detect and correct grammatical errors in the Filipino language effectively. With the adoption of GECToR (Omelianchuk et al., 2020)'s approach, three (3) Balarila models were created and fine-tuned for the task. Each model utilized the open-source pre-trained BERT Tagalog Base (BERT-Base) (Cruz and Cheng, 2019), RoBERTa Tagalog Base (RoBERTa-Base) (Cruz and Cheng, 2021), and RoBERTa Tagalog Large (RoBERTa-Large) (Cruz and Cheng, 2021) transformer encoder models respectively.

Furthermore, an error automation pipeline was also built to create a synthetic dataset of grammatically incorrect Filipino sentences. It was then utilized in fine-tuning and testing the three (3) Balarila models. Two (2) fine-tuning stages from GECToR (Omelianchuk et al., 2020) were adopted: first on a dataset of error-filled sentences then on a dataset of both error-filled and error-free sentences. The created datasets can also be used as a benchmark for Filipino grammar error detection and correction.

However, there are several limitations to this study. First is the coverage of errors. The grammatical errors that Balarila only covers are as follows: duplicate words, morphological errors, wrong use of *nang* vs. *ng*, wrong use of spaces, wrong use of hyphens, wrong use of enclitics, wrong use of punctuation marks, improper word casing, missing words, and wrong use of *ang* and *ng* pronouns.

Another limitation is the rule-based error automation. The generation of a synthetic dataset for this study was hindered by a number of problems such as the vagueness of Word Duplication and Word Deletion algorithms used for the duplicate and missing word errors.

Several recommendations are suggested based on this study's scope and findings. With the limited types of errors covered by Balarila, the first recommendation is greater error coverage. It is recommended that future researchers cover more Filipino grammatical errors in order to produce a more robust and comprehensive model.

The next recommendation is to introduce a more sophisticated error automation algorithm that will improve the performance towards the four (4) error types wherein Balarila performed poorly, as well as resolve the inconsistency towards correcting the same erroneous sentence. An example of this is to target specific words which commonly trigger duplicate and missing words errors, which could be determiners like *ang* and *mga*. Another is to introduce multiple errors upon corrupting a sentence, which was not done.

The use of real data for building and training a GEC model for the Filipino language could also help to remove the bias or inaccuracy that may have been caused by the error automation. As Balarila was trained on a synthetically generated dataset, future researchers are recommended to use a dataset collected from real-world sources in order to represent the actual diversity of data and produce more accurate corrections.

It is also recommended to perform hyperparameter tuning. As an alternative to increasing the dataset size, hyperparameter tuning can also help to improve the model's performance by finding the optimal values for the hyperparameters used during training and prediction. It can also possibly reduce training time, increase model robustness by making it less sensitive to changes in the data, and improve the model's generalization of the data to produce more accurate corrections. In short, conducting hyperparameter tuning can lead to a significant improvement in the model's GEC and GED performance.

Acknowledgements

This research is funded by the Philippine Department of Science and Technology through its 2021 Junior Level Science Scholarships MERIT program.

References

Shamil Chollampatt and Hwee Tou Ng. 2018. A multi-layer convolutional encoder-decoder neural network for grammatical error correction. In *Proceedings of the Thirty-Second AAAI Conference on Artificial Intelligence*. Association for Computational Linguistics.

Jan Christian Blaise Cruz and Charibeth Cheng. 2019. Evaluating language model finetuning techniques for low-resource languages.

Jan Christian Blaise Cruz and Charibeth Cheng. 2021. Improving large-scale language models and resources for filipino. *arXiv preprint arXiv:2111.06053*.

Jacob Devlin, Ming-Wei Chang, Kenton Lee, and Kristina Toutanova. 2018. Bert: Pre-training of deep bidirectional transformers for language understanding. *Proceedings of the 2019 Conference of the North American Chapter of the Association for Computational Linguistics: Human Language Technologies*, 1:4171–4186.

Muhammad Ali Ghufron and Fathia Rosyida. 2018. The role of grammarly in assessing english as a foreign language (efl) writing. *Lingua Cultura*.

Matthew Philip Go, Nicco Nocon, and Allan Borra. 2017. Gramatika: A grammar checker for the low-resourced filipino language. In *TENCON 2017 - 2017 IEEE Region 10 Conference*.

Matthew Phillip Go and Allan Borra. 2016. Developing an unsupervised grammar checker for Filipino using hybrid n-grams as grammar rules. pages 105–113.

Roman Grundkiewicz, Marcin Junczys-Dowmunt, and Kenneth Heafield. 2019. Neural grammatical error correction systems with unsupervised pre-training on synthetic data. In *Proceedings of the Fourteenth Workshop on Innovative Use of NLP for Building Educational Applications*, pages 252–263.

Kalpana Jayavalan and Abu Bakar Razali. 2018. Effectiveness of online grammar checker to improve secondary students' english narrative essay writing. *International Research Journal of Education and Sciences (IRJES)*.

Diederik P. Kingma and Jimmy Ba. 2015. Adam: A method for stochastic optimization.

Komisyon sa Wikang Filipino. 2013. *Ortograpiyang Pambansa*. Accessed: 2022/10/17.

Hwee Tou Ng, Siew Mei Wu, Ted Briscoe, Christian Hadiwinoto, Raymond Hendy Susanto, and Christopher Bryant. 2014. The conll-2014 shared task on grammatical error correction. In *Proceedings of the Eighteenth Conference on Computational Natural Language Learning: Shared Task*, pages 1–14.

Manolito Octaviano, Matthew Phillip Go, Allan Borra, and Nathaniel Oco. 2016. A corpus-based analysis of filipino writing errors. In *2016 International Conference on Asian Language Processing (IALP)*, pages 95–98.

Kostiantyn Omelianchuk, Vitaliy Atrasevych, Artem Chernodub, and Oleksandr Skurzhanskyi. 2020. GECToR – grammatical error correction: Tag, not rewrite. In *Proceedings of the Fifteenth Workshop on Innovative Use of NLP for Building Educational Applications*, pages 163–170, Seattle, WA, USA → Online. Association for Computational Linguistics.

Aiman Solyman, Wang Zhenyu, Tao Qian, Arafat Abdulgader Mohammed Elhag, Muhammad Toseef, and Zeinab Aleibeid. 2021. Synthetic data with neural machine translation for automatic correction in arabic grammar. *Egyptian Informatics Journal*, 22(3):303–315.

Utilizing Weak Supervision to Generate Indonesian Conservation Datasets

Mega Fransiska
mega.fransiska@datasaur.ai

Diah Pitaloka
diah.pitaloka@datasaur.ai

Saripudin
saripudin@datasaur.ai

Satrio Putra
satrio.putra@datasaur.ai

Lintang Sutawika*
lintang@eleuther.ai*

Datasaur.ai

***Eleuther.ai**

Abstract

Weak supervision has emerged as a promising approach for rapid and large-scale dataset creation in response to the increasing demand for accelerated NLP development. By leveraging labeling functions, weak supervision allows practitioners to generate datasets quickly by creating learned label models that produce soft-labeled datasets. This paper aims to show how such an approach can be utilized to build an Indonesian NLP dataset from conservation news text. We construct two types of datasets: multi-label classification and sentiment classification. We then provide baseline experiments using various pretrained language models. These baseline results demonstrate test performances of 59.79% accuracy and 55.72% F1-score for sentiment classification, 66.87% F1-score-macro, 71.5% F1-score-micro, and 83.67% ROC-AUC for multi-label classification. Additionally, we release the datasets and labeling functions used in this work for further research and exploration.

Keywords: multi-label classification, sentiment classification, weak supervision

1 Introduction

Labeled datasets play a crucial role in Natural Language Processing (NLP) tasks. However, generating large-scale labeled datasets with high quality remains a significant challenge. In addressing this challenge, weak supervision has emerged as a promising approach (Ratner et al., 2016; Zhang et al., 2022) to create labeled datasets by leveraging weak classifiers and aggregating their outputs into noisy labels that approximate the unobserved ground truth. Empirical studies (Ratner et al., 2019, 2020; Ren et al., 2020; Lan et al., 2020; Lison et al., 2021) have demonstrated the competitiveness of this approach compared to manual data collection processes. Additionally, benchmarks (Zhang et al., 2021) have been established to further evaluate new weak-supervision approaches.

The idea of weak supervision methods to create datasets is something that can be useful for under-resourced languages such as Indonesian. The current approach to manually label every sample is a painful process that realistically results in relatively small amounts of data when budgets are limited. Another approach could be crowdsourcing (Cahyawijaya et al., 2022), but this approach rests upon many contributors whose quality or theme can be vastly different. To add more resources from downstream tasks in the Indonesian language, we seek to build datasets at larger sizes by using weak supervision.

In this paper, we utilize Datasaur's weak supervision framework, Data programming, to facilitate the creation of multiple diverse Indonesian downstream datasets with conservation as the overarching theme. Our focus is leveraging the Mongabay conservation news dataset into two NLP tasks: multi-label classification and sentiment classification. We construct a hashtag classification dataset for multi-label classification, considering the importance of hashtag classification in organizing and enhancing searchability and granularity in editorial realm[1]. Then, we also use utilize hashtag classification dataset to build sentiment classification dataset by categorizing groups of hashtags into related sentiment categories (positive, neutral, negative). For building both datasets (hashtag classification and sentiment classification), we employ a range of simple labeling functions (Ratner et al., 2020) through Datasaur's Data Programming.

Our methodology encompasses dataset construction, weak-labeled dataset learnability experiments through various BERT pre-trained models, and performance analysis of labeling functions. We

* Work completed in Datasaur.ai

[1] https://whatsnewinpublishing.com/the-importance-of-tags-in-online-news-media/

Proceedings of the First Workshop in South East Asian Language Processing, pages 30–54
November 1, 2023.

further elaborate our approach, outlining dataset and labeling functions collections, along with the associated benefits and constraints.

2 Related Work

Weak Supervision. Machine learning requires a large amount of labeled data, which can be costly and difficult to scale. To reduce the cost of building a dataset, weak supervision uses a heuristic approach to generate a training set with noisy labels from multiple sources (Ratner et al., 2016, 2020; Alexander et al., 2022). The result is a dataset with probabilities as labels or what can be called soft labels. The idea behind this approach is to encode knowledge from experts into labeling functions. These labeling functions serve as a weak classifier where they individually cannot yield a good prediction but when used in tandem with many other label functions can be an effective approximation to the unobserved ground truth. The process is then concluded with a generative model that aims to model the labeling functions by taking into account the agreement and disagreement between labeling functions (Ratner et al., 2016, 2020; Alexander et al., 2022) (later on, this generative model will be called **label model**). The output of a label model is a noisy signal that estimates the true labels which can be used to predict the soft-labels of a sample. The results have shown considerable gains and are highly applicable in real-world industries for reducing the cost of hand-labeled data (Ratner et al., 2016, 2020).

These related works used (Ratner et al., 2016) version of weak supervision to build training sets. In Ratner et al. (2016), experiments were conducted using the 2014 TAC-KBP Slot Filling dataset. The results achieved 6 F1 points over a state-of-the-art LSTM. In another study, weak supervision was used to build the ORCAS dataset for user intent classification tasks (Alexander et al., 2022). The ORCAS dataset consists of query ID, query, document ID, and clicked URL. To label the dataset, a 2-million sample of data was used. The researchers conducted experiments with machine learning models and evaluated the results. The findings indicated competitive results and high efficiency in real-world problems, where labeling functions can be easily executed for every query issued. Finally, a user study showed that using the pipeline of a weak supervision framework can increase predictive performance even faster than seven hours of hand labeling (Ratner et al., 2020).

Sentiment Classification. Sentiment classification is a classification task to extract the polarity or sentiment expression in text (Davidov et al., 2010). Several works used data from social media, such as Twitter, for classification tasks and leveraged the hashtags as additional features alongside the content of the tweet (Davidov et al., 2010; Devi et al., 2019; Diao et al., 2023).
(Davidov et al., 2010) proposed a supervised sentiment classification framework using Twitter tags and 15 smileys as features. The results showed good performance in labeling data without manual annotation. Another study (Devi et al., 2019) explored the hashtag and content tweets to predict which hashtags will become trending in the future. By using machine learning approaches, hashtags as features contribute the better results of the model. Also (Diao et al., 2023) uses hashtags to provide auxiliary signals to get labels for the data. They generated hashtags from input text to produce new input for the model, with meaningful hashtags. The hashtag generator uses an encoder and decoder to predict the hashtags, and the results showed significant improvements in tweet classification tasks.

Multi-Label Classification. In comparison to other text classification research, the field of multi-label classification remains relatively underexplored. Nonetheless, it constitutes a valuable NLP task for extracting metadata from extensive textual datasets, like research papers and articles. For instance, Li and Ou (2021) leveraged a KNN-based model to address the challenges posed by multi-label classification in the context of research papers.

3 Building Dataset Using Weak Supervision

Building large datasets using weak supervision has been demonstrated to be effective and of high quality in many studies. For instance, in a recent study by Tekumalla and Banda (2022), they curated a silver standard dataset (samples of raw data sources that have good enough quality to be trained, which were collected and cleaned using weak supervision heuristics) for natural disasters using weak supervision. Similarly, another study by Painter et al. (2022) utilized weak supervision to create a silver-standard sarcasm-annotated dataset (S3D)

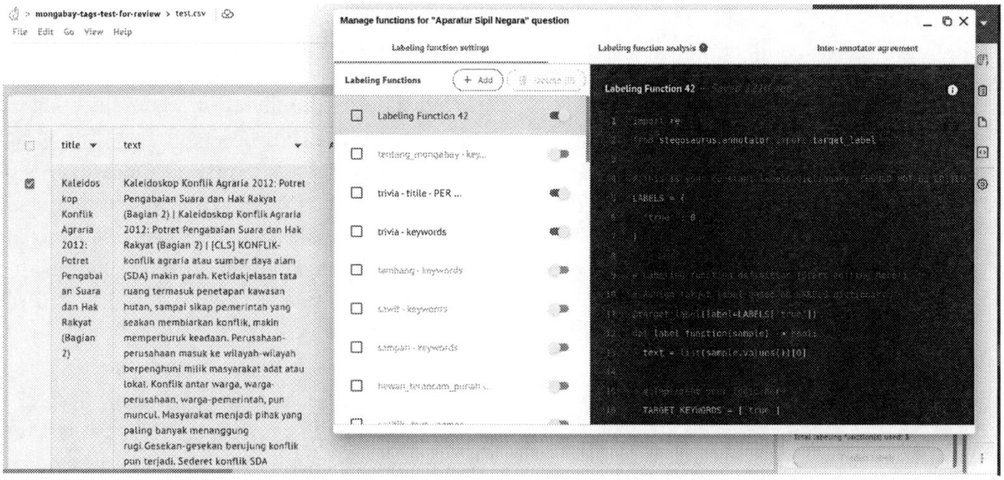

Figure 1: Integrated Labeling function editor in Datasaur workspace

containing over 100,000 tweets. This approach holds great promise for expanding the availability of labeled datasets, facilitating the development of more accurate and robust machine learning models.

Our research is focused on curating Indonesian conservation datasets using a weak supervision framework, which has been adapted from Snorkel's works (Ratner et al., 2016, 2020; Alexander et al., 2022). To make the process as user-friendly as possible, we have developed interactive weak supervision tools, known as Data Programming, in Datasaur[2] workspace. Our Data Programming is integrated with a simple code editor in the workspace, which allows users to create labeling functions interactively (figure 1). We've also provided a Python labeling function template, as detailed in A.1. The predictions generated by each labeling function are processed in the background by a label model (Ratner et al., 2019).

Our Data Programming returns two types of results: probability outputs, which are used as soft labels in the fine-tuning process, and hard-label predictions. These hard-label predictions can be reviewed and revised by human annotators directly in our workspace. In this work, we use the probability results in our training set and revise the hard-label prediction for validation and test set, as our **golden-set**.

3.1 Dataset Source

We collect articles from the Indonesian conservation news collection, Mongabay[3], in 2012 - 2023 period. The raw dataset was sampled from either the first or last 100 articles in each year. These articles were then segmented into multiple chunks, with each chunk containing a maximum of 512 tokens, The format for each data point is as follows:

```
{title} ; {chunked-article}
```

This process resulted in a total of 4896 chunked articles, which were split into 3919, 492, and 485 chunked articles as training set, validation set, and test set respectively.

3.2 Task

We categorized the scraped dataset into two primary tasks: multi-label classification and sentiment classification. The multi-label classification task aimed to depict the distribution of hashtags within the dataset. On the other hand, the sentiment classification task was undertaken to gauge the sentiment of the authors, which was still embedded in the articles. For the sentiment classification task, we constructed it based on the hashtag distribution dataset, as previously employed in these works (Devi et al., 2019; Davidov et al., 2010).

We defined 31 classes for the hashtag classification task and 3 classes for the sentiment classification task. The 31 tags were collected by our labelers through an internal analysis of popular environmental and news topics among Indonesian

[2] https://datasaur.ai/

[3] https://www.mongabay.co.id/

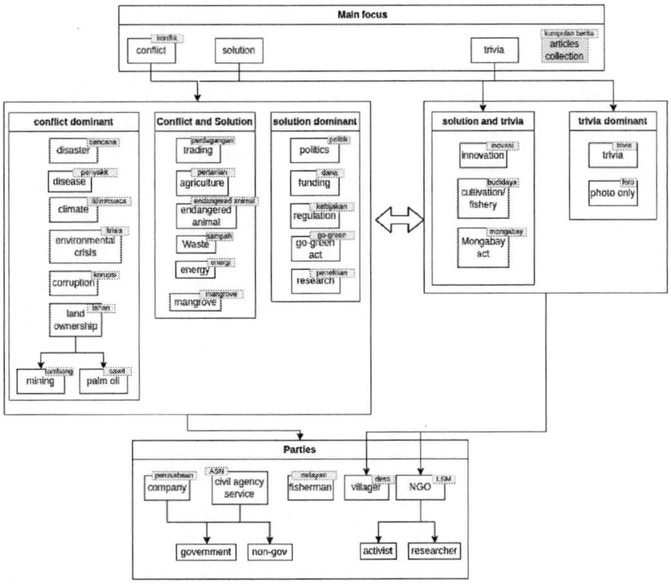

Figure 2: The representation of 31 tags in our dataset; yellow box is our tag label and green box is special class because the article consists of many different articles.

citizens, as shown in Figure 2. We acknowledge that this approach heavily depends on the knowledge and personal experience of the labelers in the field of conservation news and environmental topics. The subsequent section (Section 3.3) will offer more comprehensive insights into the dataset construction.

3.3 Dataset Construction

As mentioned in Section 3, our data programming generates hard labels and probability labels. In this work, our strategy involves using data programming for labeling the entire dataset, including the training, validation, and test sets. We use the probability outputs as our training set, while our validation and test sets use hard-label outputs that have been reviewed and revised by human annotators, forming our **golden-set**.
When reviewing the hard-label predictions, our labelers follow this simple guideline:

- **Hashtag Classification**: A hashtag is assigned to a chunked article if it is discussed in the text, even if it's mentioned as a side effect.
- **sentiment Classification**: Chunked articles are labeled as follows: 1) **negative:** If they mention any conflict or victims. 2) **neutral:** If there is no discernible sentiment tone, the article is purely descriptive, OR it contains both a conflict and its resolution. 3) **positive:** If the article discusses trivia topics or initiatives aimed at solving environmental issues.

The dataset construction processes for both hashtag classification and sentiment classification involve three key steps: **labeling function construction**, **labeling function analysis**, and **label model and final prediction**.

3.3.1 Labeling Function Construction

The labeling functions used in this study are based on collected keywords from the labeler's perspective. In certain cases, additional rules and logic were added to augment the labeling functions. For the hashtag classification task, labelers gathered relevant keywords for each collected hashtag. In the sentiment classification task, the labeling functions relied on aggregated tags on each article corresponding to positive, neutral, or negative labels.

For the sentiment classification task, we developed two versions of labeling functions: the default version, v0, which was used in the main experiment, and v1 which has more specific logic. The detailed methodology for building labeling functions in the tags classification task and sentiment classification task undertaken in this work is presented in Appendix A.1.

3.3.2 Labeling Function Analysis

To evaluate the performance of sentiment classification labeling functions, we used coverage, overlaps, and conflict statistics, which have been defined in Ratner et al. (2016). However, in tags classification, we only utilize coverage score to represent the density of tags in each article, as other metrics such as overlaps and conflict did not adequately reflect the quality of the labeling functions.

As discussed in Section 3.3.1, for the sentiment classification task, we developed v1 labeling functions with more specific logic. This resulted in higher level of inter-independence among the labeling functions, leading to lower coverage and conflict scores (Table 1). Notably, the v1 labeling functions exhibited a significantly smaller percentage of conflict/coverage (2.9%) compared to v0 (32%).

As highlighted in Ratner et al. (2016), the statistical performance of the labeling functions directly impacts the quality of the final label prediction and the performance of fine-tuned models. Hence, we conducted experiments and analyzed the influence of the quality of two labeling function versions (v0: prioritizing coverage score; v1: prioritizing less conflict) for the sentiment classification task, as analyzed in section 4.4.1.

Task	LFs Vars	Cov	Over	Conf
Sentiment	**v0**	**21.03**	**18.21**	**6.72**
	v1	10.63	11.37	4.41
Tags	-	12.35	-	-

Table 1: The performance of the labeling functions varied for each task(sentiment and tags classification). Sentiment classification labeling functions were evaluated based on coverage, overlaps, and conflict statistics. v0: prioritizing coverage score; v1: prioritizing less conflict. While tags classification labeling functions only evaluated on coverage score, which represented the density of tags

3.3.3 Label Model and Final Prediction

We employed two types of label models in this study: the Covariance Matrix-based label model, adapted from Snorkel (Ratner et al., 2016), and the Majority Voter. The main difference between them lies in their process. The Covariance Matrix requires initial training to generate the final labels using learned weights, whereas the majority voter directly predicts the final labels based on the distribution of labeling function predictions. The hyperparameters used in training Covariance Matrix label model will be provided in Table 6

4 Experiments

4.1 Constructed Dataset

From the gold-label distribution (Figure 3), it can be inferred that the sampled Mongabay articles have a bias towards negative sentiment, which is distributed to the entire tags. Refer to (fig 2), all tags from **conflict** are predominantly associated with negative articles, while a few tags from **trivia** and **solution** are more commonly found in positive articles, and other tags from **conflict and solution** were majorly included in neutral articles. It is worth noting that, each article can match with more than one tag considering the varies of author's writing style. **For example:** one article with negative sentiment can have various tags such as *go-green*, *konflik*, *korupsi*, *LSM*, which indicates the article discusses conflicts in go-green action/regulation, highlights corruption issues, and mentions the involvement of LSM (NGOs).

The format of the experimental dataset for training, validation, and testing can be seen in Table 2. Additionally, the constructed dataset, as well as the raw dataset, can be accessed in `https://huggingface.co/datasets/Datasaur/mongabay-experiment`.

4.2 Pipelines

The experiment pipelines have two main goals: 1) To compare the performance of the covariance matrix and the majority voter-generated dataset for each task, and 2) To assess the performance of different BERT pre-trained models with varying language bases when fine-tuned using the weak dataset. This comparison enables an evaluation of the effectiveness of different approaches to weak supervision for various NLP tasks.

To accomplish these objectives, the experiment pipeline is structured as follows:

- Each variation of the pre-trained models will be trained using the soft-label dataset (both the covariance matrix and the majority voter version).
- The models will be iteratively evaluated using the gold-label validation set at each epoch.
- The weight configuration yielding the best validation metrics will be tested using the gold-label test set.

This pipeline was executed for both the tags classification and sentiment classification tasks.

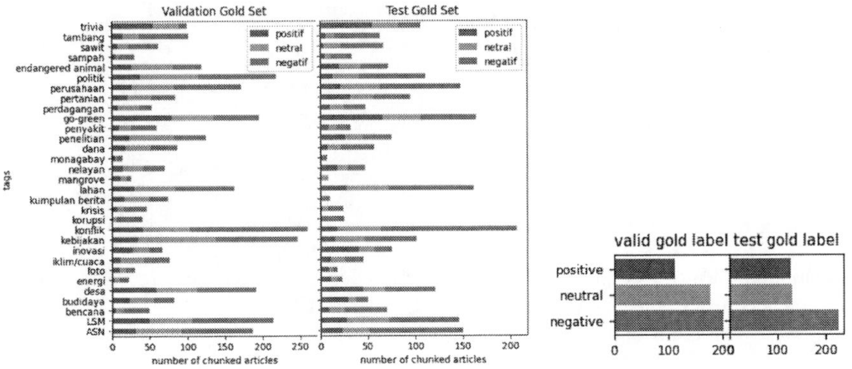

Figure 3: Distribution of validation and test set gold label for tags classification (left) and sentiment classification (right). Detailed explanation about tags definition was provided in Appendix A.3

Input	Soft-label
Pandemi, Momentum ... | [CLS] Hutan adalah gudang...	[0.108, 0.001, 0.001, ...

Input	Soft-label
Pandemi, Momentum ... | [CLS] Hutan adalah gudang...	[1.0, 1.44e-09, 1.32e-09]

Input	ASN	Desa	Konflik
Begini Nasib ... | [CLS] Maliau ingin ...	NaN	True	True

Input	Label
Begini Nasib ... | [CLS] Maliau ingin ...	negative

Table 2: Snippet of constructed dataset (top-bottom): **1:** train set sample with 31 probabilities as soft-label for tags classification experiment **2:** train set sample with 3 probabilities as soft-label for sentiment classification experiment **3:** validation set sample with 31 tags in binary label for tags classification experiment **4:** validation set sample with single-class for sentiment classification experiment

4.3 Finetuning

We utilized various BERT variations from HuggingFace's pretrained language models: `indobert-base-uncased`[4], `bert-base-multilingual-cased`[5], and `bert-base-cased`[6]. We employed these models to assess the performance of our weakly labeled dataset when learned by three distinct models: 1) Indonesian monolingual (pre-trained with the same language as our data), 2) Multilingual (pre-trained with multiple languages, including the same language as our data), 3) English monolingual (pre-trained with a language different from our data).

In finetuning hashtag classification, we utilized cross-entropy loss instead of binary-cross-entropy loss. However, in the inference session, we keep using binary-cross-entropy loss. This decision is based on the soft-label distribution of the training set obtained from the weak supervision process, which is not binary for each class, in contrast to the binary distribution of the gold labels in the validation and test sets. We utilize the hyperparameter setup outlined in (Table 7) for the fine-tuning of each task.

4.4 Analysis

The experiment results were analyzed from two key perspectives: 1) Label model comparison perspective, and 2) Dataset learnability.

From the perspective of dataset learnability, the Learning process went well by the Indobert pretrained model, represented by significantly better performance compared to the Multilingual BERT (mbert) and BERT Base models, as evident in the results presented in Table 3, Figure 4, and Table 5 In the context of label model comparison, the results vary between multi-label and sentiment classification tasks. For sentiment classification (as

[4]`https://huggingface.co/indolem/indobert-base-uncased`

[5]`https://huggingface.co/bert-base-multilingual-cased`

[6]`https://huggingface.co/bert-base-cased`

PreModel	Aggr	Acc (Val)	F1 (Val)	Acc (Test)	F1 (Test)
indobert	CM	60.77	56.37	59.79	55.72
	MV	58.74	53.97	58.97	54.12
mbert	CM	55.08	50.25	50.93	44.16
	MV	55.89	42.45	49.9	38.25
bert	CM	46.16	36.43	44.74	35.83
	MV	44.51	34.55	42.68	33.22

Table 3: Validation and test results from sentiment classification experiment, use labeling functions v0. The performance was gained from a model with the best validation score. **CM**: using Covariance Matrix as label model; **MV**: using Majority Voter as label model

LFs var	cov	over	conf	ACC (Val)	F1 (Val)	ACC test	F1 test
v0	21.03	18.21	6.72	60.77	56.37	59.79	55.72
v1	6.9	2.31	0.21	56.71	45.27	50.31	40.49

Table 4: Validation and test results from sentiment classification labeling function variations experiment using indobert and Covariance Matrix. High coverage (v0), even with high conflict, gives the best performance than more precise and accurate labeling functions result (v1)

shown in Table 3), the Covariance Matrix (CM) approximates the human judgment (gold label) more accurately. In contrast, Majority Voter (MV) predictions are more closely correlated with the gold label in multi-label classification, as indicated in Table 5.

4.4.1 Sentiment Classification

The highest performance, reaching 60% accuracy and a 56% F1-score (macro average), was achieved by utilizing the Covariance Matrix label model in conjunction with the Indobert pre-trained model, as shown in Table 3.

Detailed sentiment classification F1-scores for each label (refer to Appendix A.2.1) reveal that our fine-tuned models (Indobert and Multilingual-Bert) exhibit a tendency to predict negative articles accurately, with F1-scores exceeding 70%. This observation aligns with our dataset's characteristic (Figure 3), where negative articles are prominently distributed. However, Indobert faces challenges when predicting articles associated with the positive or neutral class, resulting in F1-scores hovering around 40%. This could be attributed to the similarity between positive and neutral-related tags (Figure 3).

Indobert also exhibits a faster learnability rate compared to other pretrained models, supported by the loss graph in Figure 4. The comparison between training and evaluation losses indicates that Indobert's loss fits well, while Multilingual-Bert displays signs of overfitting around the 15th epoch, and Bert-Base encounters difficulties in learning the dataset from the outset. Additionally, our sup-

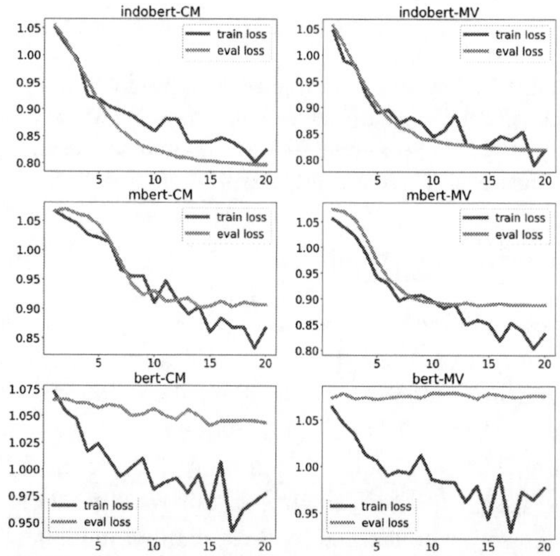

Figure 4: Train-eval loss graph of sentiment classification finetuning on 3 pre-trained models and 2 label models. **Left:** Loss graph of CovarianceMatrix across indobert, multilingual-bert (mbert), bert-base (bert) (top-bottom). **Right:** Loss graph of MajorityVoter across indobert, multilingual-bert (mbert), bert-base (bert) (top-bottom)

plementary experiment explores how the quality of labeling functions affects model performance. As shown in Table 4, despite LFs v0 having ten times higher conflict proportion compared to LFs v1, the v0 labeling functions significantly outperform v1 in fine-tuned models. This suggests that higher cov-

PreModel	Aggr	R/A (Val)	F1-ma (Val)	F1-mi (Val)	R/A (Test)	F1-ma (Test)	F1-mi (Test)
indobert	CM	82.93	73.33	78.3	81.89	65.71	69.9
	MV	85.61	76.39	81.7	83.67	66.87	71.5
mbert	CM	81.16	69.86	75	80.01	62.18	66.8
	MV	85.14	75.49	80.7	82.85	64.95	70.2
bert	CM	70.07	47.07	55	69.56	44.45	49.2
	MV	73.34	53.25	61.23	73.16	51.96	55.4

Table 5: Validation and test results from tags classification experiment. The performance was gained from a model with the best validation score. **CM**: Using Covariance Matrix as label model; **MV**: Using Majority Voter as label model. **R/A**:ROC-AUC; **F1-ma**: F1-score macro average; **F1-mi**: F1-score micro average

erage and overlaps contribute to enhanced performance in fine-tuned models, even in the presence of increased conflict. This finding is consistent with the statement in Ratner et al. (2020) that higher coverage results in higher accuracy.

4.4.2 Tags Classification

The tags classification results are depicted in micro-average F1-score and ROC-AUC due to the imbalanced distribution of tags in our dataset (Figure 3). As stated earlier in Section 4.4, Majority Voter (MV) consistently outperforms the Covariance Matrix (CM) by approximately 2-3%. This aligns with the findings in Zhang et al. (2021), which reported that Majority Voters as the label model achieved superior performance when dealing with sparse labels in tags classification. The highest performance is observed when using Majority Voter as the label model and Indobert for finetuning, resulting in a test performance of 81.89% ROC-AUC, 65.71% F1-score$_{macro_average}$, and 69.9% F1-score$_{micro_average}$.

A more detailed analysis of tags classification F1-scores for each label is provided in Appendix A.2.1. Tags associated with negative sentiment achieve F1-scores exceeding 70% with either Indobert or Multilingual-Bert. In contrast, tags primarily composed of non-negative sentiment classes do not perform as effectively. This result aligns with the sentiment classification results.

Since we utilize different losses during training and inference sessions, we cannot compare the train and eval loss in a single frame (Section 4.3).

5 Limitations

Our dataset construction using weak supervision relies heavily on our labelers' subjectivity, particularly in collecting hashtags and creating labeling functions. These functions are designed to match the unique characteristics of our dataset, and their effectiveness may not extend well to other datasets, even with similar characteristics. The low results in our experiments are attributed to biases within the dataset. However, these biases provide insights into the Indonesian environmental and conservation editorial landscape, albeit presenting challenges for future efforts in creating more equitable datasets.

Although our data programming is primarily designed for single/multi-class classification, through this work it can be utilized for multi-label classification due to the one-hot-encoded output format. However, we have not yet implemented any metrics for evaluating labeling function performance, aside from coverage, which represents the dataset's labeling density.

6 Conclusion

In conclusion, we've presented our weak supervision pipeline for creating two datasets: sentiment classification and multi-label classification. We utilized Mongabay conservation articles collection to construct our datasets and adapted Snorkel's framework in Datasaur's workspace for conducting this work. Our results show that utilizing Data Programming to curate datasets can deliver qualified datasets that are learnable by BERT pre-trained models, especially indobert. However, some limitations remain, such as labeling function subjectivity, incomplete multi-label classification labeling function metrics, and the implicit bias within this dataset. Future work will curate more datasets more robustly and reproducibly, especially for NLP datasets with underrepresented language, topic, or task.

Ethics Statement

We acknowledge the presence of implicit biases in both our dataset source and the constructed dataset. Additionally, as we utilized news datasets, they may contain certain viewpoints from editors or journalists. It is ensured that the dataset is free from harmful or offensive content, biases may still exist in our model and results. As a news dataset, it contains formal Indonesian-native content.

Acknowledgements

We extend our heartfelt gratitude to Datasaur.ai[7] for their generous financial and resource support, which was instrumental in making this research possible. Their assistance provided us with essential resources, especially computational support, and allowed us to collaborate with experts in the field. We sincerely appreciate the entire team at Datasaur.ai for their invaluable support and partnership throughout this study.

We would also thank Mongabay[8] conservation portal for providing the dataset used in this study. The extensive collection of articles rich in Indonesian environmental subjects, issues, and concerns really helps in curating our Indonesian NLP dataset based on real-world conditions.

References

Daria Alexander, Wojciech Kusa, and Arjen P. de Vries. 2022. Orcas-i: Queries annotated with intent using weak supervision. In *Proceedings of the 45th International ACM SIGIR Conference on Research and Development in Information Retrieval*. ACM.

Samuel Cahyawijaya, Holy Lovenia, Alham Fikri Aji, Genta Indra Winata, Bryan Wilie, Rahmad Mahendra, Christianto Wibisono, Ade Romadhony, Karissa Vincentio, Fajri Koto, Jennifer Santoso, David Moeljadi, Cahya Wirawan, Frederikus Hudi, Ivan Halim Parmonangan, Ika Alfina, Muhammad Satrio Wicaksono, Ilham Firdausi Putra, Samsul Rahmadani, Yulianti Oenang, Ali Akbar Septiandri, James Jaya, Kaustubh D. Dhole, Arie A. Suryani, Rifki Afina Putri, Dan Su, Keith Stevens, Made Nindyatama Nityasya, Muhammad Farid Adilazuarda, Ryan Ignatius, Ryandito Diandaru, Tiezheng Yu, Vito Ghifari, Wenliang Dai, Yan Xu, Dyah Damapuspita, Cuk Tho, Ichwanul Muslim Karo Karo, Tirana Noor Fatyanosa, Ziwei Ji, Pascale Fung, Graham Neubig, Timothy Baldwin, Sebastian Ruder, Herry Sujaini, Sakriani Sakti, and Ayu Purwarianti. 2022. Nusacrowd: Open source initiative for indonesian nlp resources. *ArXiv*, abs/2212.09648.

Dmitry Davidov, Oren Tsur, and Ari Rappoport. 2010. Enhanced sentiment learning using Twitter hashtags and smileys. In *Coling 2010: Posters*, pages 241–249, Beijing, China. Coling 2010 Organizing Committee.

P. Suthanthira Devi, R. Geetha, and S. K. Karthika. 2019. Trendingtags—classification & prediction of hashtag popularity using twitter features in machine learning approach proceedings. *Advances in Intelligent Systems and Computing*.

Shizhe Diao, Sedrick Scott Keh, Liangming Pan, Zhiliang Tian, Yan Song, and Tong Zhang. 2023. Hashtag-guided low-resource tweet classification. *Proceedings of the ACM Web Conference 2023*.

Ouyu Lan, Xiao Huang, Bill Yuchen Lin, He Jiang, Liyuan Liu, and Xiang Ren. 2020. Learning to contextually aggregate multi-source supervision for sequence labeling. In *Proceedings of the 58th Annual Meeting of the Association for Computational Linguistics*, pages 2134–2146, Online. Association for Computational Linguistics.

Shurui Li and Jiechen Ou. 2021. Multi-label classification of research papers using multi-label k-nearest neighbour algorithm. *Journal of Physics: Conference Series*, 1994(1):012031.

Pierre Lison, Jeremy Barnes, and Aliaksandr Hubin. 2021. skweak: Weak supervision made easy for nlp. In *Annual Meeting of the Association for Computational Linguistics*.

Jordan Painter, Helen Treharne, and Diptesh Kanojia. 2022. Utilizing weak supervision to create S3D: A sarcasm annotated dataset. In *Proceedings of the Fifth Workshop on Natural Language Processing and Computational Social Science (NLP+CSS)*, pages 197–206, Abu Dhabi, UAE. Association for Computational Linguistics.

Alexander Ratner, Stephen H. Bach, Henry Ehrenberg, Jason Fries, Sen Wu, and Christopher Ré. 2020. Snorkel: rapid training data creation with weak supervision. *The VLDB Journal*, 29:709–730.

Alexander Ratner, Braden Hancock, Jared Dunnmon, Frederic Sala, Shreyash Pandey, and Christopher Ré. 2019. Training complex models with multi-task weak supervision. *Proc AAAI Conf Artif Intell*, 33(1):4763–4771.

Alexander Ratner, Christopher De Sa, Sen Wu, Daniel Selsam, and Christopher Ré. 2016. Data programming: creating large training sets, quickly. In *Proceedings of the 30th International Conference on Neural Information Processing Systems*, pages 3574–3582.

Wendi Ren, Yinghao Li, Hanting Su, David Kartchner, Cassie Mitchell, and Chao Zhang. 2020. Denoising multi-source weak supervision for neural text classification. In *Findings of the Association for Computational Linguistics: EMNLP 2020*, pages 3739–3754. Association for Computational Linguistics.

Ramya Tekumalla and Juan M. Banda. 2022. TweetDIS: A large twitter dataset for natural disasters built

[7]https://datasaur.ai/

[8]https://www.mongabay.co.id/

using weak supervision. In *2022 IEEE International Conference on Big Data (Big Data)*. IEEE.

Jieyu Zhang, Cheng-Yu Hsieh, Yue Yu, Chao Zhang, and Alexander Ratner. 2022. A survey on programmatic weak supervision. *preprint arXiv*, arXiv:2202.05433. Version 2.

Jieyu Zhang, Yue Yu, Yinghao Li, Yujing Wang, Yaming Yang, Mao Yang, and Alexander Ratner. 2021. WRENCH: A comprehensive benchmark for weak supervision. In *Thirty-fifth Conference on Neural Information Processing Systems Datasets and Benchmarks Track (Round 2)*.

A Appendix

A.1 Labeling Function Construction

Our labeling functions were supported with external Python libraries, such as SpaCy[9], NLTK[10], TextBlob[11], and Stanza[12]. We have standardized the labeling functions' code into this template. So varies of Python algorithms can be implemented under `label_function`.

```
LABELS = {
  'labelA' : 0,
  'labelB' : 1,
  'labelC' : 2
}


# decorator to wrap labeling function into ready output
# to be aggregated by label model

#assign target label
@target_label(label=LABELS['labelA'])
def label_function(sample) -> bool:
  #this line created text with all columns of table
  #dataset in this case title and article columns
  text = list(sample.values())[0]

  # Implement your logic here
  TARGET_KEYWORDS = ['special keywords']
  for keyword in TARGET_KEYWORDS:
    if re.search(keyword, text, re.IGNORECASE):
      return True
  return False
```

For the simplest labeling functions, we only inserted keywords into `TARGET_KEYWORDS`, and add additional code/rules below `LABELS` when required.

A.1.1 Tag Classification

targeted tags: *pertanian, penelitian, lembaga internasional, berita internasional, Aparatur Sipil Negara, kebijakan, hewan terancam punah, bencana alam, konflik, tambang, perusahaan, pendanaan, penyelamatan lingkungan, sawit, lahan, Lembaga Swadaya Masyarakat, foto, trivia, mangrove, politik, masyarakat desa, inovasi, tentang mongabay, perdagangan, kumpulan berita, krisis, penyakit, sampah, korupsi, budidaya, nelayan, iklim/cuaca, energi*

To address the 31 tags, we developed a total of 36 labeling functions, categorized based on their complexity. The least complex labeling functions applied rules directly to the data point, which consisted of the `title` and `chunked-article`. Medium complexity labeling functions involved separate keyword searches in the `title` and `chunked-article`. The most complex labeling functions required more intricate logic and rules.

- The simplest labeling functions consists of rules that return tags labels related to obvious keywords. These tags represent specific topics and can be identified by a single or a few keywords.

```
budidaya= ['perudangan', 'pembenihan', 'budidaya', 'tambak', 'keramba', 'budi daya', 'perikanan']
energi= ['Energi', 'energi', 'bahan bakar,', 'BBM', 'batubara', 'batu bara']
foto= ['Foto', 'foto utama']
korupsi= ['korupsi', 'koruptor', 'korup']
krisis= ['krisis']
kumpulan berita= ['catatan awal tahun', 'catatan akhir tahun', 'kaleidoskop']
mangrove= ['mangrove']
nelayan= ['nelayan', 'melaut']
perdagangan= ['pemesan', 'perdagangan', 'ekspor', 'export', 'impor', 'trade', 'market']
pertanian= ['pertanian', 'bertani', 'sawah', 'ladang', 'pupuk','pestisida']
endangered animal= ['predator', 'diburu', 'populasi', 'habitat', 'peliharaan', 'penangkaran', '
    conservation', 'habitat', 'pelepasliaran', 'hutan lindung', 'langka ', 'punah', 'endangered', '
    cagar alam', 'suaka margasatwa', 'kebun binatang']
sampah= ['sampah', 'cemari', 'tercemar']
sawit= ['sawit']
tambang= ['tambang', 'nambang']
```

[9] https://spacy.io/
[10] https://www.nltk.org/
[11] https://textblob.readthedocs.io/en/dev/
[12] https://stanfordnlp.github.io/stanza/

- The medium labeling functions utilize common additional logic, such as searching for keywords in separate parts (`title` and `chunked-article`) and combining them, searching for keywords based on the case or uncased first character, or employing simple regex patterns for keyword matching.

```
def label_function(sample) -> bool:
  text = sample['title']+' | '+sample['text']

  # Implement your logic here
  TARGET_KEYWORDS_UNCASED = ['jendral', 'sekretariat', 'pasukan', 'komnas', 'dirjen', 'direktorat', '
    mahkamah', 'militer', 'aparat', 'polda', 'polres', 'polsek', 'polri', 'kepala desa', ' dinas', '
    polisi']
  TARGET_KEYWORDS_CASED = ['BPD', 'KPK', 'MA', 'MK', 'PNS', 'TNI']
  if any(re.search(keyword, text) for keyword in TARGET_KEYWORDS_CASED) or \
  any(re.search(keyword, text, re.IGNORECASE) for keyword in TARGET_KEYWORDS_UNCASED):
    return True
  return False
```

Listing 1: ASN

```
def label_function(sample) -> bool:
  text = sample['title']+' | '+sample['text']

  # Implement your logic here
  TARGET_KEYWORDS = ['Alliance', 'Liga', 'Duta', 'Yayasan', 'LSM', 'Balai', 'Society', 'Lembaga', '
    Perhimpunan', 'WWF-Indonesia', 'Greenpeace', 'Friends', 'Badan', 'Community', 'Komunitas', 'Forum'
    , 'Dewan', 'Support', 'Lovers', 'PKK']
  for keyword in TARGET_KEYWORDS:
    if re.search(keyword, text):
      if 'DPRD' in text or 'Dewan Perwakilan Rakyat' in text:
        continue
      return True
  return False
```

Listing 2: LSM

```
def label_function(sample) -> bool:
  title = sample['title']
  text = title+' | '+sample['text']

  # Implement your logic here
  TARGET_KEYWORDS_TITLE = ['Bencana', 'Mitigasi']
  TARGET_KEYWORDS = ['kebakaran', 'banjir', 'gempa', 'tsunami', 'erupsi', 'longsor']
  if any(re.search(keyword,title) for keyword in TARGET_KEYWORDS_TITLE) or \
  any(re.search(keyword, text, re.IGNORECASE) for keyword in TARGET_KEYWORDS):
    return True
  return False
```

Listing 3: bencana

```
def label_function(sample) -> bool:
  title = sample['title']
  text = sample['text']

  # Implement your logic here
  TARGET_KEYWORDS_TITLE = ['Penelitian', 'Riset', 'Studi', 'Analisis', 'Sukses', 'Inovasi', 'Alternatif
    ', 'Manfaat', 'Sains', 'Potensi', 'Asa ', 'Solusi']
  EX_KEYWORDS_TITLE = ['Tapi', 'Tidak']
  TARGET_KEYWORDS_TEXT = ['sukses', 'inisiatif', 'penghargaan']
  if any(re.search(keyword,title) for keyword in TARGET_KEYWORDS_TITLE) and all(re.search(ex_keyword,
    title)==None for ex_keyword in EX_KEYWORDS_TITLE) or\
   any(re.search(keyword, text, re.IGNORECASE) for keyword in TARGET_KEYWORDS_TEXT):
     return True
  return False
```

Listing 4: inovasi

```
def label_function(sample) -> bool:
  title = sample['title']
  text = title+' | '+sample['text']

  # Implement your logic here
  TARGET_KEYWORDS_TITLE = ['Kebijakan']
  TARGET_KEYWORDS_CASED = ['UU', 'SK', 'PP', 'REDD', 'Permen']
  TARGET_KEYWORDS_UNCASED = ['zonasi', ' perda ', 'perizinan', 'moratorium', 'lisensi', 'undang', '
    legalitas', 'revisi', 'regulasi', 'restorasi']
  if any(re.search(keyword,title) for keyword in TARGET_KEYWORDS_TITLE) or \
  any(re.search(keyword, text) for keyword in TARGET_KEYWORDS_CASED) or \
  any(re.search(keyword, text, re.IGNORECASE) for keyword in TARGET_KEYWORDS_UNCASED):
    return True
```

```
  return False
```

Listing 5: kebijakan

```
def label_function(sample) -> bool:
  title = sample['title']
  text = sample['title']+' | '+sample['text']

  # Implement your logic here
  TARGET_KEYWORDS_TITLE = ['Mangkir', 'Merana', 'Diburu', 'Merusak', 'Kesulitan', 'Disita', '
     Selundupkan', 'Memusuhi', 'Rumit', 'Perusak', 'Terpaksa', 'Kurang Gizi', 'Protes', 'Kehilangan', '
     Nestapa', 'Ilegal', 'Kriminal', 'Balada', 'Lapor ', 'Terancam', 'Usir', 'Musuh', 'Terkontaminasi',
      'Kasus']
  TARGET_KEYWORDS = ['pelanggaran hukum', 'pemaksaan', 'beracun', 'melanggar', 'kebakaran', 'muak','
     egois', 'over populasi', 'perusakan', 'membahayakan', 'kriminal', 'serakah', 'kejam', 'kelaparan',
      'tak becus', 'eksploitasi', 'pengeboman', 'penjahat', 'diracun', 'penyuapan', 'teror', '
     intimidasi', 'illegal', 'ilegal', 'polemik', 'tercemar', 'cemar', 'modus', 'diabaikan', ' tambang'
     , 'korupsi', 'koruptor', 'korup', 'nyiksa', 'siksa', 'penjara', 'aniaya', 'diancam', 'mengancam',
     'pembunuh', 'dibunuh', 'membunuh', 'terbunuh', 'tembak', 'nembak', 'miris', 'konflik', 'bentrok',
     'tuduh', 'tuding', 'tuntut', 'nuntut']
  EX_KEYWORDS_TITLE = ['Tidak Berbahaya', 'Paling', 'Konservasi', 'Ini ', 'Menentramkan', 'Karya', '
     Festival', 'Ke Alam', 'Menghijaukan', 'DNA', 'Perjuangan', 'Kerjasama', 'unik', 'Belajar', '
     Dilepasliarkan', 'Tidak Berbahaya', 'Manfaat', 'Ayo', 'Solusi', 'Restorasi', 'Inilah', 'Sayang', '
     Transparansi', 'Keren', 'Mengubah Dunia', 'Konsolidasi', 'Diselamatkan', ' Si ', 'Berjuang', '
     Evolusi', 'Foto:', 'Penyelamatan', 'Disahkan', 'Bantuan', 'Mengakhiri Penebangan Liar', 'Berhasil'
     , 'Bersihkan', 'Penjaga', 'Perkuat', 'Aplikasi', 'Sukses', 'Anti', 'Perlindungan', 'Agen Rahasia',
      'Warrior']
  EX_KEYWORDS = ['kerusakan', 'sustainable', 'teknologi canggih', 'rehabilitasi', 'bersinergi', '
     konservasi', 'presisi', 'untunglah', 'komitmen', 'edukasi', 'kredibilitas', 'citation', 'reward',
     'penghargaan', 'inisiatif', 'pulih']
  if (any(re.search(keyword, title) for keyword in TARGET_KEYWORDS_TITLE) or \
  any(re.search(keyword, text, re.IGNORECASE) for keyword in TARGET_KEYWORDS)) and \
  (all(ex_keyword not in title for ex_keyword in EX_KEYWORDS_TITLE) and \
  all(ex_keyword not in text for ex_keyword in EX_KEYWORDS)):
    return True
  return False
```

Listing 6: konflik

```
def label_function(sample) -> bool:
  title = sample['title']
  text = sample['text']

  # Implement your logic here
  TARGET_KEYWORDS_TITLE = ['tanah']
  TARGET_KEYWORDS_TEXT = ['lahan']
  if any(re.search(keyword,title) for keyword in TARGET_KEYWORDS_TITLE) or\
    any(re.search(keyword, text, re.IGNORECASE) for keyword in TARGET_KEYWORDS_TEXT):
      return True
  return False
```

Listing 7: lahan

```
def label_function(sample) -> bool:
  title = sample['title']
  text = sample['text']

  # Implement your logic here
  TITLE_KEYWORDS = ['Mongabay']
  TEXT_KEYWORDS = ['Mongabay.org']

  if any(re.search(keyword, title) for keyword in TITLE_KEYWORDS) or\
  any(re.search(keyword, text) for keyword in TEXT_KEYWORDS):
    return True
  return False
```

Listing 8: mongabay

```
def label_function(sample) -> bool:
  title = sample['title']
  text = sample['text']

  # Implement your logic here
  TARGET_KEYWORDS_TITLE = ['LIPI', 'Ahli', 'Studi', 'Kajian', 'Aplikasi', 'Pakar', 'Peneliti', 'Riset',
      'Analisis', 'Analisa', 'Inovasi', 'Alternatif', 'Sains']
  TARGET_KEYWORDS_CASED = ['LIPI', 'M.Sc', 'M.Si', 'CITATION', 'DNA', 'PhD']
  TARGET_KEYWORDS_UNCASED = ['ahli biologi', 'hasil penelitian', 'pakar ', 'peneliti ', 'universitas',
     'university', 'profesor', 'professor', 'science', 'ilmuwan', 'scientist', 'research', 'college']
  if any(re.search(keyword,title) for keyword in TARGET_KEYWORDS_TITLE) or \
  any(re.search(keyword, text) for keyword in TARGET_KEYWORDS_CASED) or \
  any(re.search(keyword, text, re.IGNORECASE) for keyword in TARGET_KEYWORDS_UNCASED) or \
  len(re.findall('ilmiah', text, re.IGNORECASE)) > 1:
    return True
```

```
    return False
```

Listing 9: penelitian

```
def label_function(sample) -> bool:
  title = sample['title']
  text = title+' | '+sample['text']

  # Implement your logic here
  TARGET_KEYWORDS_TITLE = ['penyakit', 'virus', 'parasit', 'covid', 'corona']
  TARGET_KEYWORDS = ['infeksi ', 'menular', ' medis ']
  if any(re.search(keyword, text, re.IGNORECASE) for keyword in TARGET_KEYWORDS) or \
  any(re.search(keyword, title, re.IGNORECASE) for keyword in TARGET_KEYWORDS_TITLE):
    return True
  return False
```

Listing 10: penyakit

```
def label_function(sample) -> bool:
  text = sample['title'] +' | '+ sample['text']

  # Implement your logic here
  TARGET_PATTERNS = [re.compile('\bPT '), re.compile('\bPT.'), ' PT ', ' CV ']
  TARGET_KEYWORDS = ['perusahaan','.org', 'direksi', 'badan usaha', 'industri', 'pabrik', 'produsen']

  if any(re.search(keyword, text, re.IGNORECASE) for keyword in TARGET_KEYWORDS) or \
  any(re.search(pattern, text) for pattern in TARGET_PATTERNS):
    return True
  return False
```

Listing 11: perusahaan

- The most complex labeling functions, handle tags that are related to common keywords that are also found commonly in regular content. In such cases, more detailed and complex rules need to be added in combination with keywords. This type of tags is typically handled by multiple labeling functions and may require the use of external packages, such as spaCy.

```
def label_function(sample) -> bool:
  text = sample['title']+' | '+sample['text']

  # Implement your logic here
  TARGET_KEYWORDS_CASED = ['Adat', 'Suku']
  TARGET_KEYWORDS_UNCASED = ['desa', 'dusun']

  if any(re.search(keyword, text) for keyword in TARGET_KEYWORDS_CASED) or\
  any(re.search(keyword, text, re.IGNORECASE) for keyword in TARGET_KEYWORDS_UNCASED):
    return True
  return False
```

Listing 12: desa-keywords

```
def label_function(sample) -> bool:
  text = list(sample.values())[0]

  # Implement your logic here
  first_word = text.split()[0]
  if first_word == 'Masyarakat':
    return True
  elif 'Warga' in sample['title']:
    return True
  return False
```

Listing 13: desa-title-masyarakat-logic

```
def label_function(sample) -> bool:
  text = sample['title']+' | '+sample['text']

  # Implement your logic here
  TARGET_KEYWORDS = ['iklim', 'cuaca', 'pemanasan global', 'el-nino', 'el nino', 'siklon']
  for keyword in TARGET_KEYWORDS:
    if re.search(keyword, text, re.IGNORECASE):
      return True
  return False
```

Listing 14: iklim/cuaca-keywords

```
def label_function(sample) -> bool:
  text = sample['title']+' | '+sample['text']

  # Implement your logic here
  TARGET_KEYWORDS = ['badai', 'kemarau', 'hujan']
  match_collection = []
  for keyword in TARGET_KEYWORDS:
    match_collection.extend(re.findall(keyword, text, re.IGNORECASE))

  if len(match_collection)>3:
    return True
  else:
    return False
```

Listing 15: iklim/cuaca-repetitive keywords

```
def label_function(sample) -> bool:
  text = sample['title']+' | '+sample['text']

  TARGET_PATTERNS = []
  nominal_keywords = ["juta","miliar","triliun"]
  for nominal in nominal_keywords:
    TARGET_PATTERNS.append(re.compile(r"Rp\d+[,|.]\d+ {}".format(nominal)))
    TARGET_PATTERNS.append(re.compile(r"Rp \d+[,|.]\d+ {}".format(nominal)))
    TARGET_PATTERNS.append(re.compile(r"Rp \d+ {}".format(nominal)))
    TARGET_PATTERNS.append(re.compile(r"Rp\d+ {}".format(nominal)))

  rp_2 = re.compile(r"Rp \d+.\d+")
  rp_3 = re.compile(r'Rp\d+.\d+')
  TARGET_PATTERNS.append(rp_2)
  TARGET_PATTERNS.append(rp_3)

  nominal_keywords = ["puluh","ratus","ribu","juta","miliar"]
  for nominal in nominal_keywords:
    TARGET_PATTERNS.append(re.compile(r"\d+ {} dollar [AS|Australia]".format(nominal)))
    TARGET_PATTERNS.append(re.compile(r"\d+ {} dollar".format(nominal)))
    TARGET_PATTERNS.append(re.compile(r"\$\d+[,|.]\d+ {}".format(nominal)))
    TARGET_PATTERNS.append(re.compile(r"\$ \d+[,|.]\d+ {}".format(nominal)))
    TARGET_PATTERNS.append(re.compile(r"\$ \d+ {}".format(nominal)))
    TARGET_PATTERNS.append(re.compile(r"\$\d+ {}".format(nominal)))

  dollar_2 = re.compile(r"\$ \d+.\d+")
  dollar_3 = re.compile(r'\$\d+.\d+')

  TARGET_PATTERNS.append(dollar_2)
  TARGET_PATTERNS.append(dollar_3)

  # Implement your logic here
  TARGET_KEYWORDS = [' dana', 'pendanaan', 'dollar', 'rupiah']

  if any(re.search(keyword, text, re.IGNORECASE) for keyword in TARGET_KEYWORDS) or \
  any(re.search(pattern, text) for pattern in TARGET_PATTERNS):
    return True
  return False
```

Listing 16: pendanaan-keywords-regex number

```
def label_function(sample) -> bool:
  text = sample['title']+' | '+sample['text']

  # Implement your logic here
  TARGET_KEYWORDS = ['pelestarian lingkungan', 'revitalisasi', 'melindungi hutan', 'kampanye lingkungan
    ', 'kontribusi', 'gerakan', 'ramah lingkungan', 'pegiat']

  for keyword in TARGET_KEYWORDS:
    if re.search(keyword, text, re.IGNORECASE):
      return True
  return False
```

Listing 17: go green (penyelamatan lingkungan) - keywords

```
def label_function(sample) -> bool:
  text = sample['title']

  # Implement your logic here
  TARGET_KEYWORDS = ['pelestarian', 'mengelola', 'merawat alam', 'pengelolaan', 'penghargaan', 'aksi',
    'hijau', 'kisah', 'jaga', 'selamat', 'menyelamatkan', 'penyelamat', 'aktivis', 'karya', 'ayo', '
    mengajak', 'anti-illegal', 'warior']
  EX_KEYWORDS = ['penyu', 'bunglon']
  for keyword in TARGET_KEYWORDS:
    if re.search('Ajak', text):
      return True
    elif re.search(keyword, text, re.IGNORECASE) and re.search('konflik', sample['text'], re.IGNORECASE
    )==None:
```

```
    if keyword == 'hijau':
      try:
        previous_text = text[:text.index(keyword)]
        if any(re.search(ex_keyword,previous_text,re.IGNORECASE) for ex_keyword in EX_KEYWORDS):
          continue
      except:
        pass
    return True
  return False
```

Listing 18: go green (penyelamatan lingkungan) - keywords - logic

```
def label_function(sample) -> bool:
  title = sample['title']
  text = sample['title']+' | '+sample['text']

  # Implement your logic here
  TARGET_KEYWORDS_TITLE = ['Presiden', 'Politik', 'Pemerintah']
  TARGET_KEYWORDS_CASED = ['DPR', 'MPR', 'KPK']
  TARGET_KEYWORDS_UNCASED = ['partai', 'pemilu', 'capres', 'cawapres', 'presiden indonesia', 'wali kota
    ', 'walikota', 'bupati', 'gubernur', 'menteri', 'mentri', 'pemkot', 'pemda', 'pemprov', 'pejabat',
     'parpol', 'pilkada', 'pilpres', 'politis', 'politikus']

  if any(re.search(keyword, text) for keyword in TARGET_KEYWORDS_CASED) or\
  any(re.search(keyword, text, re.IGNORECASE) for keyword in TARGET_KEYWORDS_UNCASED) or\
  any(re.search(keyword, title) for keyword in TARGET_KEYWORDS_TITLE):
    return True

  return False
```

Listing 19: politic-keywords

```
def label_function(sample) -> bool:
  text = sample['text']

  # Implement your logic here
  TARGET_KEYWORDS = ['pemerintah']
  match_collection = []
  for keyword in TARGET_KEYWORDS:
    match_collection.extend(re.findall(keyword, text, re.IGNORECASE))

  if len(match_collection)>3:
    return True
  return False
```

Listing 20: politic-text-pemerintah-logic

```
def label_function(sample) -> bool:
  text = sample['text']

  # Implement your logic here
  TARGET_KEYWORDS = ['pemerintah']
  match_collection = []
  for keyword in TARGET_KEYWORDS:
    match_collection.extend(re.findall(keyword, text, re.IGNORECASE))

  if len(match_collection)>3:
    return True
  return False
```

Listing 21: trivia-keywords

```
def label_function(sample) -> bool:
  text = sample['title']

  try:
    translated_text = TextBlob(text).translate(from_lang='id', to='en')
  except:
    translated_text = TextBlob(text)

  trans_text_split = str(translated_text).split(',')
  if len(trans_text_split) == 1:
    trans_text_split = str(translated_text).split(':')

  if len(trans_text_split) > 1:
    name_candidate = trans_text_split[0]

    spacy_pred = nlp(name_candidate)
    TARGET_KEYWORDS = []
    for token in spacy_pred.ents:
      token_label = token.label_
      if token_label in NER_LABELS:
        TARGET_KEYWORDS.append(str(token))
```

```
    # Implement your logic here
    for keyword in TARGET_KEYWORDS:
      if re.search(keyword, text, re.IGNORECASE):
        return True
  return False
```

Listing 22: trivia-title-PER-spaCy

A.1.2 Sentiment Classification

The main idea of sentiment classification labeling functions is to gather groups of tags that are related to specific sentiment classes (positive, neutral, or negative). However, we discovered that labeling functions based solely on tags often resulted in conflicts between different labeling functions. To address this issue, we created two versions of labeling functions: one that relies solely on tags (v0) and another that incorporates sentiment-related keywords (v1). The use of sentiment-related keywords in v1 enhances their precision and detail.

- v0, contains 12 labeling functions

```
@target_label(label=LABELS['negatif'])
def label_function(sample) -> bool:
  ex_tags = ['penelitian', 'penyelamatan lingkungan', 'Lembaga Swadaya Masyarakat', 'inovasi', 'trivia'
    , 'foto']
  tags = sample['tags'].split(',')
  target_tags = ['perusahaan']

  # Implement your logic here
  if 'konflik' in tags and all(ex not in tags for ex in ex_tags):
    return True
  else:
    return False
```

Listing 23: negatif-konflik

```
@target_label(label=LABELS['negatif'])
def label_function(sample) -> bool:
  tags = sample['tags'].split(',')

  # Implement your logic here
  if 'konflik' in tags and 'tambang' in tags:
    return True
  else:
    return False
```

Listing 24: negatif-konflik-tambang

```
@target_label(label=LABELS['negatif'])
def label_function(sample) -> bool:
  ex_tags = ['penelitian', 'penyelamatan lingkungan', 'inovasi', 'trivia']
  tags = sample['tags'].split(',')
  target_tags = ['perusahaan']

  # Implement your logic here
  if 'konflik' in tags and any(target in tags for target in target_tags) and all(ex not in tags for ex
    in ex_tags):
    return True
  else:
    return False
```

Listing 25: negatif-konflik-keywords

```
@target_label(label=LABELS['negatif'])
def label_function(sample) -> bool:
  tags = sample['tags'].split(',')
  target_tags = ['krisis', 'bencana alam']
  ex_tags = ['penelitian', 'penyelamatan lingkungan', 'inovasi', 'trivia']

  # Implement your logic here
  for target in target_tags:
    if target in tags and all(ex not in tags for ex in ex_tags):
      return True
  return False
```

Listing 26: negatif-krisis-bencana

```
@target_label(label=LABELS['positif'])
def label_function(sample) -> bool:
  ex_tags = ['konflik', 'bencana alam']
  tags = sample['tags'].split(',')
  target_tags = ['trivia', 'inovasi', 'tentang mongabay', 'penyelamatan lingkungan', 'penelitian']

  # Implement your logic here
  for target in target_tags:
    if target in tags and all(ex not in tags for ex in ex_tags):
      return True
  return False
```

Listing 27: positif-keywords

```
@target_label(label=LABELS['positif'])
def label_function(sample) -> bool:
  tags = sample['tags'].split(',')

  # Implement your logic here
  ex_tags = ['tambang', 'bencana alam', 'korupsi']
  if 'inovasi' in tags and all(ex not in tags for ex in ex_tags):
    return True
  else:
    return False
```

Listing 28: positif-inovasi

```
@target_label(label=LABELS['negatif'])
def label_function(sample) -> bool:
  tags = sample['tags'].split(',')

  # Implement your logic here
  if 'korupsi' in tags:
    return True
  else:
    return False
```

Listing 29: negatif-korupsi

```
@target_label(label=LABELS['negatif'])
def label_function(sample) -> bool:
  tags = sample['tags'].split(',')

  # Implement your logic here
  if 'Aparatur Sipil Negara' in tags and 'masyarakat desa' in tags:
    return True
  else:
    return False
```

Listing 30: negatif-ASN-desa

```
@target_label(label=LABELS['netral'])
def label_function(sample) -> bool:
  tags = sample['tags'].split(',')

  # Implement your logic here
  ex_tags = ['konflik', 'tambang', 'bencana alam', 'korupsi', 'inovasi']
  if all(ex not in tags for ex in ex_tags):
    return True
  else:
    return False
```

Listing 31: netral-keywords

```
@target_label(label=LABELS['netral'])
def label_function(sample) -> bool:
  tags = sample['tags'].split(',')

  # Implement your logic here
  positif_tags = ["foto", "inovasi", "tentang mongabay", "penelitian", "penyelamatan lingkungan"]
  negatif_tags = ["bencana alam", "konflik", "korupsi", "krisis"]
  n_positif = 0
  n_negatif = 0
  for pos in positif_tags:
    if pos in tags:
      n_positif += 1
  for neg in negatif_tags:
    if neg in tags:
      n_negatif += 1

  if n_positif == n_negatif:
```

```
    return True
  else:
    return False
```

Listing 32: netral-logic

```
@target_label(label=LABELS['positif'])
def label_function(sample) -> bool:
  tags = sample['tags'].split(',')

  # Implement your logic here
  positif_tags = ["foto", "inovasi", "tentang mongabay", "penelitian", "penyelamatan lingkungan"]
  negatif_tags = ["bencana alam", "konflik", "korupsi", "krisis"]
  n_positif = 0
  n_negatif = 0
  for pos in positif_tags:
    if pos in tags:
      n_positif += 1
  for neg in negatif_tags:
    if neg in tags:
      n_negatif += 1

  if n_positif > n_negatif:
    return True
  else:
    return False
```

Listing 33: positif-logic

```
@target_label(label=LABELS['negatif'])
def label_function(sample) -> bool:
  tags = sample['tags'].split(',')

  # Implement your logic here
  positif_tags = ["foto", "inovasi", "tentang mongabay", "penelitian", "penyelamatan lingkungan"]
  negatif_tags = ["bencana alam", "konflik", "korupsi", "krisis"]
  n_positif = 0
  n_negatif = 0
  for pos in positif_tags:
    if pos in tags:
      n_positif += 1
  for neg in negatif_tags:
    if neg in tags:
      n_negatif += 1

  if n_positif < n_negatif:
    return True
  else:
    return False
```

Listing 34: negatif-logic

- v1, contains 16 labeling functions. In this collection, we design various rules of labeling functions, but most of them are combination of keywords with tags condition

```
@target_label(label=LABELS['netral'])
def label_function(sample) -> bool:

  tags = sample['tags']

  # Implement your logic here
  if len(tags)<=1:
    return True
  else:
    return False
```

Listing 35: netral-abstain

```
# Labeling function definition (Start editing here!)
POSITIF = ['inovasi', 'penyelamatan lingkungan']
NEGATIF = ['konflik', 'krisis', 'tambang', 'korupsi', 'penyakit', 'sampah', 'hewan terancam punah']
# Assign target label based on LABELS dictionary
@target_label(label=LABELS['netral'])
def label_function(sample) -> bool:
  tags = sample['tags'].split(',')

  # Implement your logic here
  if len(tags) == 1:
    tag = tags[0]
    if tag not in POSITIF and tag not in NEGATIF:
      return True
```

```
  return False
```

Listing 36: netral-1tag

```
# Labeling function definition (Start editing here!)
POSITIF = ['inovasi', 'penyelamatan lingkungan']
NEGATIF = ['konflik', 'krisis', 'tambang', 'korupsi', 'penyakit', 'sampah', 'hewan terancam punah']
# Assign target label based on LABELS dictionary
@target_label(label=LABELS['positif'])
def label_function(sample) -> bool:
  tags = sample['tags'].split(',')

  # Implement your logic here
  if len(tags) == 1:
    tag = tags[0]
    if tag in POSITIF:
      return True
  return False
```

Listing 37: positif-1tag

```
# Labeling function definition (Start editing here!)
POSITIF = ['inovasi', 'penyelamatan lingkungan']
NEGATIF = ['konflik', 'krisis', 'tambang', 'korupsi', 'penyakit', 'sampah', 'hewan terancam punah']
EX_KEYWORDS = ['Tahukah Anda?']
# Assign target label based on LABELS dictionary
@target_label(label=LABELS['negatif'])
def label_function(sample) -> bool:
  tags = sample['tags'].split(',')

  # Implement your logic here
  if len(tags) == 1 and all(re.search(ex, sample['title'], re.IGNORECASE)==None for ex in EX_KEYWORDS):
    tag = tags[0]
    if tag in NEGATIF:
      return True
  return False
```

Listing 38: negatif-1tag

```
@target_label(label=LABELS['netral'])
def label_function(sample) -> bool:
  text = sample['title']

  # Implement your logic here
  TARGET_KEYWORDS = ['Tahukah Anda?']
  for keyword in TARGET_KEYWORDS:
    if type(keyword) == str:
      if re.search(keyword, text):
        return True
    if type(keyword) == list:
      if all(key in text for key in keyword):
        return True
  return False
```

Listing 39: netral-keywords

```
@target_label(label=LABELS['positif'])
def label_function(sample) -> bool:
  tags = sample['tags'].split(',')
  EX_TAGS = ['kebijakan', 'konflik', 'bencana alam'] #['hewan terancam punah', 'konflik', 'pendanaan']

  # Implement your logic here
  if 'inovasi' in tags and all(ex not in tags for ex in EX_TAGS) and 'APP' not in sample['text']:
    return True
  return False
```

Listing 40: positif-inovasi

```
@target_label(label=LABELS['netral'])
def label_function(sample) -> bool:
  tags = sample['tags'].split(',')
  COMB_TAGS = ['kebijakan', 'konflik', 'bencana alam']
  EX_TAGS = [] #['hewan terancam punah', 'konflik', 'pendanaan']

  # Implement your logic here

  if 'inovasi' in tags and any(comb in tags for comb in COMB_TAGS):
    return True
  return False
```

Listing 41: netral-inovasi

```
@target_label(label=LABELS['negatif'])
def label_function(sample) -> bool:
  tags = sample['tags'].split(',')
  PRIME_TAGS = ['konflik', 'krisis', 'korupsi']
  COMB_TAGS = ['kumpulan berita', 'tambang', 'bencana alam', 'sampah', 'lahan', 'sawit', 'penyakit']
  EX_TAGS = ['inovasi', 'penyelamatan lingkungan']
  SPECIAL_TAGS = [['tambang', 'sawit'], ['sampah', 'sawit', 'tambang', 'bencana alam']]
  SPECIAL_EX_TAGS = [['kebijakan'], ['trivia', 'Lembaga Swadaya Masyarakat']]
  EX_KEYWORDS_TITLE = ['Menyelamatkan', 'Unggulan', 'Asa ', 'Ekologi','Persatuan', 'Amankan', '
    Kemandirian', 'Berdampingan', 'Penghormatan', 'Ekowisata', 'Mitigasi ', 'Si ', 'Tahukah Anda?']
  EX_KEYWORDS = ['menjaga laut', 'memuji', 'menjaga hutan', 'alhamdulillah', 'sertifikasi', '
    melestarikan', 'sinergi']

  # Implement your logic here
  if len(tags) == 2:
    if any(prime in tags for prime in PRIME_TAGS):
      return True

  elif len(tags) == 3:
    if any(prime in tags for prime in PRIME_TAGS) and all(comb not in tags for comb in ['inovasi']):
      return True

  elif any(prime in tags for prime in PRIME_TAGS) and any(key in sample['title'] for key in ['Konflik',
      'Ironi', 'Polemik', 'Penyumbang Masalah', 'Belum Aman']):
      return True

  n = 0
  for tag in tags:
    if tag in PRIME_TAGS:
      n += 1

  if all(ex not in tags for ex in EX_TAGS) and all(ex not in sample['title'] for ex in
    EX_KEYWORDS_TITLE):
    for s_tag, s_ex in zip(SPECIAL_TAGS, SPECIAL_EX_TAGS):
      if any(prime in tags for prime in PRIME_TAGS) and all(special not in tags for special in s_tag)
     and all(ex in tags for ex in s_ex):
        return False
      elif any(prime in tags for prime in PRIME_TAGS) and any(tag in tags for tag in s_tag) and all(ex
     in tags for ex in s_ex):
        if any(ex_kw in sample['text'].lower() for ex_kw in EX_KEYWORDS):
          return False

    if n>=2:
      return True
    elif n ==1 and any(comb in tags for comb in COMB_TAGS):
      return True
    elif n==1 and 'tambang' in tags and 'penyelamatan lingkungan' in tags:
      return True

  return False
```

Listing 42: negatif-konflik-tags

```
@target_label(label=LABELS['negatif'])
def label_function(sample) -> bool:
  tags = sample['tags'].split(',')
  PRIME_TAGS = ['korupsi']
  EX_TAGS = ['inovasi', 'tentang mongabay']
  EX_KEYWORDS = ['mengurangi korupsi', 'Tahukah anda?']

  if any(prime in tags for prime in PRIME_TAGS) and all(ex not in tags for ex in EX_TAGS) and all(ex
    not in sample['title']+' | '+sample['text'] for ex in EX_KEYWORDS):
    return True
  return False
```

Listing 43: negatif-korupsi

```
@target_label(label=LABELS['negatif'])
def label_function(sample) -> bool:
  tags = sample['tags'].split(',')
  PRIME_TAGS = ['konflik']
  COMBS = [['bencana alam', 'lahan'], ['bencana alam', 'masyarakat desa'],['bencana alam', 'sampah'],['
    hewan terancam punah'],['perdagangan', 'hewan terancam punah'],['pendanaan'],['Aparatur Sipil
    Negara','masyarakat desa'],['perusahaan', 'masyarakat desa'],['Aparatur Sipil Negara','perusahaan'
    ],['Aparatur Sipil Negara','tambang']]
  EX_TAGS = ['inovasi', 'tentang mongabay'] #'penyelamatan lingkungan']
  EX_KEYWORDS_TITLE = ['Menyelamatkan', 'Ekologi', ' Asa ', 'Ajak', 'Semangat', 'Kisah', 'Pentingnya',
    'Pelestarian', 'Defender', 'Menghentikan Tambang', 'Persatuan', 'Amankan', 'Kemandirian', '
    Berdampingan', 'Penghormatan', 'Ekowisata', 'Mitigasi ', 'Si ', 'Tahukah Anda?']
  EX_KEYWORDS = [] #['menjaga laut', 'memuji', 'menjaga hutan', 'alhamdulillah', 'sertifikasi', '
    melestarikan', 'sinergi']

  # Implement your logic here
  for comb in COMBS:
```

```
    if any(prime in tags for prime in PRIME_TAGS) and all(c in tags for c in comb) and all(ex not in
    tags for ex in EX_TAGS) and all(ex not in sample['title'] for ex in EX_KEYWORDS_TITLE) and all(ex
    not in sample['text'] for ex in EX_KEYWORDS):
      return True
    elif any(prime in tags for prime in PRIME_TAGS) and 'Konflik' in sample['title']:
      return True
  return False
```

Listing 44: negatif-konflik

```
@target_label(label=LABELS['netral'])
def label_function(sample) -> bool:
  tags = sample['tags'].split(',')
  PRIME_TAGS = ['konflik', 'krisis']
  COMBS = [['kebijakan','politik'],['kebijakan','perdagangan'],['kebijakan', 'Lembaga Swadaya
    Masyarakat'], ['penyelamatan lingkungan'],['kebijakan','budidaya']]
  EX_COMBS = [['bencana alam', 'lahan'], ['bencana alam', 'masyarakat desa'],['bencana alam', 'sampah'
    ],['hewan terancam punah'],['perdagangan', 'hewan terancam punah'],['pendanaan'],['Aparatur Sipil
    Negara','masyarakat desa'],['perusahaan', 'masyarakat desa'],['Aparatur Sipil Negara','perusahaan'
    ],['Aparatur Sipil Negara','tambang'],['Aparatur Sipil Negara','Lembaga Swadaya Masyarakat']]
  EX_KEYWORDS = ['Belum Aman', 'Penyumbang Masalah', 'Polemik', 'Ironi', 'Konflik', 'Intimidasi', '
    Perompakan', 'Lestari', 'Unggulan', 'Ajak', 'Semangat', 'Kisah', 'Pentingnya', 'Pelestarian', '
    Defender', 'Menghentikan Tambang', 'Persatuan', 'Amankan', 'Kemandirian', 'Berdampingan', '
    Penghormatan']
  EX_TAGS = ['inovasi', 'korupsi', 'tambang', 'krisis', 'hewan terancam punah'] #['hewan terancam punah
    ', 'konflik', 'pendanaan']

  # Implement your logic here
  if all(ex not in tags for ex in EX_TAGS) and all(ex not in sample['title'] for ex in EX_KEYWORDS):
    if all(all(ex_c not in tags for ex_c in ex_comb) and any(prime in tags for prime in PRIME_TAGS) for
      ex_comb in EX_COMBS):
      for comb in COMBS:
        if any(prime in tags for prime in PRIME_TAGS) and all(c in tags for c in comb):
          return True
  return False
```

Listing 45: netral-konflik

```
@target_label(label=LABELS['positif'])
def label_function(sample) -> bool:
  tags = sample['tags'].split(',')
  COMBS = [] #['kumpulan berita', 'tambang', 'bencana alam', 'sampah', 'lahan', 'sawit']
  PRIME_TAGS = ['konflik', 'krisis']
  KEYWORDS = ['Lestari', 'Unggulan', 'Ajak', 'Semangat', 'Kisah', 'Pentingnya', 'Pelestarian', '
    Defender', 'Menghentikan Tambang', 'Persatuan', 'Amankan', 'Kemandirian', 'Berdampingan', '
    Penghormatan']
  # Implement your logic here
  if any(prime in tags for prime in PRIME_TAGS) and any(key in sample['title'] for key in KEYWORDS):
    return True
  return False
```

Listing 46: positif-konflik

```
@target_label(label=LABELS['negatif'])
def label_function(sample) -> bool:
  tags = sample['tags'].split(',')
  PRIME_TAGS = ['krisis']
  EX_TAGS = ['konflik', 'inovasi', 'tentang mongabay']
  EX_KEYWORDS = []

  if any(prime in tags for prime in PRIME_TAGS) and all(ex not in tags for ex in EX_TAGS) and all(ex
    not in sample['title']+' | '+sample['text'] for ex in EX_KEYWORDS):
    if any(tag in tags for tag in ['politik', 'pendanaan', 'tambang', 'sawit', 'lahan']):
      return True
  return False
```

Listing 47: negatif-krisis

```
@target_label(label=LABELS['positif'])
def label_function(sample) -> bool:
  tags = sample['tags'].split(',')
  EX_TAGS = ['konflik', 'krisis', 'korupsi', 'sampah', 'inovasi']
  POS_TAGS = [['penyelamatan lingkungan', 'Lembaga Swadaya Masyarakat'], ['penyelamatan lingkungan', '
    pertanian'],['penyelamatan lingkungan', 'hewan terancam punah']]
  POS_EX_TAGS = [['hewan terancam punah', 'kebijakan', 'perdagangan', 'pendanaan', 'sawit', 'tambang'],
     ['hewan terancam punah', 'kebijakan', 'perdagangan', 'pendanaan', 'tambang'], ['kebijakan', '
    perdagangan', 'pendanaan', 'tambang']]
  NEG_TAGS = [['perdagangan', 'hewan terancam punah'], ['tambang']]
  NETRAL_TAGS = ['hewan terancam punah', 'kebijakan', 'perdagangan', 'pendanaan']

  if all(tag not in EX_TAGS for tag in tags):
    if any(all(pos in tags for pos in pos_tags) and all(ex not in tags for ex in pos_ex_tags) for (
      pos_tags, pos_ex_tags) in zip(POS_TAGS, POS_EX_TAGS)):
```

```
    return True
  elif any(all(neg in tags for neg in neg_tags) for neg_tags in NEG_TAGS):
    return False
  else:
    return False
return False
```

Listing 48: positif-tags

```
@target_label(label=LABELS['negatif'])
def label_function(sample) -> bool:
  tags = sample['tags'].split(',')
  EX_TAGS = ['konflik', 'krisis', 'korupsi', 'sampah', 'inovasi']
  POS_TAGS = [['penyelamatan lingkungan', 'Lembaga Swadaya Masyarakat'], ['penyelamatan lingkungan', '
    pertanian'],['penyelamatan lingkungan', 'hewan terancam punah']]
  POS_EX_TAGS = [['hewan terancam punah', 'kebijakan', 'perdagangan', 'pendanaan', 'sawit', 'tambang'],
     ['hewan terancam punah', 'kebijakan', 'perdagangan', 'pendanaan', 'tambang'], ['kebijakan', '
    perdagangan', 'pendanaan', 'tambang']]
  NEG_TAGS = [['perdagangan', 'hewan terancam punah'], ['tambang']]
  NETRAL_TAGS = ['hewan terancam punah', 'kebijakan', 'perdagangan', 'pendanaan']

  if all(tag not in EX_TAGS for tag in tags):
    if any(all(pos in tags for pos in pos_tags) and all(ex not in tags for ex in pos_ex_tags) for (
     pos_tags, pos_ex_tags) in zip(POS_TAGS, POS_EX_TAGS)):
      return False
    elif any(all(neg in tags for neg in neg_tags) for neg_tags in NEG_TAGS):
      return True
    else:
      return False
  return False
```

Listing 49: negatif-tags

```
@target_label(label=LABELS['netral'])
def label_function(sample) -> bool:
  tags = sample['tags'].split(',')
  EX_TAGS = ['konflik', 'krisis', 'korupsi', 'sampah', 'inovasi']
  POS_TAGS = [['penyelamatan lingkungan', 'Lembaga Swadaya Masyarakat'], ['penyelamatan lingkungan', '
    pertanian'],['penyelamatan lingkungan', 'hewan terancam punah']]
  POS_EX_TAGS = [['hewan terancam punah', 'kebijakan', 'perdagangan', 'pendanaan', 'sawit', 'tambang'],
     ['hewan terancam punah', 'kebijakan', 'perdagangan', 'pendanaan', 'tambang'], ['kebijakan', '
    perdagangan', 'pendanaan', 'tambang']]
  NEG_TAGS = [['perdagangan', 'hewan terancam punah'], ['tambang']]
  NETRAL_TAGS = ['hewan terancam punah', 'kebijakan', 'perdagangan', 'pendanaan']

  if all(tag not in EX_TAGS for tag in tags):
    if any(all(pos in tags for pos in pos_tags) and all(ex not in tags for ex in pos_ex_tags) for (
     pos_tags, pos_ex_tags) in zip(POS_TAGS, POS_EX_TAGS)):
      return False
    elif any(all(neg in tags for neg in neg_tags) for neg_tags in NEG_TAGS):
      return False
    else:
      return True
  return False
```

Listing 50: netral-tags

A.2 Hyperparameter

Hyper-Params	Value
optimizer	Adam
l2 regularization	0.01
epoch	2
batch size	5000
lr	1e-2

Table 6: Label model training Hyperparams

Hyper-Params	Tags	Sentiment
epoch	20	20
train batch size	32	32
eval batch size	1	1
optimizer	Adam	Adam
adam beta1	0.9	0.9
adam beta 2	0.95	0.95
adam epsilon	1e-8	1e-8
lr	1e-6	1e-4
warmup ratio	0.03	0.03
lr scheduler type	cosine,linear	cosine,linear

Table 7: Model finetuning Hyperparams

A.2.1 F1-Score per label

Label	indobert		mbert		bert	
	CM	MV	CM	MV	CM	MV
positive	44.1	37.5	24.8	0	7	0
neutral	46.3	48.2	37.4	44.3	38.5	42.5
negative	76.7	76.7	70.3	70.4	61.9	57.1

Table 8: F1-score per label for sentiment classification task

Tag	indobert		mbert		bert	
	CM	MV	CM	MV	CM	MV
ASN	84.5	88.1	83.3	85.6	56.3	54.5
LSM	69.3	72.6	71.9	74.4	41	47.5
bencana	82.4	86.1	83.8	82.7	36.5	42.7
budidaya	50.5	51.7	47.3	48.6	36.7	43.6
desa	42.9	43.6	42.1	43.5	42.1	44.6
energi	73.5	70.8	75.6	65.1	59.1	65
foto	55.8	55.8	50	59.1	64.9	65
iklim/cuaca	87.6	90.1	84.1	86	59.5	64.9
inovasi	48.1	52.3	21.7	41.5	27.1	25.3
kebijakan	46.9	48.5	44.9	49.1	42	48.4
konflik	77.3	80.2	73.4	79.5	62.9	63
korupsi	32.3	37.5	36.4	36.4	0	27.6
krisis	78	76.2	74.4	76.2	40.9	50
news-bulk	0	0	0	0	0	0
lahan	82.7	85.6	77.8	87.3	53.2	62.3
mangrove	94.7	94.7	88.9	85.7	94.7	90
nelayan	0	0	0	0	0	0
mongabay	88.4	89.7	89.7	89.7	51.5	73.4
dana	69.2	70.4	65.8	67.5	32.1	50.4
penelitian	72	67.7	68.7	69.8	58.8	57.4
penyakit	61.4	62.6	63.3	60.8	23.2	41
go-green	41.4	43.6	40.5	46.9	33.7	43.6
perdagangan	75.6	73.9	71.4	74.5	45.9	57.9
pertanian	85.2	84.6	79.3	81.3	49.5	62.9
perusahaan	78.3	83.3	78.2	83.4	58.4	68.8
politik	70.5	71.5	70	70.4	61.8	63.2
end-animal	68.2	65.6	43.5	49.3	38.4	52.3
sampah	76.9	79.5	67.5	78.5	20.7	41.4
sawit	89.8	93.2	88.4	94	75.2	85.7
tambang	89.3	92.8	89.7	93.5	55.7	72.1
trivia	64.3	60.4	56.3	53.2	56	46.2

Table 9: F1-score per tag for tags classification task

A.3 Tags Explanation

Tags	Explanation
ASN	Civil Service Agency that took part in the event of the news
LSM	Non-Governmental Organizations (NGO) that took action in the event of the news (commonly in go-green/conservation action)
bencana	disaster that was discussed in the news
budidaya	plant cultivation/fishery that was discussed in the news
desa	villager/village life that becomes the subject of the news
energi	energy issue/solution that was discussed in the news
foto	short news that discusses the photo, commonly the uniqueness of ethnic animals/culture/moment that was captured in the photo
iklim/cuaca	weather/climate issues that discussed in the news
inovasi	innovation of an action/product/rule that was discussed in the news (commonly comes from citizens)
kebijakan	policy related to conservation or environment that commonly comes up from government
konflik	conflict between two or more parties that were included/narrated in the news
korupsi	corruption/bribery case that was discussed in the news (commonly related to manipulation of conservation funding)
krisis	crisis (environment/weather/hunger/war) that was discussed in the news (commonly was narrated from a third-party point of view, sometimes it was the indirect impact of conflict/disaster
kumpulan berita	bulk of news articles from various topics that were delivered as a long-list article
lahan	regulatory of parts of land that were discussed in the news (commonly narrated as a conflict between regulatory/company and citizens/NGO)
mangrove	mangrove topics/action/issue that was discussed in the news
nelayan	fisherman life/conflict/related-policy that was discussed in the news
mongabay	news that raised redaction (Mongabay) action/event/concern related to conservation
dana	funding (in relation to conservation) that was discussed in the news
penelitian	research/exploration in nature field (solution proposal/announce newest species/point out risk analysis) that was discussed in the news.
penyakit	disease that become impact/concern/impact in the news
go-green	conservation/go-green/endangered-animal-saving related action/campaign, commonly proposed by NGO/citizens
perdagangan	trading activities related to conservation that was pointed out in the news
pertanian	agriculture issue/solution/concern that was discussed in the news
perusahaan	company/corporation that was involved in conservation-related regulation/activities
politik	politics/government activities/regulation/candidacy/scandal that were mentioned in the news
endangered animal	endangered animal that was concerned in the news
sampah	waste issue/solution/action that was discussed in the news
sawit	any event/regulation/conflict/solution related to palm oil (in terms of one of fuel resources)
tambang	any event/regulation/conflict/solution related to mining activities
trivia	trivia/non-serious event/topic that was raised in the news (commonly related to fun-fact, biography, culture activities, etc)

InstructAlign: High-and-Low Resource Language Alignment via Continual Crosslingual Instruction Tuning

Samuel Cahyawijaya, Holy Lovenia, Tiezheng Yu, Willy Chung, Pascale Fung
Hong Kong University of Science and Technology
Clear Water Bay, Hong Kong
scahyawijaya@connect.ust.hk

Abstract

Large language models (LLMs) that are tuned with instructions have demonstrated remarkable capabilities in various tasks and languages. However, their ability to generalize to underrepresented languages is limited due to the scarcity of available data. Additionally, directly adapting new languages to instruction-tuned LLMs can result in catastrophic forgetting, which leads to the loss of multitasking ability. To address this issue, we propose InstructAlign which uses continual crosslingual instruction tuning to enable LLMs to align new unseen languages with previously learned high-resource languages. Our results demonstrate the effectiveness of InstructAlign in enabling the model to understand low-resource languages with limited parallel data while preventing catastrophic forgetting. Our work contributes to the advancement of language adaptation methods, particularly for adapting instruction-tuned LLMs to underrepresented languages. We will release our code publicly upon acceptance.

1 Introduction

Instruction-tuned Large language models (LLMs) have demonstrated their generalization capability of solving various tasks expressed in natural language without requiring any explicit training on the corresponding task (Brown et al., 2020; Smith et al., 2022; Rae et al., 2022; Thoppilan et al., 2022; Chowdhery et al., 2022; Scao et al., 2022; Zeng et al., 2022). This generalization capability is further improved with various tuning methods, such as instruction tuning (Sanh et al., 2022; Wei et al., 2022a; Chung et al., 2022; Muennighoff et al., 2022). However, LLMs and their instruction-tuned variants face difficulties in generalizing across various languages, leading to a disparity in performances(Xue et al., 2021; Gehrmann et al., 2022; Scao et al., 2022; Chowdhery et al., 2022; Yong et al., 2023; Zhang et al., 2023; Asai et al., 2023; Kabra et al., 2023). Moreover, these models have limited language coverage, mostly in the Indo-European language family as indicated in Figure 1. For instance, BLOOM (Scao et al., 2022) and BLOOMZ (Muennighoff et al., 2022), the largest community-driven open-source multilingual pretrained LLM, only covers 46 languages during pretraining, excluding some high-resource languages with hundreds of millions of speakers, such as German, Japanese, Korean, and Russian, as well as many more low-resource languages with millions of speakers, such as Serbian, Finnish, Amharic, Sinhala, Lao, Javanese, Sundanese, etc.

Expanding the language repertoire of LLMs is essential for promoting inclusivity and diversity in Natural Language Processing (NLP) technology, particularly for languages that are underrepresented and low-resource. Recent studies, including Wilie et al. (2020); Cahyawijaya et al. (2021); Aji et al. (2022); Adelani et al. (2021, 2022); Kakwani et al. (2020); Kumar et al. (2022); Ebrahimi et al. (2022); **?**); Cahyawijaya et al. (2023b,a); Song et al. (2023) have emphasized the importance of this issue. To address this concern, previous research (Yong et al., 2022) has demonstrated that continual pretraining (Chau et al., 2020; Muller et al., 2021; Ebrahimi and Kann, 2021) and parameter-efficient fine-tuning (PEFT) methods, like MAD-X (Pfeiffer et al., 2020) and $(IA)^3$ (Liu et al., 2022), can be utilized to swiftly integrate the knowledge of unseen languages into LLMs using monolingual corpora of the new languages by conducting masked language modeling (MLM) (Devlin et al., 2019). However, these methods become ineffective when applied directly to instruction-tuned LLMs due to catastrophic forgetting (French, 1993) which prevents them from solving general natural language tasks after the language adaptation phase (Yong et al., 2022). Moreover, adapter-based approaches, such as MAD-X (Pfeiffer et al., 2020), result in the loss of multilingual inference capability due to modularity (Adilazuarda et al., 2023).

Proceedings of the First Workshop in South East Asian Language Processing, pages 55–78
November 1, 2023.

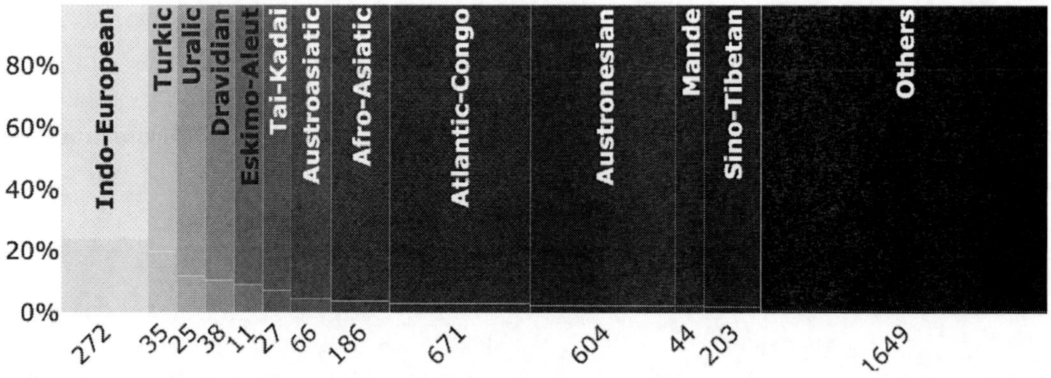

Figure 1: The number of languages supported by existing LLMs (green region) per language family[1]. Existing LLMs only support a fraction of languages around the globe. Most of them are within the Indo-European language family, while most other language families are underrepresented or even unexplored.

To solve this problem, we introduce InstructAlign, a continual instruction tuning framework to seamlessly align newly adapted low-resource languages (L2) with the pre-trained high-resource languages (L1) of an instruction-tuned LLM through crosslingual alignment. InstructAlign compels LLMs to perform crosslingual alignments between pre-trained and novel languages through alignment-based crosslingual instruction tuning, enabling the model to grasp L2 with only a limited amount of parallel data. To further prevent catastrophic forgetting, InstructAlign incorporates experience replay (Chaudhry et al., 2019b; Rolnick et al., 2019), which adds past data during the instruction tuning.

In summary, our work presents the following major contributions:

- We propose InstructAlign, a crosslingual continual instruction tuning method that allows instruction-tuned LLMs to understand L2 with minimal degradation on L1 while retaining their zero-shot prompting capability.
- We propose alignment-based crosslingual instruction tuning, which enables LLMs to align L2 to L1 allowing better L2 acquisition with only a limited amount of parallel data.
- We evaluate the effectiveness of InstructAlign on Indonesian local languages datasets, and demonstrate that InstructAlign can significantly improve the performance on L2 by 5-10% F1 while maintaining the original performance on L1 and its multitask capability.
- We analyze the correlation between the performance of L2 and other unseen languages (L3), suggesting the zero-shot generalization of InstructAlign to L3 particularly when the languages are related. [2]

2 Related Work

2.1 Instruction Tuning in LLMs

Early works (Wei et al., 2022a; Chung et al., 2022; Sanh et al., 2022; Ouyang et al., 2022) have shown the effectiveness of instruction-tuned LLMs, which significantly improves the zero-shot generalization capability over the corresponding non-instruction-tuned LLMs by a huge margin. Since then, various instruction-tuned LLMs have been released, including T0 (Sanh et al., 2022), InstructGPT (Ouyang et al., 2022), FLAN-GPT (Wei et al., 2022a), FLAN-T5 (Chung et al., 2022), FLAN-PaLM (Chung et al., 2022), mT0 (Muennighoff et al., 2022), BLOOMZ (Muennighoff et al., 2022), Alpaca (Taori et al., 2023), etc. However, most of these models are only pre-trained on a single or few languages, with the exception of mT0 and BLOOMZ which are adapted from models pre-trained on 101 languages, i.e., mT5 (Xue et al., 2021), and pre-trained on 46 languages, i.e., BLOOM (Scao et al., 2022), respectively. In this work, we utilize BLOOMZ (Muennighoff et al., 2022) as the backbone in of InstructAlign.

[1]We gather the language and language family information from URIEL (Littell et al., 2017; Malaviya et al., 2017).

[2]We use the terms L1, L2, and L3 to denote the first, second, and third language acquisition (Hammarberg, 2001, 2014). In our context, L1 denotes the pre-trained languages in LLMs, L2 denotes the newly adapted languages, and L3denotes other languages that have not been seen after tuning with InstructAlign, which are only used in the evaluation.

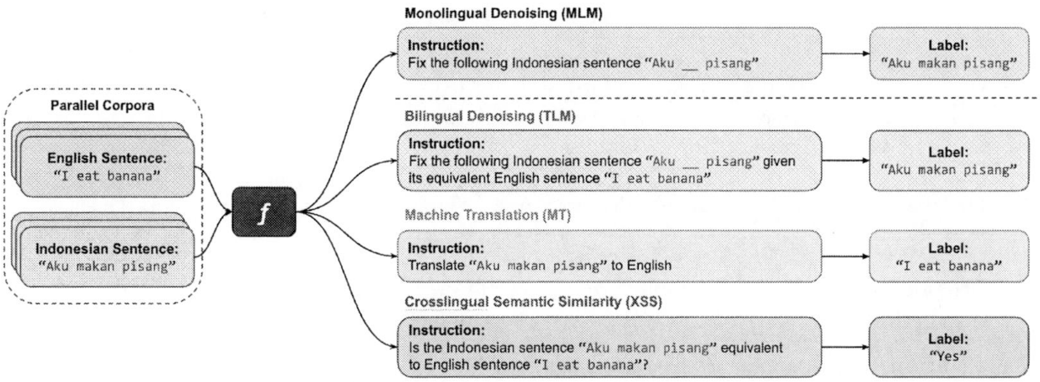

Figure 2: Example of the alignment-based crosslingual instruction prompts, i.e., bilingual denoising (TLM), machine translation (MT), and crosslingual semantic similarity (XSS) in comparison to the monolingual denoising (MLM).

2.2 Crosslingual Alignment

Crosslingual alignment is a widely explored concept that allows language models (LMs) to align, commonly at a word/sentence level, across different languages. Crosslingual alignment allows the models to perform crosslingual inference without requiring any tuning on the target task. Fung (1997, 1998) a bilingual lexicon extraction method through word-to-word alignment from word relation matrix. Fung and Cheung (2004) introduces a bilingual lexicon and parallel sentence extraction method from aligning sentences from non-parallel data via Bootstrapping and EM. Lample et al. (2018b); Cao et al. (2020) introduces align bilingual lexicon method that requires no parallel data by performing embedding alignment across different languages. This is then utilized to deal with unsupervised machine translation Lample et al. (2018a). A crosslingual pre-training objective for building LMs, namely translation language modeling (TLM) (Conneau and Lample, 2019), has also been explored which enforces token-level alignment between languages allowing the model to learn aligned representation across multiple languages. In this work, we perform crosslingual alignment through instruction by introducing bilingual denoising instruction which is equivalent to token-level alignment in TLM, and translation instruction which serves as sentence-level alignment across different languages.

2.3 Continual Learning for Language Models

Continual learning is a paradigm to learn various tasks gradually allowing the model to acquire new knowledge over time(Delange et al., 2021). Using a naive fine-tuning approach for continual learning causes the model to suffer from catastrophic forgetting (CF) (French, 1999). Therefore, various methods have been introduced to prevent CF. Regularization-based methods (Kirkpatrick et al., 2017; Liu et al., 2018; Aljundi et al., 2018) add a regularization in the loss function to prevent the model to be updated into a direction that causes CF. Replay-based methods (Rolnick et al., 2019; Lopez-Paz and Ranzato, 2017; Chaudhry et al., 2019a) add samples from previous tasks to be incorporated during learning the new task, which helps regularize the model to avoid CF. Parameter isolation methods (Aljundi et al., 2017; Serrà et al., 2018; Mallya and Lazebnik, 2018) prevent the model from CF by learning new tasks using a new set of parameters while keeping the other parameters frozen during fine-tuning. In this work, we apply experience replay (Rolnick et al., 2019), which is a simple replay-based method by adding tasks from previously learned languages when training new languages without any loss modification.

3 Methodology

InstructAlign is a continual crosslingual instruction tuning framework that allows the model to align high-to-low resource languages through instruction tuning. InstructAlign introduces two components, i.e., 1) crosslingual alignment through instruction tuning, which allows the model to align pre-trained languages with the new languages through crosslingual alignment, and 2) continual instruction tuning, which applies continual learning into instruction tuning to avoid catastrophic forgetting.

Dataset	Task	#Lang.	#L1	#L2	#L3	#Test
NusaX	Sentiment Analysis	12	2	7	3	4400
NusaTranslation	Sentiment Analysis	11+1	1	3	8	10400
NusaParagraph	Emotion Recognition	10	0	4	6	5700
NusaParagraph	Topic Classification	10	0	4	6	6250

Table 1: Statistics of all datasets used in the experiments. **#Lang.** denotes the #languages in each dataset.

3.1 Crosslingual Alignment through Instruction

Given a parallel text pair (x, y) from two languages, the goal of crosslingual alignment is to learn a mapping function $f(.)$ parameterized by θ such that $f(x, \theta) = f(y, \theta)$. The (x, y) text pair commonly comes in the form of a word pair or a phrase pair (Lample et al., 2018b,a), but in theory, it should be able to generalize to a sentence pair or even a paragraph. With the goal of aligning two parallel texts from two different languages, InstructAlign defines a set of alignment-based crosslingual instructions by exploiting multiple alignment objectives that can be achieved through a parallel sentence. Specifically, we explore three different objectives, i.e., bilingual denoising / translation language modeling (**TLM**), machine translation (**MT**) and crosslingual semantic similarity (**XSS**).

We first define a parallel sentence pair ($X = \{x_1, x_2, \ldots, x_m\}, Y = \{y_1, y_2, \ldots, y_n\}$), where x_i and y_i denote the i-th token of the sentence X and Y, respectively. For bilingual denoising (**TLM**), we model the problem as a conditional denoising task. InstructAlign first applies a perturbation function $g^{tlm}(.)$ to the target sentence Y that masks out part of the tokens in order to get $\tilde{Y} = g^{tlm}(Y)$. The pair $(X, \tilde{Y})$ is then used to generate a prompt using $h(X, \tilde{Y}, T^{tlm})$, resulting in an input-output data pair for prompting $(h^{tlm}(X, \tilde{Y}, T^{tlm}), Y)$, where $h^{tlm}(.)$ denotes a bilingual denoising prompt generator and T^{tlm} the prompt template.

For the machine translation (**MT**) objective, we define the input-output data pair as $(h^{mt}(X, T^{mt}), Y)$, where $h^{mt}(.)$ denotes a machine translation prompt generator and T^{mt} denotes a machine translation prompt template. As for the crosslingual semantic similarity (**XSS**) objective, we models the problem as an inference task to predict whether two parallel sentences X and Y are semantically similar. Specifically, we define the input-output data pair as $(h^{xss}(X, Y, T^{xss}), l)$ where $h^{xss}(.)$ is a semantic similarity prompt generator, T^{xss} denotes a semantic similarity prompt template and l the binary label regarding whether the sentences are semantically related or not. The examples of the crosslingual alignment objectives are shown in Figure 2.

3.2 Continual Instruction Tuning through Experience Replay

Within the continual instruction tuning phase of InstructAlign, experience replay (Rolnick et al., 2019) is employed to minimize the catastrophic forgetting problem. mhamdi-etal-2023-cross Experience replay works by storing some of the past training data and using them during the optimization step of the new data. These past data serve as a regularization term that prevents the models to forget past knowledge when learning from the new data. The past data is collected from the instruction tuning data used when developing the corresponding instruction-tuned model, which are all supervised.

During the continual instruction tuning, InstructAlign takes only r randomly sampled data from the past instruction tuning data. The sampled past data is used during continual-instruction tuning with a balanced sampling between the past data and new data. More formally, we define a past dataset $\mathcal{D}^{old}$ and a newly generated crosslingual instruction dataset $\mathcal{D}^{cli}$. On each optimization step, InstructAlign samples data in an interleaving manner resulting in a batch data $\mathcal{B} = \{s_1^{\mathcal{D}^{old}}, s_1^{\mathcal{D}^{new}}, s_2^{\mathcal{D}^{old}}, s_2^{\mathcal{D}^{new}}, \ldots, s_n^{\mathcal{D}^{old}}, s_n^{\mathcal{D}^{new}}\}$ with $2n$ samples, where $s_i^{\mathcal{D}^{old}}$ and $s_i^{\mathcal{D}^{new}}$ denote a sample that is taken randomly from $\mathcal{D}^{old}$ and $\mathcal{D}^{new}$, respectively. Since the samples are all supervised, the optimization can be done by optimizing the cross-entropy loss (Good, 1952) from all the samples in the batch.

4 Experiment Setting

4.1 Continual-Instruction Tuning Dataset

During the InstructAlign tuning, we train the model on 7 L2 languages from Malayo-Polynesian lan-

Method	L2 Weighted F1 (%)					L1 Weighted F1 (%)			
	NT-S	NX-S	NP-E	NP-T	Avg.	NX-S En	NX-S Id	NT-S Id	Avg.
BLOOM & BLOOMZ Baseline									
BLOOM-560M	57.62	21.80	2.80	5.34	21.89	29.26	21.13	61.47	37.29
BLOOM-1.1B	59.18	22.02	2.80	5.35	22.34	22.02	22.54	58.81	34.46
BLOOM-3B	44.98	21.21	2.80	5.35	18.59	24.03	21.17	58.30	34.50
BLOOMZ-560M	46.83	33.73	2.80	5.35	22.18	58.24	55.59	69.81	61.21
BLOOMZ-1.1B	64.01	41.50	2.80	5.35	28.42	57.41	58.58	80.40	65.46
BLOOMZ-3B	69.41	45.82	2.80	5.73	30.94	62.65	**63.21**	**81.38**	**69.08**
InstructAlign-Tuned BLOOMZ-560M									
MLM r=100k	66.51	42.51	2.80	5.52	29.34	60.97	60.01	70.93	63.97
MT Obj. r=100k	66.42	41.20	2.82	5.40	28.96	60.96	58.09	64.18	61.08
TLM r=100k	69.24	42.91	2.87	5.43	30.11	61.65	58.52	72.40	64.19
XSS r=100k	68.10	45.83	2.84	5.53	30.58	61.89	58.22	71.27	63.79
InstructAlign-Tuned BLOOMZ-1.1B									
MLM r=100k	71.46	45.73	2.84	5.49	31.38	61.30	60.83	73.25	65.13
MT Obj. r=100k	66.15	44.93	2.84	5.40	29.91	61.68	59.18	65.28	62.05
TLM r=100k	70.29	**49.25**	**3.17**	**6.34**	32.26	63.26	60.54	74.66	66.15
XSS r=100k	**71.89**	49.23	3.08	5.81	**32.50**	**63.78**	59.34	75.74	66.29

Table 2: Evaluation results of InstructAlign with BLOOMZ-560M and BLOOMZ-1.1B backbones. Compared to BLOOM and BLOOMZ baselines, All InstructAlign-tuned models improve the zero-shot crosslingual performance in L2 while also retaining the performance in L1.

guage family group, i.e., Sundanese (sun), Javanese (jav), Balinese (ban), Minangkabau (min), Buginese (bug), Acehnese (ace), and Banjarese (bjn). For the L1 languages, we utilize English (eng), as English covers the majority of the pre-training data in most LLMs, and Indonesian (ind), as the language isclosely related to the target L2 languages. For the dataset, we utilize FLORES-200 dataset (Goyal et al., 2021; Team et al., 2022) as the source of the parallel data where we combine the validation and the test set producing a total of $\sim$2000 parallel sentences for each language pair which is orders of magnitude smaller compared the data size used for language adaptation used in prior works(Pfeiffer et al., 2020; Cahyawijaya et al., 2021; Alabi et al., 2022; Yong et al., 2022).

4.2 Models & Hyperparameters

We utilize BLOOMZ (Muennighoff et al., 2022) as the backbone model. Specifically, we explore InstructAlign on two model size, i.e., BLOOMZ-560M and BLOOMZ-1.1B. For InstructAlign, we evaluate three crosslingual alignment objectives, i.e., **TLM**, **XSS**, and **MT**. The list of prompts used for instruction tuning is described in Appendix A. We use English prompts in all experiments. We run all experiments with an initial learning rate of 1e-5 with a linear learning rate decay and a batch size of 32 for a fixed optimization step of 50,000. We run the InstructAlign on a single RTX3090 GPU (24GB) using the AdamW optimizer (Loshchilov and Hutter, 2019) and mixed-precision training (Micikevicius et al., 2018). We use a fixed number of replay samples r = 100000.

4.3 Evaluation Setting

After tuning with InstructAlign, the model is then evaluated in a zero-shot crosslingual inference setting, in which the model has never seen the task on the target languages, but might have seen the task on other seen languages. To retrieve the classification label, we compute the joint probability of the prompt with each label in the dataset and pick the label which prompt the highest joint probability. We consider 3 different prompts in English for the zero-shot inference and take the average accuracy and weighted F1 scores as the evaluation metrics. The list of the prompts used in our evaluation is shown in Appendix A. We use a single RTX1080Ti GPU (11GB) to run the evaluation for all models. To reduce the memory bottleneck during inference, we run the evaluations using 8-bit inference via

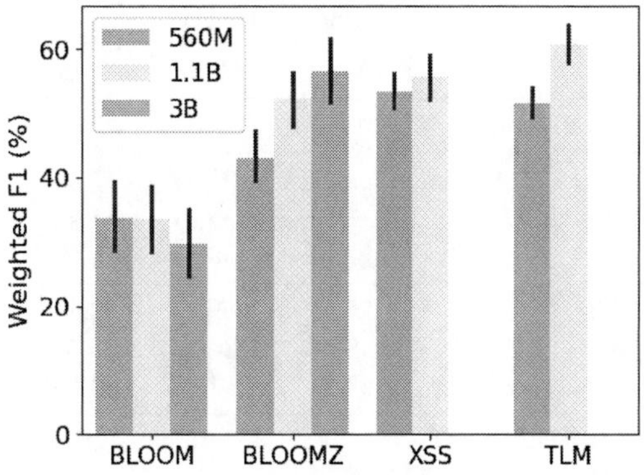

Figure 3: Average performance of various models across different model scales on the L1 and L2 languages subsets of the **NT-S** and **NX-S** datasets.

LLM.int8() (Dettmers et al., 2022). We provide the performance comparison between 8-bit and 32-bit evaluation in Appendix B.

Zero-Shot Evaluation Datasets For evaluating the effectiveness of InstructAlign, we utilize four multilingual Indonesian local languages datasets, i.e., the sentiment analysis task from NusaX (**NX-S**) (Winata et al., 2022), the sentiment analysis task from NusaTranslation (**NT-S**) (Cahyawijaya et al., 2023a), the topic classification task from NusaParagraph (**NP-T**) (Cahyawijaya et al., 2023a), and the paragraph-level emotion recognition task from NusaParagraph (**NP-E**) (Cahyawijaya et al., 2023a). The detailed per-dataset statistics are shown in Table 1. NusaX covers 12 languages including 2 L1 languages: English (eng) and Indonesian (ind), 7 L2 languages: Acehnese (ace), Balinese (ban), Buginese (bug), Banjarese (ban), Javanese (jav), Minangkabau (min), and Sundanese (sun), and 3 L3 languages: Toba Batak (bbc), Madurese (mad), and Ngaju (nij). While NusaTranslation covers 11 languages, which includes 3 L2 languages: Javanese (jav), Sundanese (sun), and Minangkabau (min), and 8 L3 languages: Ambon (abs), Batak (btk), Betawi (bew), Bima (bhp), Madurese (mad), Makassarese (mak), Musi (mui), and Rejang (rej). NusaParagraph covers 10 languages, which includes 4 L2 languages: Sundanese, Javanese (jav), Minangkabau (min), and, and 6 L3 languages: Batak (btk), Betawi (bew), Madurese (mad), Makassarese (mak), Musi (mui), Rejang (rej). To expand the evaluation dataset for L1, we add the Indonesian sentiment analaysis data from IndoLEM (Koto et al., 2020) [3] as the Indonesian (ind) subset of **NT-S**. More details about each dataset can be found in Appendix C.

[3]The source translation data of NusaTranslation

Method	L2	L1
Baselines		
Random	40.28	30.88
Majority	32.34	21.17
BLOOMZ-560M	37.66	**61.21**
Single Objective		
Monolingual Denoising (MLM)	36.71	53.14
Machine Translation (MT)	35.43	47.95
Bilingual Denoising (TLM)	45.48	53.28
Crosslingual Semantic Similarity (XSS)	44.55	54.05
Multi Objectives		
MLM + MT	40.09	47.67
TLM + MT	42.93	48.75
XSS + MT	43.32	50.66
MLM + TLM	43.46	53.16
MLM + XSS	42.82	53.90
TLM + XSS	**45.83**	54.01

Table 3: Averaged Weighted F1 scores from various InstructAlign objectives in the **NT-S** and **NX-S** datasets. We use BLOOMZ-560M as the backbone.

4.4 Baselines

For our baselines, we conduct zero-shot prompting using four different sizes of BLOOMZ, i.e., BLOOMZ-560M, BLOOMZ-1.1B, BLOOMZ-1.7B, and BLOOMZ-3B, without any additional language adaptation phase. In addition, to compare the effectiveness of the crosslingual alignment, we add continual instruction-tuned baselines that incorporate only monolingual denoising instructions, which is equivalent to performing language adaptation using MLM (Devlin et al., 2019).

5 Experiment Result

Effectiveness of InstructAlign Table 2 shows the result of InstructAlign on both L1 and L2 languages. InstructAlign-tuned models with MT, TLM, and XSS objectives significantly outperform the comparable-sized BLOOM and BLOOMZ baselines on L2 languages while retaining a similar performance level as the original BLOOMZ models on L1 languages. Surprisingly, InstructAlign with MLM objectives is also effective, yielding a similar performance on L2 languages compared to the crosslingual objectives. In § 6.1, we show that this improvement only occurs after combining the MLM objective with the experience replay, demonstrating the importance of continual instruc-

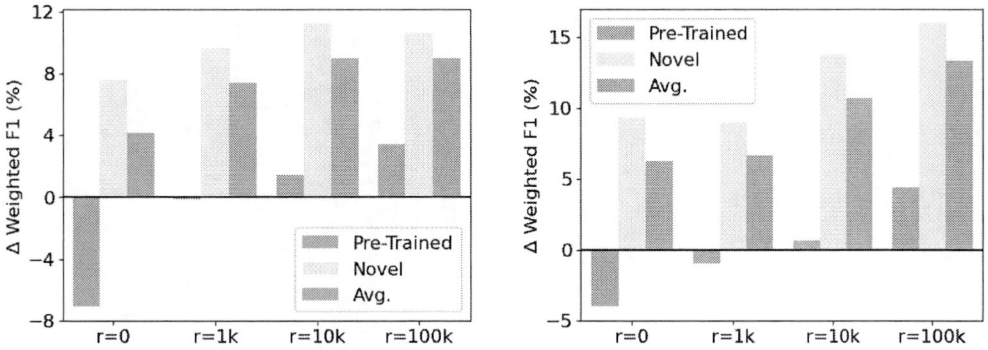

Figure 4: Δ weighted F1 of InstructAlign tuned BLOOMZ-560M with **(left)** TLM and **(right)** XSS objectives various continual instruction-tuned approaches compared to the original BLOOMZ-560M baseline. Negative scores indicate that the model performs worse compared to the baseline.

tion tuning during language adaption. While in the NusaParagraph emotion recognition (**NP-E**) and topic classification (**NP-T**) tasks, all baselines yield a very low score, suggesting that the ability to solve long text classification tasks do not emerge on that scale (Wei et al., 2022b). Interestingly, InstructAlign tuned models indicate consistent improvement, although marginal, on these tasks, demonstrating that an early emergence in L2 languages is possible through InstructAlign.

Effect of Model Scaling As shown in Figure 3, we observe that scaling increases the zero-shot performance of BLOOMZ on both L1 and L2, but the same does not apply to BLOOM, suggesting the benefit of instruction tuning for better generalization to unseen tasks and languages. Moreover, applying InstructAlign on larger BLOOMZ results in higher overall zero-shot performance on both L1 and L2. Specifically, InstructAlign-tuned models with 1.1 billion parameters yield ~2% higher performance compared to the 560 million parameters InstructAlign-tuned models and even perform competitively with the original 3 billion parameters BLOOMZ model. This suggests that the scaling law of language models (Kaplan et al., 2020; Hoffmann et al., 2022) also apply after InstructAlign where larger-sized models tend to perform better compared to their smaller counterpart. Detailed experiment results are described in Appendix D.

6 Analysis and Discussion

6.1 Alignment Objectives

To better understand the effectiveness of each alignment objective, we conduct experiments by using a single objective, i.e., monolingual denoising (MLM), machine translation (MT), bilingual denoising (TLM) and crosslingual semantic similarity (XSS), as well as multi objectives on various combinations. We also test zero-shot prompting without any additional language adaption phase as a baseline for comparison. Note that continual instruction tuning through experience replay is not applied (r=0) in these experiments since we focused on the effect of alignment objectives.

As shown in Table 3, BLOOMZ 560M zero-shot performs better than the random baseline on L1 while achieving a lower score on L2, showing that BLOOMZ 560M is unable to be directly applied to these L2 languages. For InstructAlign with a single objective, similar to the result from prior work (Yong et al., 2022), applying the MLM objective decays the performance of the model. Similarly, using MT objective also decreases the performance of both L1 and L2. Nevertheless, as shown in Table 2, this problem can be mitigated by applying continual learning. On the other hand, both TLM and XSS help improve the model on L2, indicating that these objectives are effective for aligning L1 and L2 languages. Additionally, the performance in L1 languages is also retained the most when using the TLM and XSS objectives.

When combining multiple objectives during InstructAlign, we observe the highest score when combining TLM and XSS. Interestingly, adding the MLM and MT objectives during InstructAlign consistently yields a lower score compared to the single TLM and XSS objectives for both L2 and L1 languages. These facts suggest that cross-lingual objectives such as XSS and TLM, are effective for learning new languages through cross-lingual instruction-tuning with limited data.

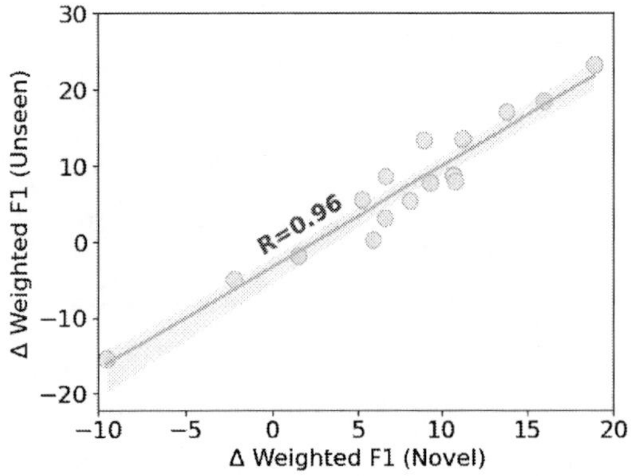

Figure 5: Correlation of Δ weighted F1 from the InstructAlign tuned models to the corresponding BLOOMZ backbone models on novel and unseen languages. R denotes the Pearson correlation coefficient.

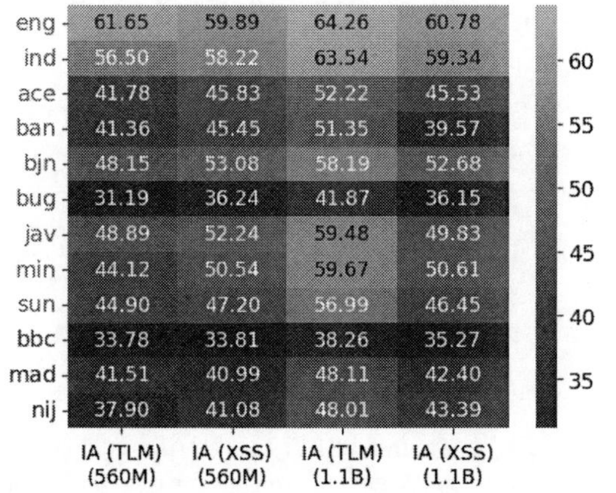

Figure 6: Per language results of InstructAlign tuned models in NusaX. red denotes L1 languages. teal denotes L2 languages. purple denotes L3 languages

6.2 Continual Instruction Tuning

In order to assess the effectiveness of continual instruction tuning through experience replay, we conduct an experiment exploring the effect of different numbers of replay samples r used in continual instruction tuning. Specifically, we explore 4 settings of r, i.e., $r = [0, 1000, 10000, 100000]$. Figure 4 shows the performance of the InstructAlign tuned models across different ranges of replay examples r. When using no experience replay (r=0), the performance of the **pre-trained** languages drops significantly, and even further, the performances on the **novel** languages also drop which suggests that the multitask prompting capability for both of these methods are degraded (Yong et al., 2022). When r increases, a much smaller performance degradation is observed on the L1 languages. Interestingly, the performance on **novel** languages also improved when r increases which in the end, increases the performance of the model across all languages. These facts demonstrate the importance of the experience replays for avoiding catastrophic forgetting in continual instruction tuning.

6.3 Impact of InstructAlign on L3 Languages

We further assess the impact of aligning L2 languages through InstructAlign to other unseen Indonesian languages which are within the same language family group (L3). To assess the effectiveness of transferability from the L2 languages to L3 languages, we compute the correlation coefficient between Δ weighted F1 score on the L2 and L3 languages for each model compared to the corresponding baseline, and measure the Pearson's correlation coefficient (Rodgers and Nicewander, 1988; Freedman et al., 2007).

As shown in Figure 5, the correlation coefficient between the performance improvement of L2 and L3 languages is high with a Pearson's correlation coefficient of 0.96. This indicates the effectiveness of the InstructAlign approach for not only adapting to L2 languages but also to related L3 languages. Nevertheless, the improvement for unseen language still depends on the language distances as shown in Figure 6, where performance on Toba Batak (bbc) and Buginese (bug) yield much lower scores compares the other languages. This result aligns with the analysis from NusaX (Winata et al., 2022) which shows that the performances of Buginese (bug) and Toba Batak (bbc) are the lowest for both the multitask and zero-shot crosslingual settings due to the relatively low vocabulary overlapping compared to other languages in NusaX. This suggests that by performing , the model can also understand unseen languages that are related to the novel-adapted language, indicating the generalization of the crosslingual transfer from pre-trained languages to novel and unseen languages

6.4 Conclusion

In this work, we address the challenge of increasing the language coverage of instruction-tuned LLMs by introducing a crosslingual continual instruction tuning method, InstructAlign. We demonstrate that InstructAlign allows an instruction-tuned LLM to effectively learn novel languages through alignment-based crosslingual instruction tuning objectives while retaining the existing multitask and multilingual abilities. Based on our experiment results on four Indonesian local languages datasets, InstructAlign effectively improves the understanding of novel Indonesian local languages, improving the language understanding performance on novel languages by ~5-10% weighted F1 score and also demonstrates a better forward transfer performance to other unseen Indonesian local languages by a significant margin. In addition, we analyze various objectives of InstructAlign and demonstrate the effectiveness of alignment-based crosslingual instruction tuning objectives compared to the traditional masked language modeling (MLM) for learning novel languages with a limited amount of data. Our work contributes to the advancement of language adaptation methods for instruction-tuned LLMs, especially for underrepresented languages.

7 Limitation and Future Works

7.1 Other Model Architectures

Despite the effectiveness of InstructAlign on BLOOMZ, its effectiveness has not been explored for different model architectures such as encoder-decoder or other model architectures. Due to the limited computing budget, we can only run the InstructAlign experiment on a decoder-only model, i.e., BLOOMZ, We encourage future works to explore the experiment in other model architectures.

7.2 Scaling to Larger LLMs

As described in §5, we hypothesize that InstructAlign-tuned models follow the scaling laws of language models (Kaplan et al., 2020; Hoffmann et al., 2022). Nevertheless, we can only empirically show this scaling effect of InstructAlign in BLOOMZ-560M and BLOOMZ-1.1B due to the limited computing budget. We expect future works to expand the exploration to larger-scale models.

7.3 Other Continual Learning Methods

In terms of continual learning methods, we only explore a single approach, i.e., experience replay (Rolnick et al., 2019), due to the efficient memory requirement of this method. Further analysis and examination of other potential continual learning approaches, such as A-GEM (Chaudhry et al., 2019a) and EWC (Liu et al., 2018), is another potential research direction to be explored in future works.

7.4 Underrepresented Languages from Other Language Family

There are many other underrepresented languages such as indigenous languages of the Americas (Ebrahimi et al., 2022), African (Adelani et al., 2021, 2022), Indic (Kakwani et al., 2020; Kumar et al., 2022), Austronesian (Winata et al., 2022; Cahyawijaya et al., 2023b), and many others all around the world. In this work, we only explore InstructAlign for Malayo-Polynesian language family group under the Austronesian language family, specifically for Indonesian local languages. For future work, we are eager to explore the generalization of InstructAlign and other language adaptation methods on other underrepresented and low-resource languages.

Ethical Consideration

Our work highlights the importance of inclusivity in LLM technology for underrepresented and extremely low-resource languages. During our study, we are well aware of the ethical responsibility associated with language research and the potential impact it can have on communities. Our ultimate goal is to promote linguistic diversity and contribute to a more inclusive NLP landscape. We encourage further collaboration and engagement with underrepresented and low-resource language communities to ensure that their voices are heard and their needs are addressed in future language technology development. We remain committed to the principles of ethical research, diversity, inclusivity, and fairness, striving to mitigate biases and promote social good through our work in the field of NLP.

8 Acknowledgements

We thank Bryan Wilie and Yong Zheng Xin for the fruitful discussions and suggestions. This work has been partially funded by PhD Fellowship Award, the Hong Kong University of Science and Technology; and PF20-43679 Hong Kong PhD Fellowship Scheme, Research Grant Council, Hong Kong.

References

David Adelani, Graham Neubig, Sebastian Ruder, Shruti Rijhwani, Michael Beukman, Chester Palen-Michel, Constantine Lignos, Jesujoba Alabi, Shamsuddeen Muhammad, Peter Nabende, Cheikh M. Bamba Dione, Andiswa Bukula, Rooweither Mabuya, Bonaventure F. P. Dossou, Blessing Sibanda, Happy Buzaaba, Jonathan Mukiibi, Godson Kalipe, Derguene Mbaye, Amelia Taylor, Fatoumata Kabore, Chris Chinenye Emezue, Anuoluwapo Aremu, Perez Ogayo, Catherine Gitau, Edwin Munkoh-Buabeng, Victoire Memdjokam Koagne, Allahsera Auguste Tapo, Tebogo Macucwa, Vukosi Marivate, Mboning Tchiaze Elvis, Tajuddeen Gwadabe, Tosin Adewumi, Orevaoghene Ahia, Joyce Nakatumba-Nabende, Neo Lerato Mokono, Ignatius Ezeani, Chiamaka Chukwuneke, Mofetoluwa Oluwaseun Adeyemi, Gilles Quentin Hacheme, Idris Abdulmumin, Odunayo Ogundepo, Oreen Yousuf, Tatiana Moteu, and Dietrich Klakow. 2022. MasakhaNER 2.0: Africa-centric transfer learning for named entity recognition. In *Proceedings of the 2022 Conference on Empirical Methods in Natural Language Processing*, pages 4488–4508, Abu Dhabi, United Arab Emirates. Association for Computational Linguistics.

David Ifeoluwa Adelani, Jade Abbott, Graham Neubig, Daniel D'souza, Julia Kreutzer, Constantine Lignos, Chester Palen-Michel, Happy Buzaaba, Shruti Rijhwani, Sebastian Ruder, Stephen Mayhew, Israel Abebe Azime, Shamsuddeen H. Muhammad, Chris Chinenye Emezue, Joyce Nakatumba-Nabende, Perez Ogayo, Aremu Anuoluwapo, Catherine Gitau, Derguene Mbaye, Jesujoba Alabi, Seid Muhie Yimam, Tajuddeen Rabiu Gwadabe, Ignatius Ezeani, Rubungo Andre Niyongabo, Jonathan Mukiibi, Verrah Otiende, Iroro Orife, Davis David, Samba Ngom, Tosin Adewumi, Paul Rayson, Mofetoluwa Adeyemi, Gerald Muriuki, Emmanuel Anebi, Chiamaka Chukwuneke, Nkiruka Odu, Eric Peter Wairagala, Samuel Oyerinde, Clemencia Siro, Tobius Saul Bateesa, Temilola Oloyede, Yvonne Wambui, Victor Akinode, Deborah Nabagereka, Maurice Katusiime, Ayodele Awokoya, Mouhamadane MBOUP, Dibora Gebreyohannes, Henok Tilaye, Kelechi Nwaike, Degaga Wolde, Abdoulaye Faye, Blessing Sibanda, Orevaoghene Ahia, Bonaventure F. P. Dossou, Kelechi Ogueji, Thierno Ibrahima DIOP, Abdoulaye Diallo, Adewale Akinfaderin, Tendai Marengereke, and Salomey Osei. 2021. MasakhaNER: Named Entity Recognition for African Languages. *Transactions of the Association for Computational Linguistics*, 9:1116–1131.

Muhammad Farid Adilazuarda, Samuel Cahyawijaya, and Ayu Purwarianti. 2023. The obscure limitation of modular multilingual language models.

Alham Fikri Aji, Genta Indra Winata, Fajri Koto, Samuel Cahyawijaya, Ade Romadhony, Rahmad Mahendra, Kemal Kurniawan, David Moeljadi, Radityo Eko Prasojo, Timothy Baldwin, Jey Han Lau, and Sebastian Ruder. 2022. One country, 700+ languages: NLP challenges for underrepresented languages and dialects in Indonesia. In *Proceedings of the 60th Annual Meeting of the Association for Computational Linguistics (Volume 1: Long Papers)*, pages 7226–7249, Dublin, Ireland. Association for Computational Linguistics.

Jesujoba O. Alabi, David Ifeoluwa Adelani, Marius Mosbach, and Dietrich Klakow. 2022. Adapting pre-trained language models to African languages via multilingual adaptive fine-tuning. In *Proceedings of the 29th International Conference on Computational Linguistics*, pages 4336–4349, Gyeongju, Republic of Korea. International Committee on Computational Linguistics.

Rahaf Aljundi, Francesca Babiloni, Mohamed Elhoseiny, Marcus Rohrbach, and Tinne Tuytelaars. 2018. Memory aware synapses: Learning what (not) to forget. In *Computer Vision – ECCV 2018*, pages 144–161. Springer International Publishing.

Rahaf Aljundi, Punarjay Chakravarty, and Tinne Tuytelaars. 2017. Expert gate: Lifelong learning with a network of experts. In *2017 IEEE Conference on Computer Vision and Pattern Recognition (CVPR)*. IEEE.

Akari Asai, Sneha Kudugunta, Xinyan Velocity Yu, Terra Blevins, Hila Gonen, Machel Reid, Yulia Tsvetkov, Sebastian Ruder, and Hannaneh Hajishirzi. 2023. Buffet: Benchmarking large language models for few-shot cross-lingual transfer.

Tom Brown, Benjamin Mann, Nick Ryder, Melanie Subbiah, Jared D Kaplan, Prafulla Dhariwal, Arvind Neelakantan, Pranav Shyam, Girish Sastry, Amanda Askell, Sandhini Agarwal, Ariel Herbert-Voss, Gretchen Krueger, Tom Henighan, Rewon Child, Aditya Ramesh, Daniel Ziegler, Jeffrey Wu, Clemens Winter, Chris Hesse, Mark Chen, Eric Sigler, Mateusz Litwin, Scott Gray, Benjamin Chess, Jack Clark, Christopher Berner, Sam McCandlish, Alec Radford, Ilya Sutskever, and Dario Amodei. 2020. Language models are few-shot learners. In *Advances in Neural Information Processing Systems*, volume 33, pages 1877–1901. Curran Associates, Inc.

Samuel Cahyawijaya, Fajri Koto Holy Lovenia, Dea Adhista, Emmanuel Dave, Sarah Oktavianti, Salsabil Maulana Akbar, Jhonson Lee, Nuur Shadieq, Tjeng Wawan Cenggoro, Hanung Linuwih, Bryan Wilie, Galih Pradipta Muridan, Alham Fikri Aji, Genta Indra Winata, David Moeljadi, Ayu Purwarianti, and Pascale Fung. 2023a. Nusawrites: Constructing high-quality corpora for underrepresented and extremely low-resource languages. Anonymous preprint under review.

Samuel Cahyawijaya, Holy Lovenia, Alham Fikri Aji, Genta Indra Winata, Bryan Wilie, Rahmad Mahendra, Christian Wibisono, Ade Romadhony, Karissa Vincentio, Fajri Koto, Jennifer Santoso, David Moeljadi,

Cahya Wirawan, Frederikus Hudi, Ivan Halim Parmonangan, Ika Alfina, Muhammad Satrio Wicaksono, Ilham Firdausi Putra, Samsul Rahmadani, Yulianti Oenang, Ali Akbar Septiandri, James Jaya, Kaustubh D. Dhole, Arie Ardiyanti Suryani, Rifki Afina Putri, Dan Su, Keith Stevens, Made Nindyatama Nityasya, Muhammad Farid Adilazuarda, Ryan Ignatius, Ryandito Diandaru, Tiezheng Yu, Vito Ghifari, Wenliang Dai, Yan Xu, Dyah Damapuspita, Cuk Tho, Ichwanul Muslim Karo Karo, Tirana Noor Fatyanosa, Ziwei Ji, Pascale Fung, Graham Neubig, Timothy Baldwin, Sebastian Ruder, Herry Sujaini, Sakriani Sakti, and Ayu Purwarianti. 2023b. Nusacrowd: Open source initiative for indonesian nlp resources.

Samuel Cahyawijaya, Genta Indra Winata, Bryan Wilie, Karissa Vincentio, Xiaohong Li, Adhiguna Kuncoro, Sebastian Ruder, Zhi Yuan Lim, Syafri Bahar, Masayu Khodra, Ayu Purwarianti, and Pascale Fung. 2021. IndoNLG: Benchmark and resources for evaluating Indonesian natural language generation. In *Proceedings of the 2021 Conference on Empirical Methods in Natural Language Processing*, pages 8875–8898, Online and Punta Cana, Dominican Republic. Association for Computational Linguistics.

Steven Cao, Nikita Kitaev, and Dan Klein. 2020. Multilingual alignment of contextual word representations. In *International Conference on Learning Representations*.

Ethan C. Chau, Lucy H. Lin, and Noah A. Smith. 2020. Parsing with multilingual BERT, a small corpus, and a small treebank. In *Findings of the Association for Computational Linguistics: EMNLP 2020*, pages 1324–1334, Online. Association for Computational Linguistics.

Arslan Chaudhry, Marc'Aurelio Ranzato, Marcus Rohrbach, and Mohamed Elhoseiny. 2019a. Efficient lifelong learning with a-gem. In *ICLR*.

Arslan Chaudhry, Marcus Rohrbach, Mohamed Elhoseiny, Thalaiyasingam Ajanthan, Puneet K. Dokania, Philip H. S. Torr, and Marc'Aurelio Ranzato. 2019b. On tiny episodic memories in continual learning.

Aakanksha Chowdhery, Sharan Narang, Jacob Devlin, Maarten Bosma, Gaurav Mishra, Adam Roberts, Paul Barham, Hyung Won Chung, Charles Sutton, Sebastian Gehrmann, Parker Schuh, Kensen Shi, Sasha Tsvyashchenko, Joshua Maynez, Abhishek Rao, Parker Barnes, Yi Tay, Noam Shazeer, Vinodkumar Prabhakaran, Emily Reif, Nan Du, Ben Hutchinson, Reiner Pope, James Bradbury, Jacob Austin, Michael Isard, Guy Gur-Ari, Pengcheng Yin, Toju Duke, Anselm Levskaya, Sanjay Ghemawat, Sunipa Dev, Henryk Michalewski, Xavier Garcia, Vedant Misra, Kevin Robinson, Liam Fedus, Denny Zhou, Daphne Ippolito, David Luan, Hyeontaek Lim, Barret Zoph, Alexander Spiridonov, Ryan Sepassi, David Dohan, Shivani Agrawal, Mark Omernick, Andrew M. Dai, Thanumalayan Sankaranarayana Pillai, Marie Pellat, Aitor Lewkowycz, Erica Moreira, Rewon Child, Oleksandr Polozov, Katherine Lee, Zongwei Zhou, Xuezhi Wang, Brennan Saeta, Mark Diaz, Orhan Firat, Michele Catasta, Jason Wei, Kathy Meier-Hellstern, Douglas Eck, Jeff Dean, Slav Petrov, and Noah Fiedel. 2022. Palm: Scaling language modeling with pathways.

Hyung Won Chung, Le Hou, Shayne Longpre, Barret Zoph, Yi Tay, William Fedus, Yunxuan Li, Xuezhi Wang, Mostafa Dehghani, Siddhartha Brahma, Albert Webson, Shixiang Shane Gu, Zhuyun Dai, Mirac Suzgun, Xinyun Chen, Aakanksha Chowdhery, Alex Castro-Ros, Marie Pellat, Kevin Robinson, Dasha Valter, Sharan Narang, Gaurav Mishra, Adams Yu, Vincent Zhao, Yanping Huang, Andrew Dai, Hongkun Yu, Slav Petrov, Ed H. Chi, Jeff Dean, Jacob Devlin, Adam Roberts, Denny Zhou, Quoc V. Le, and Jason Wei. 2022. Scaling instruction-finetuned language models.

Alexis Conneau and Guillaume Lample. 2019. *Cross-Lingual Language Model Pretraining*. Curran Associates Inc., Red Hook, NY, USA.

Matthias Delange, Rahaf Aljundi, Marc Masana, Sarah Parisot, Xu Jia, Ales Leonardis, Greg Slabaugh, and Tinne Tuytelaars. 2021. A continual learning survey: Defying forgetting in classification tasks. *IEEE Transactions on Pattern Analysis and Machine Intelligence*, pages 1–1.

Tim Dettmers, Mike Lewis, Younes Belkada, and Luke Zettlemoyer. 2022. Llm.int8(): 8-bit matrix multiplication for transformers at scale.

Jacob Devlin, Ming-Wei Chang, Kenton Lee, and Kristina Toutanova. 2019. BERT: Pre-training of deep bidirectional transformers for language understanding. In *Proceedings of the 2019 Conference of the North American Chapter of the Association for Computational Linguistics: Human Language Technologies, Volume 1 (Long and Short Papers)*, pages 4171–4186, Minneapolis, Minnesota. Association for Computational Linguistics.

Abteen Ebrahimi and Katharina Kann. 2021. How to adapt your pretrained multilingual model to 1600 languages. In *Proceedings of the 59th Annual Meeting of the Association for Computational Linguistics and the 11th International Joint Conference on Natural Language Processing (Volume 1: Long Papers)*, pages 4555–4567, Online. Association for Computational Linguistics.

Abteen Ebrahimi, Manuel Mager, Arturo Oncevay, Vishrav Chaudhary, Luis Chiruzzo, Angela Fan, John Ortega, Ricardo Ramos, Annette Rios, Ivan Vladimir Meza Ruiz, Gustavo Giménez-Lugo, Elisabeth Mager, Graham Neubig, Alexis Palmer, Rolando Coto-Solano, Thang Vu, and Katharina Kann. 2022. AmericasNLI: Evaluating zero-shot natural language understanding of pretrained multilingual models in truly low-resource languages. In *Proceedings of the 60th Annual Meeting of the Association for Computational Linguistics (Volume 1: Long Papers)*, pages 6279–6299, Dublin, Ireland. Association for Computational Linguistics.

David Freedman, Robert Pisani, and Roger Purves. 2007. Statistics (international student edition). *Pisani, R. Purves, 4th edn. WW Norton & Company, New York.*

R French. 1999. Catastrophic forgetting in connectionist networks. *Trends in Cognitive Sciences*, 3(4):128–135.

Robert M. French. 1993. Catastrophic interference in connectionist networks: Can it be predicted, can it be prevented? In *Proceedings of the 6th International Conference on Neural Information Processing Systems*, NIPS'93, page 1176–1177, San Francisco, CA, USA. Morgan Kaufmann Publishers Inc.

Pascale Fung. 1997. Finding terminology translations from non-parallel corpora. In *Fifth Workshop on Very Large Corpora, VLC 1997, Beijing, China and Hong Kong, August 18 and August 20, 1997.*

Pascale Fung. 1998. A statistical view on bilingual lexicon extraction: From parallel corpora to non-parallel corpora. In *Machine Translation and the Information Soup, Third Conference of the Association for Machine Translation in the Americas, AMTA '98, Langhorne, PA, USA, October 28-31, 1998, Proceedings*, volume 1529 of *Lecture Notes in Computer Science*, pages 1–17. Springer.

Pascale Fung and Percy Cheung. 2004. Mining very-non-parallel corpora: Parallel sentence and lexicon extraction via bootstrapping and E. In *Proceedings of the 2004 Conference on Empirical Methods in Natural Language Processing , EMNLP 2004, A meeting of SIGDAT, a Special Interest Group of the ACL, held in conjunction with ACL 2004, 25-26 July 2004, Barcelona, Spain*, pages 57–63. ACL.

Sebastian Gehrmann, Abhik Bhattacharjee, Abinaya Mahendiran, Alex Wang, Alexandros Papangelis, Aman Madaan, Angelina Mcmillan-major, Anna Shvets, Ashish Upadhyay, Bernd Bohnet, Bingsheng Yao, Bryan Wilie, Chandra Bhagavatula, Chaobin You, Craig Thomson, Cristina Garbacea, Dakuo Wang, Daniel Deutsch, Deyi Xiong, Di Jin, Dimitra Gkatzia, Dragomir Radev, Elizabeth Clark, Esin Durmus, Faisal Ladhak, Filip Ginter, Genta Indra Winata, Hendrik Strobelt, Hiroaki Hayashi, Jekaterina Novikova, Jenna Kanerva, Jenny Chim, Jiawei Zhou, Jordan Clive, Joshua Maynez, João Sedoc, Juraj Juraska, Kaustubh Dhole, Khyathi Raghavi Chandu, Laura Perez Beltrachini, Leonardo F . R. Ribeiro, Lewis Tunstall, Li Zhang, Mahim Pushkarna, Mathias Creutz, Michael White, Mihir Sanjay Kale, Moussa Kamal Eddine, Nico Daheim, Nishant Subramani, Ondrej Dusek, Paul Pu Liang, Pawan Sasanka Ammanamanchi, Qi Zhu, Ratish Puduppully, Reno Kriz, Rifat Shahriyar, Ronald Cardenas, Saad Mahamood, Salomey Osei, Samuel Cahyawijaya, Sanja Štajner, Sebastien Montella, Shailza Jolly, Simon Mille, Tahmid Hasan, Tianhao Shen, Tosin Adewumi, Vikas Raunak, Vipul Raheja, Vitaly Nikolaev, Vivian Tsai, Yacine Jernite, Ying Xu, Yisi Sang, Yixin Liu, and Yufang Hou. 2022. GEMv2: Multilingual NLG benchmarking in a single line of code. In *Proceedings of the 2022 Conference on Empirical Methods in Natural Language Processing: System Demonstrations*, pages 266–281, Abu Dhabi, UAE. Association for Computational Linguistics.

I. J. Good. 1952. Rational decisions. *Journal of the Royal Statistical Society. Series B (Methodological)*, 14(1):107–114.

Naman Goyal, Cynthia Gao, Vishrav Chaudhary, Peng-Jen Chen, Guillaume Wenzek, Da Ju, Sanjana Krishnan, Marc'Aurelio Ranzato, Francisco Guzmán, and Angela Fan. 2021. The flores-101 evaluation benchmark for low-resource and multilingual machine translation.

Björn Hammarberg. 2001. Chapter 2. roles of l1 and l2 in l3 production and acquisition. In *Cross-Linguistic Influence in Third Language Acquisition*, pages 21–41. Multilingual Matters.

Björn Hammarberg. 2014. 1. problems in defining the concepts of l1, l2 and l3. In *Teaching and Learning in Multilingual Contexts*, pages 3–18. Multilingual Matters.

Jordan Hoffmann, Sebastian Borgeaud, Arthur Mensch, Elena Buchatskaya, Trevor Cai, Eliza Rutherford, Diego de las Casas, Lisa Anne Hendricks, Johannes Welbl, Aidan Clark, Tom Hennigan, Eric Noland, Katherine Millican, George van den Driessche, Bogdan Damoc, Aurelia Guy, Simon Osindero, Karen Simonyan, Erich Elsen, Oriol Vinyals, Jack William Rae, and Laurent Sifre. 2022. An empirical analysis of compute-optimal large language model training. In *Advances in Neural Information Processing Systems*.

Arfinda Ilmania, Abdurrahman, Samuel Cahyawijaya, and Ayu Purwarianti. 2018. Aspect detection and sentiment classification using deep neural network for indonesian aspect-based sentiment analysis. In *2018 International Conference on Asian Language Processing (IALP)*, pages 62–67.

Anubha Kabra, Emmy Liu, Simran Khanuja, Alham Fikri Aji, Genta Winata, Samuel Cahyawijaya, Anuoluwapo Aremu, Perez Ogayo, and Graham Neubig. 2023. Multi-lingual and multi-cultural figurative language understanding. In *Findings of the Association for Computational Linguistics: ACL 2023*, pages 8269–8284, Toronto, Canada. Association for Computational Linguistics.

Divyanshu Kakwani, Anoop Kunchukuttan, Satish Golla, Gokul N.C., Avik Bhattacharyya, Mitesh M. Khapra, and Pratyush Kumar. 2020. IndicNLPSuite: Monolingual corpora, evaluation benchmarks and pre-trained multilingual language models for Indian languages. In *Findings of the Association for Computational Linguistics: EMNLP 2020*, pages 4948–4961, Online. Association for Computational Linguistics.

Jared Kaplan, Sam McCandlish, Tom Henighan, Tom B. Brown, Benjamin Chess, Rewon Child, Scott Gray, Alec Radford, Jeffrey Wu, and Dario Amodei. 2020. Scaling laws for neural language models.

James Kirkpatrick, Razvan Pascanu, Neil Rabinowitz, Joel Veness, Guillaume Desjardins, Andrei A. Rusu, Kieran Milan, John Quan, Tiago Ramalho, Agnieszka Grabska-Barwinska, Demis Hassabis, Claudia Clopath, Dharshan Kumaran, and Raia Hadsell. 2017. Overcoming catastrophic forgetting in neural networks. *Proceedings of the National Academy of Sciences*, 114(13):3521–3526.

Fajri Koto, Afshin Rahimi, Jey Han Lau, and Timothy Baldwin. 2020. IndoLEM and IndoBERT: A benchmark dataset and pre-trained language model for Indonesian NLP. In *Proceedings of the 28th International Conference on Computational Linguistics*, pages 757–770, Barcelona, Spain (Online). International Committee on Computational Linguistics.

Aman Kumar, Himani Shrotriya, Prachi Sahu, Amogh Mishra, Raj Dabre, Ratish Puduppully, Anoop Kunchukuttan, Mitesh M. Khapra, and Pratyush Kumar. 2022. IndicNLG benchmark: Multilingual datasets for diverse NLG tasks in Indic languages. In *Proceedings of the 2022 Conference on Empirical Methods in Natural Language Processing*, pages 5363–5394, Abu Dhabi, United Arab Emirates. Association for Computational Linguistics.

Guillaume Lample, Alexis Conneau, Ludovic Denoyer, and Marc'Aurelio Ranzato. 2018a. Unsupervised machine translation using monolingual corpora only. In *International Conference on Learning Representations*.

Guillaume Lample, Alexis Conneau, Marc'Aurelio Ranzato, Ludovic Denoyer, and Hervé Jégou. 2018b. Word translation without parallel data. In *International Conference on Learning Representations*.

Patrick Littell, David R Mortensen, Ke Lin, Katherine Kairis, Carlisle Turner, and Lori Levin. 2017. Uriel and lang2vec: Representing languages as typological, geographical, and phylogenetic vectors. In *Proceedings of the 15th Conference of the European Chapter of the Association for Computational Linguistics: Volume 2, Short Papers*, volume 2, pages 8–14.

Haokun Liu, Derek Tam, Muqeeth Mohammed, Jay Mohta, Tenghao Huang, Mohit Bansal, and Colin Raffel. 2022. Few-shot parameter-efficient fine-tuning is better and cheaper than in-context learning. In *Advances in Neural Information Processing Systems*.

Xialei Liu, Marc Masana, Luis Herranz, Joost Van de Weijer, Antonio M. López, and Andrew D. Bagdanov. 2018. Rotate your networks: Better weight consolidation and less catastrophic forgetting. In *2018 24th International Conference on Pattern Recognition (ICPR)*, pages 2262–2268.

David Lopez-Paz and Marc'Aurelio Ranzato. 2017. Gradient episodic memory for continual learning. In *Proceedings of the 31st International Conference on Neural Information Processing Systems*, NIPS'17, page 6470–6479, Red Hook, NY, USA. Curran Associates Inc.

Ilya Loshchilov and Frank Hutter. 2019. Decoupled weight decay regularization. In *International Conference on Learning Representations*.

Rahmad Mahendra, Alham Fikri Aji, Samuel Louvan, Fahrurrozi Rahman, and Clara Vania. 2021. IndoNLI: A natural language inference dataset for Indonesian. In *Proceedings of the 2021 Conference on Empirical Methods in Natural Language Processing*, pages 10511–10527, Online and Punta Cana, Dominican Republic. Association for Computational Linguistics.

Chaitanya Malaviya, Graham Neubig, and Patrick Littell. 2017. Learning language representations for typology prediction. In *Conference on Empirical Methods in Natural Language Processing (EMNLP)*, Copenhagen, Denmark.

Arun Mallya and Svetlana Lazebnik. 2018. Packnet: Adding multiple tasks to a single network by iterative pruning. In *Proceedings of the IEEE conference on Computer Vision and Pattern Recognition*, pages 7765–7773.

Paulius Micikevicius, Sharan Narang, Jonah Alben, Gregory Diamos, Erich Elsen, David Garcia, Boris Ginsburg, Michael Houston, Oleksii Kuchaiev, Ganesh Venkatesh, and Hao Wu. 2018. Mixed precision training.

Niklas Muennighoff, Thomas Wang, Lintang Sutawika, Adam Roberts, Stella Biderman, Teven Le Scao, M Saiful Bari, Sheng Shen, Zheng-Xin Yong, Hailey Schoelkopf, Xiangru Tang, Dragomir Radev, Alham Fikri Aji, Khalid Almubarak, Samuel Albanie, Zaid Alyafeai, Albert Webson, Edward Raff, and Colin Raffel. 2022. Crosslingual generalization through multitask finetuning.

Benjamin Muller, Antonios Anastasopoulos, Benoît Sagot, and Djamé Seddah. 2021. When being unseen from mBERT is just the beginning: Handling new languages with multilingual language models. In *Proceedings of the 2021 Conference of the North American Chapter of the Association for Computational Linguistics: Human Language Technologies*, pages 448–462, Online. Association for Computational Linguistics.

Long Ouyang, Jeff Wu, Xu Jiang, Diogo Almeida, Carroll L. Wainwright, Pamela Mishkin, Chong Zhang, Sandhini Agarwal, Katarina Slama, Alex Ray, John Schulman, Jacob Hilton, Fraser Kelton, Luke Miller, Maddie Simens, Amanda Askell, Peter Welinder, Paul Christiano, Jan Leike, and Ryan Lowe. 2022. Training language models to follow instructions with human feedback.

Jonas Pfeiffer, Ivan Vulić, Iryna Gurevych, and Sebastian Ruder. 2020. MAD-X: An Adapter-Based Framework for Multi-Task Cross-Lingual Transfer. In *Proceedings of the 2020 Conference on Empirical Methods in Natural Language Processing (EMNLP)*, pages 7654–7673, Online. Association for Computational Linguistics.

Ayu Purwarianti and Ida Ayu Putu Ari Crisdayanti. 2019. Improving bi-lstm performance for indonesian sentiment analysis using paragraph vector. In *2019 International Conference of Advanced Informatics: Concepts, Theory and Applications (ICAICTA)*, pages 1–5.

Oddy Virgantara Putra, Fathin Muhammad Wasmanson, Triana Harmini, and Shoffin Nahwa Utama. 2020. Sundanese twitter dataset for emotion classification. In *2020 International Conference on Computer Engineering, Network, and Intelligent Multimedia (CENIM)*, pages 391–395.

Jack W. Rae, Sebastian Borgeaud, Trevor Cai, Katie Millican, Jordan Hoffmann, Francis Song, John Aslanides, Sarah Henderson, Roman Ring, Susannah Young, Eliza Rutherford, Tom Hennigan, Jacob Menick, Albin Cassirer, Richard Powell, George van den Driessche, Lisa Anne Hendricks, Maribeth Rauh, Po-Sen Huang, Amelia Glaese, Johannes Welbl, Sumanth Dathathri, Saffron Huang, Jonathan Uesato, John Mellor, Irina Higgins, Antonia Creswell, Nat McAleese, Amy Wu, Erich Elsen, Siddhant Jayakumar, Elena Buchatskaya, David Budden, Esme Sutherland, Karen Simonyan, Michela Paganini, Laurent Sifre, Lena Martens, Xiang Lorraine Li, Adhiguna Kuncoro, Aida Nematzadeh, Elena Gribovskaya, Domenic Donato, Angeliki Lazaridou, Arthur Mensch, Jean-Baptiste Lespiau, Maria Tsimpoukelli, Nikolai Grigorev, Doug Fritz, Thibault Sottiaux, Mantas Pajarskas, Toby Pohlen, Zhitao Gong, Daniel Toyama, Cyprien de Masson d'Autume, Yujia Li, Tayfun Terzi, Vladimir Mikulik, Igor Babuschkin, Aidan Clark, Diego de Las Casas, Aurelia Guy, Chris Jones, James Bradbury, Matthew Johnson, Blake Hechtman, Laura Weidinger, Iason Gabriel, William Isaac, Ed Lockhart, Simon Osindero, Laura Rimell, Chris Dyer, Oriol Vinyals, Kareem Ayoub, Jeff Stanway, Lorrayne Bennett, Demis Hassabis, Koray Kavukcuoglu, and Geoffrey Irving. 2022. Scaling language models: Methods, analysis & insights from training gopher.

Joseph Lee Rodgers and W. Alan Nicewander. 1988. Thirteen ways to look at the correlation coefficient. *The American Statistician*, 42(1):59–66.

David Rolnick, Arun Ahuja, Jonathan Schwarz, Timothy Lillicrap, and Gregory Wayne. 2019. Experience replay for continual learning. In *Advances in Neural Information Processing Systems*, volume 32. Curran Associates, Inc.

Victor Sanh, Albert Webson, Colin Raffel, Stephen Bach, Lintang Sutawika, Zaid Alyafeai, Antoine Chaffin, Arnaud Stiegler, Arun Raja, Manan Dey, M Saiful Bari, Canwen Xu, Urmish Thakker, Shanya Sharma Sharma, Eliza Szczechla, Taewoon Kim, Gunjan Chhablani, Nihal Nayak, Debajyoti Datta, Jonathan Chang, Mike Tian-Jian Jiang, Han Wang, Matteo Manica, Sheng Shen, Zheng Xin Yong, Harshit Pandey, Rachel Bawden, Thomas Wang, Trishala Neeraj, Jos Rozen, Abheesht Sharma, Andrea Santilli, Thibault Fevry, Jason Alan Fries, Ryan Teehan, Teven Le Scao, Stella Biderman, Leo Gao, Thomas Wolf, and Alexander M Rush. 2022. Multitask prompted training enables zero-shot task generalization. In *International Conference on Learning Representations*.

Teven Le Scao, Angela Fan, Christopher Akiki, Ellie Pavlick, Suzana Ilić, Daniel Hesslow, Roman Castagné, Alexandra Sasha Luccioni, François Yvon, Matthias Gallé, Jonathan Tow, Alexander M. Rush, Stella Biderman, Albert Webson, Pawan Sasanka Ammanamanchi, Thomas Wang, Benoît Sagot, Niklas Muennighoff, Albert Villanova del Moral, Olatunji Ruwase, Rachel Bawden, Stas Bekman, Angelina McMillan-Major, Iz Beltagy, Huu Nguyen, Lucile Saulnier, Samson Tan, Pedro Ortiz Suarez, Victor Sanh, Hugo Laurençon, Yacine Jernite, Julien Launay, Margaret Mitchell, Colin Raffel, Aaron Gokaslan, Adi Simhi, Aitor Soroa, Alham Fikri Aji, Amit Alfassy, Anna Rogers, Ariel Kreisberg Nitzav, Canwen Xu, Chenghao Mou, Chris Emezue, Christopher Klamm, Colin Leong, Daniel van Strien, David Ifeoluwa Adelani, Dragomir Radev, Eduardo González Ponferrada, Efrat Levkovizh, Ethan Kim, Eyal Bar Natan, Francesco De Toni, Gérard Dupont, Germán Kruszewski, Giada Pistilli, Hady Elsahar, Hamza Benyamina, Hieu Tran, Ian Yu, Idris Abdulmumin, Isaac Johnson, Itziar Gonzalez-Dios, Javier de la Rosa, Jenny Chim, Jesse Dodge, Jian Zhu, Jonathan Chang, Jörg Frohberg, Joseph Tobing, Joydeep Bhattacharjee, Khalid Almubarak, Kimbo Chen, Kyle Lo, Leandro Von Werra, Leon Weber, Long Phan, Loubna Ben allal, Ludovic Tanguy, Manan Dey, Manuel Romero Muñoz, Maraim Masoud, María Grandury, Mario Šaško, Max Huang, Maximin Coavoux, Mayank Singh, Mike Tian-Jian Jiang, Minh Chien Vu, Mohammad A. Jauhar, Mustafa Ghaleb, Nishant Subramani, Nora Kassner, Nurulaqilla Khamis, Olivier Nguyen, Omar Espejel, Ona de Gibert, Paulo Villegas, Peter Henderson, Pierre Colombo, Priscilla Amuok, Quentin Lhoest, Rheza Harliman, Rishi Bommasani, Roberto Luis López, Rui Ribeiro, Salomey Osei, Sampo Pyysalo, Sebastian Nagel, Shamik Bose, Shamsuddeen Hassan Muhammad, Shanya Sharma, Shayne Longpre, Somaieh Nikpoor, Stanislav Silberberg, Suhas Pai, Sydney Zink, Tiago Timponi Torrent, Timo Schick, Tristan Thrush, Valentin Danchev, Vassilina Nikoulina, Veronika Laippala, Violette Lepercq, Vrinda Prabhu, Zaid Alyafeai, Zeerak Talat, Arun Raja, Benjamin Heinzerling, Chenglei Si, Elizabeth Salesky, Sabrina J. Mielke, Wilson Y. Lee, Abheesht Sharma, Andrea Santilli, Antoine Chaffin, Arnaud Stiegler, Debajyoti Datta, Eliza Szczechla, Gunjan Chhablani, Han Wang, Harshit Pandey, Hendrik Strobelt, Jason Alan Fries, Jos Rozen, Leo Gao, Lintang Sutawika, M Saiful Bari, Maged S. Al-shaibani, Matteo Manica, Nihal Nayak, Ryan Teehan, Samuel Albanie, Sheng Shen, Srulik Ben-David, Stephen H. Bach, Taewoon Kim, Tali Bers, Thibault Fevry, Trishala Neeraj, Urmish Thakker, Vikas Raunak, Xiangru Tang, Zheng-Xin Yong, Zhiqing Sun, Shaked Brody, Yallow Uri, Hadar Tojarieh, Adam Roberts, Hyung Won Chung, Jaesung Tae, Jason Phang, Ofir Press, Conglong Li, Deepak Narayanan, Hatim Bourfoune, Jared Casper, Jeff Rasley, Max Ryabinin, Mayank Mishra, Minjia Zhang, Mohammad Shoeybi, Myriam Peyrounette, Nicolas Patry, Nouamane Tazi, Omar Sanseviero, Patrick von Platen, Pierre Cornette, Pierre François Lavallée, Rémi Lacroix, Samyam Rajbhandari, Sanchit Gandhi, Shaden Smith, Stéphane Requena, Suraj Patil, Tim Dettmers, Ahmed Baruwa, Amanpreet Singh, Anastasia Cheveleva, Anne-Laure Ligozat, Arjun Subramonian, Aurélie Névéol, Charles Lovering, Dan Garrette, Deepak Tunuguntla, Ehud Reiter, Ekaterina Taktasheva, Ekaterina Voloshina, Eli Bogdanov, Genta Indra Winata, Hailey Schoelkopf, Jan-Christoph Kalo, Jekaterina Novikova, Jessica Zosa Forde, Jordan Clive, Jungo Kasai, Ken Kawamura, Liam Hazan, Marine Carpuat, Miruna Clinciu, Najoung Kim, Newton Cheng, Oleg Serikov, Omer Antverg, Oskar van der Wal, Rui Zhang, Ruochen Zhang, Sebastian Gehrmann, Shani Pais, Tatiana Shavrina, Thomas Scialom, Tian Yun, Tomasz Limisiewicz, Verena Rieser, Vitaly Protasov, Vladislav Mikhailov, Yada Pruksachatkun, Yonatan Belinkov, Zachary Bamberger, Zdeněk Kasner, Alice Rueda, Amanda Pestana, Amir Feizpour, Ammar Khan, Amy Faranak, Ana Santos, Anthony Hevia, Antigona Unldreaj, Arash Aghagol, Arezoo Abdollahi, Aycha Tammour, Azadeh HajiHosseini, Bahareh Behroozi, Benjamin Ajibade, Bharat Saxena, Carlos Muñoz Ferrandis, Danish Contractor, David Lansky, Davis David, Douwe Kiela, Duong A. Nguyen, Edward Tan, Emi Baylor, Ezinwanne Ozoani, Fatima Mirza, Frankline Ononiwu, Habib Rezanejad, Hessie Jones, Indrani Bhattacharya, Irene Solaiman, Irina Sedenko, Isar Nejadgholi, Jesse Passmore, Josh Seltzer, Julio Bonis Sanz, Karen Fort, Livia Dutra, Mairon Samagaio, Maraim Elbadri, Margot Mieskes, Marissa Gerchick, Martha Akinlolu, Michael McKenna, Mike Qiu, Muhammed Ghauri, Mykola Burynok, Nafis Abrar, Nazneen Rajani, Nour Elkott, Nour Fahmy, Olanrewaju Samuel, Ran An, Rasmus Kromann, Ryan Hao, Samira Alizadeh, Sarmad Shubber, Silas Wang, Sourav Roy, Sylvain Viguier, Thanh Le, Tobi Oyebade, Trieu Le, Yoyo Yang, Zach Nguyen, Abhinav Ramesh Kashyap, Alfredo Palasciano, Alison Callahan, Anima Shukla, Antonio Miranda-Escalada, Ayush Singh, Benjamin Beilharz, Bo Wang, Caio Brito, Chenxi Zhou, Chirag Jain, Chuxin Xu, Clémentine Fourrier, Daniel León Periñán, Daniel Molano, Dian Yu, Enrique Manjavacas, Fabio Barth, Florian Fuhrimann, Gabriel Altay, Giyaseddin Bayrak, Gully Burns, Helena U. Vrabec, Imane Bello, Ishani Dash, Jihyun Kang, John Giorgi, Jonas Golde, Jose David Posada, Karthik Rangasai Sivaraman, Lokesh Bulchandani, Lu Liu, Luisa Shinzato, Madeleine Hahn de Bykhovetz, Maiko Takeuchi, Marc Pàmies, Maria A Castillo, Marianna Nezhurina, Mario Sänger, Matthias Samwald, Michael Cullan, Michael Weinberg, Michiel De Wolf, Mina Mihaljcic, Minna Liu, Moritz Freidank, Myungsun Kang, Natasha Seelam, Nathan Dahlberg, Nicholas Michio Broad, Nikolaus Muellner, Pascale Fung, Patrick Haller, Ramya Chandrasekhar, Renata Eisenberg, Robert Martin, Rodrigo Canalli, Rosaline Su, Ruisi Su, Samuel Cahyawijaya, Samuele Garda, Shlok S Deshmukh, Shubhanshu Mishra, Sid Kiblawi, Simon Ott, Sinee Sang-aroonsiri, Srishti Kumar, Stefan Schweter, Sushil Bharati, Tanmay Laud, Théo Gigant, Tomoya Kainuma, Wojciech Kusa, Yanis Labrak, Yash Shailesh Bajaj, Yash Venkatraman, Yifan Xu, Yingxin Xu, Yu Xu, Zhe Tan, Zhongli Xie, Zifan Ye, Mathilde Bras, Younes Belkada, and Thomas Wolf. 2022. Bloom: A 176b-parameter open-access multilingual language model.

Joan Serrà, Dídac Surís, Marius Miron, and Alexandros Karatzoglou. 2018. Overcoming catastrophic forgetting with hard attention to the task. In *ICML*.

Shaden Smith, Mostofa Patwary, Brandon Norick, Patrick LeGresley, Samyam Rajbhandari, Jared Casper, Zhun Liu, Shrimai Prabhumoye, George Zerveas, Vijay Korthikanti, Elton Zhang, Rewon Child, Reza Yazdani Aminabadi, Julie Bernauer, Xia Song, Mohammad Shoeybi, Yuxiong He, Michael Houston, Saurabh Tiwary, and Bryan Catanzaro. 2022. Using deepspeed and megatron to train megatron-turing nlg 530b, a large-scale generative language model.

Yueqi Song, Catherine Cui, Simran Khanuja, Pengfei Liu, Fahim Faisal, Alissa Ostapenko, Genta Indra Winata, Alham Fikri Aji, Samuel Cahyawijaya, Yulia Tsvetkov, Antonios Anastasopoulos, and Graham Neubig. 2023. Globalbench: A benchmark for global progress in natural language processing.

Rohan Taori, Ishaan Gulrajani, Tianyi Zhang, Yann Dubois, Xuechen Li, Carlos Guestrin, Percy Liang, and Tatsunori B. Hashimoto. 2023. Stanford alpaca: An instruction-following llama model. `https://github.com/tatsu-lab/stanford_alpaca`.

NLLB Team, Marta R. Costa-jussà, James Cross, Onur Çelebi, Maha Elbayad, Kenneth Heafield, Kevin Heffernan, Elahe Kalbassi, Janice Lam, Daniel Licht, Jean Maillard, Anna Sun, Skyler Wang, Guillaume Wenzek, Al Youngblood, Bapi Akula, Loic Barrault, Gabriel Mejia Gonzalez, Prangthip Hansanti, John Hoffman, Semarley Jarrett, Kaushik Ram Sadagopan, Dirk Rowe, Shannon Spruit, Chau Tran, Pierre Andrews, Necip Fazil Ayan, Shruti Bhosale, Sergey Edunov, Angela Fan, Cynthia Gao, Vedanuj Goswami, Francisco Guzmán, Philipp Koehn, Alexandre Mourachko, Christophe Ropers, Safiyyah Saleem, Holger Schwenk, and Jeff Wang. 2022. No language left behind: Scaling human-centered machine translation.

Romal Thoppilan, Daniel De Freitas, Jamie Hall, Noam Shazeer, Apoorv Kulshreshtha, Heng-Tze Cheng, Alicia Jin, Taylor Bos, Leslie Baker, Yu Du, YaGuang Li, Hongrae Lee, Huaixiu Steven Zheng, Amin Ghafouri, Marcelo Menegali, Yanping Huang, Maxim Krikun, Dmitry Lepikhin, James Qin, Dehao Chen, Yuanzhong Xu, Zhifeng Chen, Adam Roberts, Maarten Bosma, Vincent Zhao, Yanqi Zhou, Chung-Ching Chang, Igor Krivokon, Will Rusch, Marc Pickett, Pranesh Srinivasan, Laichee Man, Kathleen Meier-Hellstern, Meredith Ringel Morris, Tulsee Doshi, Renelito Delos Santos, Toju Duke, Johnny Soraker, Ben Zevenbergen, Vinodkumar Prabhakaran, Mark Diaz, Ben Hutchinson, Kristen Olson, Alejandra Molina, Erin Hoffman-John, Josh Lee, Lora Aroyo, Ravi Rajakumar, Alena Butryna, Matthew Lamm, Viktoriya Kuzmina, Joe Fenton, Aaron Cohen, Rachel Bernstein, Ray Kurzweil, Blaise Aguera-Arcas, Claire Cui, Marian Croak, Ed Chi, and Quoc Le. 2022. Lamda: Language models for dialog applications.

Jason Wei, Maarten Bosma, Vincent Y. Zhao, Kelvin Guu, Adams Wei Yu, Brian Lester, Nan Du, Andrew M. Dai, and Quoc V. Le. 2022a. Finetuned language models are zero-shot learners.

Jason Wei, Yi Tay, Rishi Bommasani, Colin Raffel, Barret Zoph, Sebastian Borgeaud, Dani Yogatama, Maarten Bosma, Denny Zhou, Donald Metzler, Ed H. Chi, Tatsunori Hashimoto, Oriol Vinyals, Percy Liang, Jeff Dean, and William Fedus. 2022b. Emergent abilities of large language models. *Transactions on Machine Learning Research*. Survey Certification.

Bryan Wilie, Karissa Vincentio, Genta Indra Winata, Samuel Cahyawijaya, Xiaohong Li, Zhi Yuan Lim, Sidik Soleman, Rahmad Mahendra, Pascale Fung, Syafri Bahar, and Ayu Purwarianti. 2020. IndoNLU: Benchmark and resources for evaluating Indonesian natural language understanding. In *Proceedings of the 1st Conference of the Asia-Pacific Chapter of the Association for Computational Linguistics and the 10th International Joint Conference on Natural Language Processing*, pages 843–857, Suzhou, China. Association for Computational Linguistics.

Genta Indra Winata, Alham Fikri Aji, Samuel Cahyawijaya, Rahmad Mahendra, Fajri Koto, Ade Romadhony, Kemal Kurniawan, David Moeljadi, Radityo Eko Prasojo, Pascale Fung, et al. 2022. Nusax: Multilingual parallel sentiment dataset for 10 indonesian local languages. *arXiv preprint arXiv:2205.15960*.

Wilson Wongso, David Samuel Setiawan, and Derwin Suhartono. 2021. Causal and masked language modeling of javanese language using transformer-based architectures. In *2021 International Conference on Advanced Computer Science and Information Systems (ICACSIS)*, pages 1–7.

Linting Xue, Noah Constant, Adam Roberts, Mihir Kale, Rami Al-Rfou, Aditya Siddhant, Aditya Barua, and Colin Raffel. 2021. mT5: A massively multilingual pre-trained text-to-text transformer. In *Proceedings of the 2021 Conference of the North American Chapter of the Association for Computational Linguistics: Human Language Technologies*, pages 483–498, Online. Association for Computational Linguistics.

Zheng-Xin Yong, Hailey Schoelkopf, Niklas Muennighoff, Alham Fikri Aji, David Ifeoluwa Adelani, Khalid Almubarak, M Saiful Bari, Lintang Sutawika, Jungo Kasai, Ahmed Baruwa, Genta Indra Winata, Stella Biderman, Dragomir Radev, and Vassilina Nikoulina. 2022. Bloom+1: Adding language support to bloom for zero-shot prompting.

Zheng-Xin Yong, Ruochen Zhang, Jessica Zosa Forde, Skyler Wang, Samuel Cahyawijaya, Holy Lovenia, Genta Indra Winata, Lintang Sutawika, Jan Christian Blaise Cruz, Long Phan, et al. 2023. Prompting multilingual large language models to generate code-mixed texts: The case of south east asian languages. *arXiv preprint arXiv:2303.13592*.

Aohan Zeng, Xiao Liu, Zhengxiao Du, Zihan Wang, Hanyu Lai, Ming Ding, Zhuoyi Yang, Yifan Xu, Wendi Zheng, Xiao Xia, Weng Lam Tam, Zixuan Ma, Yufei Xue, Jidong Zhai, Wenguang Chen, Peng Zhang, Yuxiao Dong, and Jie Tang. 2022. Glm-130b: An open bilingual pre-trained model.

Ruochen Zhang, Samuel Cahyawijaya, Jan Christian Blaise Cruz, and Alham Fikri Aji. 2023. Multilingual large language models are not (yet) code-switchers.

A Prompt List

In this section, we provide the list of the prompt used in our experiment. For InstructAlign, we use 6 prompts for each objective. The prompt list for bilingual denoising (**TLM**), machine translation (**MT**), crosslingual semantic similarity (**XSS**), and monolingual denoising (**MLM**) are shown in Table 4, Table 5, Table 6, and Table 7, respectively. For the evaluation, we employ 3 English prompts for each task. The prompt list for sentiment analysis, emotion recognition, and topic classification tasks are described in Table 8, Table 9, and Table 10, respectively.

B Comparison Between LLM-int8() and Full Precision Inference

We run all inference within our experiment with 8-bit quantization using LLM.int8() (Dettmers et al., 2022). To the best of our knowledge, the effectiveness of LLM.int8() (Dettmers et al., 2022) has never been evaluated on zero-shot prompting in low-resource language cases. We evaluate datasets from various Indonesian and local languages spoken in Indonesian which are listed in IndoNLU (Wilie et al., 2020) and NusaCrowd (Cahyawijaya et al., 2023b). Specifically, we evaluate on 10 languages in NusaX (Winata et al., 2022), Javanese IMDB (Wongso et al., 2021), IndoLEM Sentiment (Koto et al., 2020), IndoNLI (Mahendra et al., 2021), SmSA (Purwarianti and Crisdayanti, 2019), CASA (Ilmania et al., 2018), and Sundanese Twitter Dataset for Emotion (Putra et al., 2020) datasets. Based on the result shown in Table 11, there is only a marginal performance different between 8-bit quantization with LLM.int8() compared to the full precision models, which suggests the generalization of LLM.int8() (Dettmers et al., 2022) for zero-shot prompting in low-resource languages.

C Datasets Details

In this section, we describe the statistics for each dataset use in the experiment. Table 12 shows the statistics for the sentiment analysis task of NusaTranslation (Cahyawijaya et al., 2023a). For the Indonesian subset, we take the first fold of the IndoLEM sentiment (Koto et al., 2020), which is the Indonesian sentiment analysis dataset used as the source sentences in the NusaTranslation (Cahyawijaya et al., 2023a). Table 13 shows the statistics for the sentiment analysis task of NusaX (Winata et al., 2022). Table 14 and Table 15 display the statistics for the emotion recognition and topic classification tasks of NusaParagraph (Cahyawijaya et al., 2023a), respectively.

D Detailed Experiment Results

In this section, we provide the complete experimental result per dataset. Table 16 shows the experiment results on the sentiment analysis task of NusaTranslation. Table 17 shows the experiment results on the sentiment analysis task of NusaX (Winata et al., 2022). Table 18 and Table 19 show the experiment results on the emotion recognition and topic classification tasks of NusaParagraph, respectively.

Prompt in Bilingual Denoising (TLM) Task
[INPUT_TEXT]. Denoise the previous [INPUT_LANG] text to its equivalent sentence in [CONTEXT_LANG]: [CONTEXT]\n[LABEL_TEXT]
Context in [CONTEXT_LANG]: [CONTEXT]\nFix the following [INPUT_LANG] text "[INPUT_TEXT]" ensuring the meaning is equivalent with the context. [LABEL_TEXT]
Context in [CONTEXT_LANG]: [CONTEXT]\nNoisy text in [INPUT_LANG]: [INPUT_TEXT]\nHow would you fix the [INPUT_LANG] sentence to make the meaning the same as the context? [LABEL_TEXT]
[INPUT_TEXT]. Denoise the previous [INPUT_LANG] sentence to it equivalent sentence: [CONTEXT]\n[LABEL_TEXT]
Context: [CONTEXT]\nFix the following [INPUT_LANG] text "[INPUT_TEXT]" ensuring the meaning is equivalent with the context. [LABEL_TEXT]
Context: [CONTEXT]\nNoisy text in [INPUT_LANG]: [INPUT_TEXT]\nHow would you fix the [INPUT_LANG] sentence to make the meaning the same as the [CONTEXT_LANG] sentence? [LABEL_TEXT]

Table 4: Prompt used for Bilingual Denoising (**TLM**) task

Prompt in Machine Translation (MT) Task
Translate the following text from [SOURCE_LANG] to [TARGET_LANG].\nText: [SOURCE_TEXT]\nTranslation: [TARGET_TEXT]
[SOURCE_TEXT]\nTranslate the text above from [SOURCE_LANG] to [TARGET_LANG]. [TARGET_TEXT]
Text in [SOURCE_LANG]: [SOURCE_TEXT]\nHow would you translate that in [TARGET_LANG]? [TARGET_TEXT]
Translate the following text to [TARGET_LANG].\nText: [SOURCE_TEXT]\nTranslation: [TARGET_TEXT]
[SOURCE_TEXT]\nTranslate the text above to [TARGET_LANG]. [TARGET_TEXT]
Input text: [SOURCE_TEXT]\nHow would you translate that into [TARGET_LANG]? [TARGET_TEXT]

Table 5: Prompt used for Machine Translation (**MT**) task

Prompt in Crosslingual Semantic Similarity (XSS) Task
[SOURCE_LANG] sentence: [SOURCE_TEXT]\n[TARGET_LANG] sentence: [TARGET_TEXT]\nDo the two sentences have the same meaning? [LABEL]
Sentence A: [SOURCE_TEXT]\nSentence B: [TARGET_TEXT]\nDo sentence A and sentence B have the same meaning? [LABEL]
[SOURCE_LANG] sentence: [SOURCE_TEXT]\n[TARGET_LANG] sentence: [TARGET_TEXT]\nAre the two sentences equivalent? [LABEL]
Sentence A: [SOURCE_TEXT]\nSentence B: [TARGET_TEXT]\nAre sentence A and sentence B equivalent? [LABEL]
Is the [SOURCE_LANG] sentence "[SOURCE_TEXT]" equivalent to the [TARGET_LANG] sentence "[TARGET_TEXT]"? [LABEL]
Is the sentence "[SOURCE_TEXT]" equivalent to the sentence "[TARGET_TEXT]"? [LABEL]

Table 6: Prompt used for Crosslingual Semantic Similarity (**XSS**) task

Prompt in Monolingual Denoising (MLM) Task
Denoise the following noisy [SOURCE_LANG] text: "[SOURCE_TEXT]", to make a correct sentence. [TARGET_TEXT]
Fix and complete the following [SOURCE_LANG] sentence: [SOURCE_TEXT]\n[TARGET_TEXT]
Sentence in [SOURCE_LANG]: [SOURCE_TEXT]\nHow would you fix the sentence to make a correct sentence? [TARGET_TEXT]
Denoise the following noisy text "[SOURCE_TEXT]" to make a correct [SOURCE_LANG] sentence. [TARGET_TEXT]
Fix and complete the following sentence: [SOURCE_TEXT]\n[TARGET_TEXT]
Input text: [SOURCE_TEXT]\nHow would you fix the sentence to make a correct [SOURCE_LANG] sentence? [TARGET_TEXT]

Table 7: Prompt used for Monolingual Denoising (**MLM**) task

Prompt in Sentiment Analysis Task
[INPUT]\nWhat would be the sentiment of the text above? [OPTIONS]? [LABELS_CHOICE]
What is the sentiment of this text?\nText: [INPUT]\nAnswer with [OPTIONS]: [LABELS_CHOICE]
Text: [INPUT]\n\nPlease classify the sentiment of above text. Answer with [OPTIONS]: [LABELS_CHOICE]

Table 8: Prompt used for Sentiment Analysis task

Prompt in Emotion Recognition Task
[INPUT]\nWhat would be the emotion of the text above? [OPTIONS]? [LABELS_CHOICE]
What is the emotion of this text?\nText: [INPUT]\nAnswer with [OPTIONS]: [LABELS_CHOICE]
Text: [INPUT]\n\nPlease classify the emotion of above text. Answer with [OPTIONS]: [LABELS_CHOICE]

Table 9: Prompt used for Emotion Recognition task

Prompt in Topic Classification Task
[INPUT]\nWhat would be the topic of the text above? [OPTIONS]? [LABELS_CHOICE]
What is the topic of this text?\nText: [INPUT]\nAnswer with [OPTIONS]: [LABELS_CHOICE]
Text: [INPUT]\n\nPlease classify the topic of above text. Answer with [OPTIONS]: [LABELS_CHOICE]

Table 10: Prompt used for the Topic Classification task

Model	Prompt Lang.	Acc	Macro F1	Macro Prec.	Macro Rec.
Full Precision					
BLOOMZ-560M	EN	47.58	33.25	37.97	43.11
BLOOMZ-560M	ID	44.37	29.78	37.79	40.28
BLOOMZ-1B1	EN	52.26	37.90	40.48	45.79
BLOOMZ-1B1	ID	52.88	39.28	46.42	46.67
BLOOMZ-1B7	EN	51.44	36.90	41.90	45.10
BLOOMZ-1B7	ID	52.68	41.20	50.81	48.03
8-Bit Quantization					
BLOOMZ-560M	EN	47.56	34.67	40.94	42.97
BLOOMZ-560M	ID	43.64	33.30	42.90	39.68
BLOOMZ-1B1	EN	50.68	37.52	40.37	44.56
BLOOMZ-1B1	ID	51.23	38.69	43.53	45.34
BLOOMZ-1B7	EN	49.71	35.05	42.11	43.57
BLOOMZ-1B7	ID	52.61	41.87	51.74	48.15
BLOOMZ-3B	EN	54.80	40.78	46.59	48.24
BLOOMZ-3B	ID	56.75	44.34	45.16	51.12

Table 11: Evaluation of full precision and 8-bit quantization on various Indonesian local languages datasets.

Status	Language	Train	Valid.	Test
Pre-trained	Indonesian (ind)	3638	399	1011
Seen	Javanese (jav)	3400	448	1200
	Sundanese (sun)	3400	448	1200
	Minangkabau (min)	3400	448	1200
Unseen	Ambon (abs)	250	98	500
	Batak (btk)	3400	448	1200
	Betawi (bew)	3400	448	1200
	Bima (bhp)	260	100	500
	Madurese (mad)	3400	448	1200
	Makassarese (mak)	3400	448	1200
	Musi (mui)	250	91	500
	Rejang (rej)	250	78	500

Table 12: Statistics of NusaTranslation sentiment analysis dataset. **Pre-trained** denotes languages that are already seen before the InstructAlign tuning. **Seen** denotes languages that are seen during the InstructAlign.**Unseen** denotes languages that are still unseen after the InstructAlign.

Status	Language	Train	Valid.	Test
Pre-trained	English (eng)	500	100	400
	Indonesia (ind)	500	100	400
Seen	Aceh (ace)	500	100	400
	Bali (ban)	500	100	400
	Banjar (bjn)	500	100	400
	Bugis (bug)	500	100	400
	Minang (min)	500	100	400
	Javanese(jav)	500	100	400
	Sunda (sun)	500	100	400
Unseen	Madura (mad)	500	100	400
	Ngaju (nij)	500	100	400
	Bataknese (bbc)	500	100	400

Table 13: Statistics of NusaX sentiment analysis dataset. **Pre-trained** denotes languages that are already seen before the InstructAlign. **Seen** denotes languages that are seen during the InstructAlign.**Unseen** denotes languages that are still unseen after the InstructAlign.

Status	Language	Train	Valid.	Test
Unseen	Javanese (jav)	2800	440	800
	Minangkabau (min)	2000	357	800
	Sundanese (sun)	2400	400	800
	Buginese (bug)	87	50	300
Seen	Batak (btk)	1150	292	500
	Betawi (bew)	2700	430	800
	Madurese (mad)	1000	263	500
	Makassarese(mak)	1500	304	500
	Musi (mui)	200	75	400
	Rejang (rej)	136	50	300

Table 14: Statistics of NusaParagraph emotion recognition dataset. **Pre-trained** denotes languages that are already seen before InstructAlign. **Seen** denotes languages that are seen during InstructAlign.**Unseen** denotes languages that are still unseen after InstructAlign.

Status	Language	Train	Valid.	Test
Unseen	Javanese (jav)	2650	448	800
	Minangkabau (min)	2400	399	800
	Sundanese (sun)	2800	468	900
	Buginese (bug)	93	50	300
Seen	Batak (btk)	1350	275	500
	Betawi (bew)	2650	435	800
	Madurese (mad)	1800	367	700
	Makassarese(mak)	1500	376	700
	Musi (mui)	168	80	400
	Rejang (rej)	105	50	350

Table 15: Statistics of NusaParagraph topic classification dataset. **Pre-trained** denotes languages that are already seen before InstructAlign. **Seen** denotes languages that are seen during InstructAlign.**Unseen** denotes languages that are still unseen after InstructAlign.

Model	L1	L2			L3							
	ind	jav	min	sun	abs	bew	bhp	btk	mad	mak	mui	rej
BLOOM 560m	61.47	56.09	58.13	58.63	62.53	58.42	49.72	56.05	54.02	53.97	60.27	55.55
BLOOM 1b1	58.81	59.05	59.33	59.16	47.87	58.23	60.85	58.95	58.79	58.83	54.92	57.73
BLOOM 3b	58.30	44.84	45.48	44.61	46.08	45.61	44.54	43.62	43.36	44.03	45.05	43.15
BLOOMZ 560m	69.81	43.00	50.97	46.51	45.23	47.87	33.13	36.69	36.84	35.30	61.42	36.21
BLOOMZ 1b1	80.40	61.32	68.95	61.75	61.07	66.94	46.18	50.20	49.71	50.66	70.31	52.01
BLOOMZ 3b	81.38	68.05	71.76	68.43	69.57	69.76	67.73	65.09	64.37	63.14	69.08	64.05
MLM BLOOMZ 560m	65.68	23.29	21.11	22.31	20.86	22.00	20.40	19.04	21.10	20.59	28.82	19.50
MLM BLOOMZ 560m-r=100k	71.93	63.89	69.37	66.27	64.46	65.38	56.12	62.68	58.20	56.51	67.73	58.12
MLM BLOOMZ 1b1-r=100k	73.25	71.18	72.24	70.95	62.67	67.65	56.07	59.22	58.60	60.38	68.10	60.27
MT BLOOMZ 560m	55.20	41.87	39.00	38.16	36.88	39.29	36.07	34.74	36.97	33.81	41.72	37.70
MT BLOOMZ 560m-r=100k	74.46	70.73	69.94	70.00	66.81	67.65	64.58	66.53	65.10	61.35	68.43	63.23
MT BLOOMZ 1b1-r=100k	70.86	59.62	62.22	61.63	54.37	57.97	49.95	50.22	51.31	52.22	60.25	50.30
TLM BLOOMZ 560m	71.57	66.74	66.05	66.94	63.06	65.64	59.00	61.07	61.31	61.13	65.30	63.17
TLM BLOOMZ 560m-r=1k	70.52	61.73	62.76	62.01	54.34	56.31	48.52	49.44	49.21	47.95	61.11	49.22
TLM BLOOMZ 560m-r=10k	72.82	66.27	66.22	66.76	62.29	63.32	59.61	61.27	60.35	60.32	63.60	60.49
TLM BLOOMZ 560m-r=100k	72.40	61.05	59.43	62.11	54.51	56.44	46.68	50.72	50.56	45.02	63.27	48.39
TLM BLOOMZ 1b1-r=100k	75.66	70.05	70.12	70.70	64.47	67.07	62.92	61.87	60.96	61.86	68.11	61.53
XSS BLOOMZ 560m	64.48	57.65	52.18	54.13	52.40	53.59	48.55	48.06	49.59	44.01	58.03	49.43
XSS BLOOMZ 560m-r=1k	69.34	63.55	62.84	65.45	65.20	64.15	59.11	60.53	62.34	61.58	63.51	58.36
XSS BLOOMZ 560m-r=10k	72.22	67.89	67.81	67.25	62.76	64.42	62.83	61.98	62.02	62.21	65.38	59.27
XSS BLOOMZ 560m-r=100k	71.27	68.34	67.89	68.07	61.58	68.69	62.66	65.73	63.44	58.24	70.24	64.92
XSS BLOOMZ 1b1-r=100k	76.75	72.40	71.40	71.87	63.75	65.45	60.27	61.27	60.10	63.21	66.16	60.49

Table 16: Experiment result on the sentiment analysis task of the NusaTranslation dataset

Model	L1		L2							L3		
	eng	ind	ace	ban	bjn	bug	jav	min	sun	bbc	mad	nij
BLOOM 560m	29.26	21.13	21.35	21.93	21.35	23.21	21.86	21.82	21.04	22.28	22.13	21.11
BLOOM 1b1	22.02	22.54	21.47	22.62	22.27	21.34	22.97	21.92	21.55	22.10	21.65	21.53
BLOOM 3b	24.03	21.17	21.31	21.17	21.18	21.35	21.17	21.17	21.17	21.19	21.20	21.17
BLOOMZ 560m	58.24	55.59	31.18	32.40	37.17	27.79	35.86	39.29	32.44	29.49	32.80	38.15
BLOOMZ 1b1	57.41	58.58	43.31	43.02	44.72	31.12	46.52	42.59	39.20	26.82	41.92	40.76
BLOOMZ 3b	62.65	63.21	48.81	48.40	55.27	23.47	54.26	51.11	39.41	32.42	38.88	41.68
MLM BLOOMZ 560m	49.99	49.33	31.74	28.37	34.32	25.76	33.89	31.27	29.20	28.43	32.08	30.98
MLM BLOOMZ 560m-R-100000	61.32	60.01	42.69	41.69	50.95	31.53	44.28	44.30	42.11	33.18	41.05	40.15
MLM BLOOMZ 1b1-R-100000	61.30	59.73	43.11	43.02	50.71	31.31	53.66	51.05	47.27	31.13	42.02	39.83
MT BLOOMZ 560m	47.24	41.41	31.78	33.78	34.69	28.44	35.47	35.15	36.01	26.86	26.69	27.49
MT BLOOMZ 560m-R-100000	60.09	54.18	39.11	42.59	46.22	34.50	43.37	41.31	41.31	35.95	38.54	39.84
MT BLOOMZ 1b1-R-100000	59.18	53.69	43.97	45.40	50.16	38.65	48.37	45.97	41.98	37.97	40.90	40.60
TLM BLOOMZ 560m	44.72	46.02	33.59	34.26	41.16	25.36	41.76	38.72	37.40	25.67	30.88	29.98
TLM BLOOMZ 560m-R-1000	58.05	54.59	43.03	37.06	46.55	34.02	43.21	43.24	39.59	33.99	38.16	37.39
TLM BLOOMZ 560m-R-10000	57.38	57.73	43.43	36.76	45.99	35.06	44.38	43.30	40.83	34.06	42.46	40.00
TLM BLOOMZ 560m-R-100000	61.65	56.50	41.78	41.36	48.15	31.19	48.89	44.12	44.90	33.78	41.51	37.90
TLM BLOOMZ 1b1-R-100000	64.26	63.54	52.22	51.35	58.19	41.87	59.48	59.67	56.99	38.26	48.11	48.01
XSS BLOOMZ 560m	53.93	53.19	43.60	41.73	47.09	37.79	47.29	45.36	43.42	32.59	41.66	40.79
XSS BLOOMZ 560m-R-1000	56.57	54.90	36.78	40.28	42.20	28.56	45.67	41.33	39.80	27.30	31.67	32.20
XSS BLOOMZ 560m-R-10000	55.62	57.84	44.24	44.03	50.04	32.87	48.92	45.55	45.64	36.38	40.36	43.12
XSS BLOOMZ 560m-R-100000	59.89	58.22	45.53	39.57	52.68	36.15	49.83	50.61	46.45	35.27	42.40	43.39
XSS BLOOMZ 1b1-R-100000	60.78	59.34	45.83	45.45	53.08	36.24	52.24	50.54	47.20	33.81	40.99	41.08

Table 17: Experiment result on the sentiment analysis task of the NusaX dataset

Model	L2				L3					
	bug	jav	min	sun	bew	btk	mad	mak	mui	rej
BLOOM 560m	1.19	2.42	4.54	3.05	4.37	2.56	0.59	1.42	1.11	2.66
BLOOM 1b1	1.19	2.42	4.54	3.05	4.29	2.57	0.59	1.42	1.11	2.44
BLOOM 3b	1.19	2.42	4.54	3.05	4.29	2.57	0.59	1.42	1.11	2.44
BLOOMZ 560m	2.36	2.93	4.71	3.52	4.35	3.33	1.41	3.09	1.28	4.10
BLOOMZ 1b1	1.19	2.42	4.54	3.05	4.29	2.57	0.59	1.42	1.11	2.44
BLOOMZ 3b	1.19	2.42	4.54	3.05	4.29	2.57	0.59	1.42	1.11	2.44
MLM BLOOMZ 560m	1.19	2.51	4.63	3.04	4.29	2.57	0.59	1.42	1.11	2.44
MLM BLOOMZ 560m-R-100000	1.19	2.41	4.54	3.05	4.29	2.57	0.59	1.42	1.11	2.44
MLM BLOOMZ 1b1-R-100000	1.19	2.42	4.71	3.05	4.29	2.57	0.59	1.42	1.11	2.44
MT BLOOMZ 1b1-R-100000	1.60	2.76	4.77	3.54	4.27	2.56	0.59	1.42	1.12	2.44
MT BLOOMZ 560m	1.41	2.58	9.14	5.63	4.45	2.57	0.59	1.56	2.10	2.44
MT BLOOMZ 560m-R-100000	1.19	2.51	4.54	3.04	4.29	2.70	0.59	1.42	1.11	2.44
TLM BLOOMZ 560m	1.19	2.58	4.88	3.54	4.29	2.57	0.59	1.42	1.11	2.44
TLM BLOOMZ 560m-R-1000	1.19	2.50	5.10	3.14	4.29	2.57	0.59	1.42	1.12	2.44
TLM BLOOMZ 560m-R-10000	1.19	2.67	5.12	4.34	4.29	2.57	0.73	1.42	1.11	2.66
TLM BLOOMZ 560m-R-100000	1.40	2.42	4.54	3.13	4.29	2.71	0.73	1.42	1.11	2.44
TLM BLOOMZ 1b1-R-100000	1.19	2.41	4.63	3.13	4.29	2.57	0.59	1.42	1.12	2.44
XSS BLOOMZ 560m	1.54	3.12	4.65	3.77	4.29	2.71	0.59	1.42	1.11	2.44
XSS BLOOMZ 560m-R-1000	1.56	2.82	5.16	3.54	4.37	2.69	0.73	1.42	1.11	2.44
XSS BLOOMZ 560m-R-10000	1.39	2.84	5.56	4.10	4.29	2.57	0.59	1.43	1.28	2.44
XSS BLOOMZ 560m-R-100000	1.19	2.42	4.54	3.05	4.29	2.57	0.59	1.42	1.11	2.42
XSS BLOOMZ 1b1-R-100000	1.19	2.67	4.63	3.84	4.29	2.57	0.59	1.42	1.11	2.44

Table 18: Experiment result on the emotion recognition task of the NusaParagraph dataset

Model	L2				L3					
	bug	**jav**	**min**	**sun**	**bew**	**btk**	**mad**	**mak**	**mui**	**rej**
BLOOM-560m	7.68	3.50	6.36	3.80	5.42	7.92	11.25	9.07	3.91	5.80
BLOOM-1b1	7.72	3.50	6.36	3.81	5.42	7.93	11.26	9.09	3.91	5.82
BLOOM-3b	7.72	3.50	6.36	3.81	5.42	7.93	11.26	9.09	3.91	5.82
BLOOMZ-560m	9.13	4.10	6.86	4.29	6.07	8.75	11.71	9.45	4.09	6.04
BLOOMZ-1b1	7.72	3.50	6.36	3.81	5.51	7.93	11.26	9.09	3.91	5.82
BLOOMZ-3b	7.72	4.21	6.70	4.30	7.55	8.33	11.28	9.19	7.30	5.82
MLM BLOOMZ-560m	8.15	3.50	6.36	3.81	5.42	7.93	11.26	9.09	3.91	5.82
MLM BLOOMZ-560m r=100000	7.72	3.49	6.52	4.36	5.51	7.93	11.27	9.09	4.08	5.82
MLM BLOOMZ-1b1 r=100000	7.72	3.50	6.36	3.81	5.42	7.93	11.26	9.09	3.91	5.82
MT BLOOMZ-560m	7.72	3.50	6.36	3.81	5.42	7.93	11.26	9.09	3.92	5.82
MT BLOOMZ-560m r=100000	7.72	3.58	6.37	3.93	5.52	7.94	11.22	9.19	3.92	5.82
MT BLOOMZ-1b1 r=100000	8.61	4.59	7.08	5.08	5.71	8.20	11.52	9.29	4.63	6.01
TLM BLOOMZ-560m	9.43	3.83	7.27	7.11	5.42	7.93	11.28	9.18	3.92	5.82
TLM BLOOMZ-560m r=1000	14.08	11.46	17.31	16.55	10.35	12.61	11.92	12.04	9.34	5.96
TLM BLOOMZ-560m r=10000	8.37	4.23	7.66	5.40	5.43	8.05	11.20	9.28	4.25	5.96
TLM BLOOMZ-560m r=100000	7.75	3.50	6.34	3.80	5.51	7.93	11.35	9.18	4.23	5.78
TLM BLOOMZ-1b1 r=100000	7.71	3.67	6.55	4.05	5.42	7.93	11.27	9.08	3.91	5.82
XSS BLOOMZ-560m	8.38	3.57	6.46	3.88	5.42	7.94	11.26	9.09	3.91	5.82
XSS BLOOMZ-560m r=1000	6.14	4.21	4.34	6.14	4.38	7.29	11.21	8.39	5.52	6.63
XSS BLOOMZ-560m r=10000	8.06	4.24	7.46	5.07	5.41	8.23	11.32	9.10	4.08	5.85
XSS BLOOMZ-560m r=100000	7.73	3.50	6.67	4.23	5.50	7.93	11.26	9.09	3.92	5.82
XSS BLOOMZ-1b1 r=100000	8.00	4.05	7.40	4.62	5.67	8.08	11.55	9.19	4.08	5.83

Table 19: Experiment result on the topic classification task of the NusaParagraph dataset

SentMix-3L: A Bangla-English-Hindi Code-Mixed Dataset for Sentiment Analysis

Md Nishat Raihan*, **Dhiman Goswami***, **Antara Mahmud**
Antonios Anstasopoulos, **Marcos Zampieri**
George Mason University, USA
{mraihan2, dgoswam, amahmud4, antonis, mzampier}@gmu.edu

Abstract

Code-mixing is a well-studied linguistic phenomenon when two or more languages are mixed in text or speech. Several datasets have been build with the goal of training computational models for code-mixing. Although it is very common to observe code-mixing with multiple languages, most datasets available contain code-mixed between only two languages. In this paper, we introduce SentMix-3L, a novel dataset for sentiment analysis containing code-mixed data between three languages Bangla, English, and Hindi . We carry out a comprehensive evaluation using SentMix-3L. We show that zero-shot prompting with GPT-3.5 outperforms all transformer-based models on SentMix-3L.

1 Introduction

Code-mixing and code-switching are very commonly observed in both text and speech. Code-mixing means the practice of using words from multiple languages within a single utterance, sentence, or discourse, and code-switching refers to the deliberate alteration between multiple languages within the same context (Thara and Poornachandran, 2018). The first case is spontaneous and the second case is purposeful. However, both are widely observed in bilingual and multilingual communities.

According to Anastassiou (2017), several factors are behind these two phenomena, which include social, convenience, linguistic, and cognitive reasons. Socially, this often serves as a sign of group identity which allows individuals to navigate multiple social and cultural affiliations. In terms of linguistics, it is a very common scenario to not be able to find any word for a specific term in one language, whereas another word from another language can help to communicate better. Additionally, there are several cases even in a monolingual community, when Code-mixing might be the convenient way to express something.

In most occurrences, code-mixing is bilingual. In an early research, Byers-Heinlein and Lew-Williams (2013) states that, it is very likely that by the year 2035, over half of the children enrolled in kindergarten will have grown up speaking a language other than English. Another study conducted by Jeffery and van Beuningen (2020) shows that it is very common in European countries like Germany, Spain, and Italy to use bilingualism in practice. However, in cosmopolitan cities and areas like New York, London, Singapore, and others, code-mixing with three or even more languages is fairly common. This is also observed in countries and states like Luxembourg, Kolkata, and several South-East Indian regions where more than two languages are very commonly used on a daily basis.

Several research works have been conducted on building code-mixed datasets and performing several downstream tasks on such datasets. These datasets include both synthetic and natural ones. However, most of them are bilingual in nature. In this paper, we present SentMix-3L, a Bangla-English-Hindi dataset annotated for sentiment analysis.

The main contributions of our work are as follows:

- We introduce SentMix-3L, a novel three-language code-mixed test dataset with gold standard labels in Bangla-Hindi-English for the task of Sentiment Analysis, containing 1,007 instances.[1]
- We provide a comprehensive experimental analysis with several monolingual, bilingual, and multilingual models on SentMix-3L.

We are presenting this dataset exclusively as a test set due to the unique and specialized nature of

*These two authors contributed equally to this work.

[1]https://github.com/LanguageTechnologyLab/SentMix-3L

Proceedings of the First Workshop in South East Asian Language Processing, pages 79–84
November 1, 2023.

the task. Such data is very difficult to gather and requires significant expertise to access. The size of the dataset, while limiting for training purposes, offers a high-quality testing environment with gold-standard labels that can serve as a benchmark in this domain. Given the scarcity of similar datasets and the challenges associated with data collection, SentMix-3L provides an important resource for the rigorous evaluation of text-based models, filling a critical gap in multi-level Code-mixing research. In our experiments, we also prepare a synthetic train and a development dataset to evaluate several models.

2 Related Work

There have been some works conducted on Bangla-English, Hindi-English, and Bangla-Hindi Code-mixing and Code-switching separately. Most of them are case studies and surveys that show the common occurrences of Bangla-English (Alam, 2006; Hasan et al., 2015; Hossain and Bar, 2015; Begum and Haque, 2013; Mahbub-ul Alam and Quyyum, 2016), Hindi-English (Singh, 1985; Bali et al., 2014; Thara and Poornachandran, 2018) and Bangla-Hindi (Ali et al., 2019; Jose et al., 2020) Code-mixing in a wide variety of areas and situations.

Few works are done on sentiment analysis tasks for these types of cases. The work of Khan et al. (2022) presents a Bangla-English Sentiment Analysis dataset primarily related to COVID-19. Their dataset is called CoVaxBD and it contains 1113 samples. Their experiments show that the best result of the dataset is generated by BERT with a development accuracy of 97.3%. However, a lot of the data are purely in Bangla and they only experiment using the BERT and multilingual BERT model (Devlin et al., 2019) while only providing development accuracy as the performance metric. Another recent work by Tareq et al. (2023), consists of 18,074 Bangla-English Code-mixed data from online for the purpose of sentiment analysis. They augment the dataset using their own approach and achieve their best result of an 87% weighted F1 score by implementing XGBoost with Fasttext embedding. Their experiments lack the evaluation of transformer-based models.

An early work by Sitaram et al. (2015) focuses on Hindi-English Code-mixing dataset for Sentiment Analysis. However, it contains 345 data samples in total and only 180 of them are code-mixed. They get their best results of 91.01% accuracy using Recursive Neural Tensor Network (RNTN). Joshi et al. (2016) compile a dataset of 3879 texts and get their best results using a subword-LSTM approach. Also, the work of (Yadav et al., 2020) includes a dataset of 6357 texts and Bi-LSTM helps them to get their optimal result. However, none of these works present how the transformer-based models perform on their datasets.

In summary, there are no works or datasets on sentiment analysis for code-mixed Bangla-English-Hindi altogether. SentMix-3L is a novel addition in this particular domain of research.

3 The *SentMix-3L* Dataset

In generating the dataset, we choose a controlled data collection method, asking the volunteers to freely contribute data in Bangla, English, and Hindi. This decision stems from several challenges of extracting such specific code-mixed data from the vast corpus available on social media or other online platforms. While the data are not rare, identifying and isolating them from large, unstructured corpora is a very labor-intensive and error-prone process. Our approach ensures data quality and sidesteps the ethical concerns associated with using publicly available online data. Such types of datasets are often used when it is very difficult to mine them from existing corpora. As examples, for fine-tuning LLMs on instructions and conversations, semi-natural datasets like Databricks (2023) and Nie (2023) have become popular.

Data Collection A group of 10 undergraduate students who are fluent in all 3 languages in all four language skills - listening, reading, writing, and speaking. We ask each of them to prepare 250 to 300 social media posts or tweets. They are allowed to use any language including Bangla, English, and Hindi to prepare posts on several daily topics like politics, sports, education, social media rumors, etc. We also ask them to switch languages if and wherever they feel comfortable doing it. The inclusion of emojis, hashtags, and transliteration are also encouraged. The students had the flexibility to prepare the data as naturally as possible. Upon completion of this stage, we filter 1863 samples that contain at least one word or subword from each of the three languages using langdetect (Mazzocchi, 2012) an open-sourced Python tool for language detection.

Data Annotation We annotate the dataset in two steps to prepare high-quality labels for the dataset. First, we recruit three students from social science, computer science, and linguistics as annotators who are also fluent in all 3 languages in all four language skills. They annotate all the 1863 samples with one of the three labels (Positive, Neutral, and Negative) with a raw agreement of 65.3%. We only take these 1182 data, where all three annotators agree on the labels. Second, we gather a second group of annotators consisting of two NLP researchers with the same level of fluency and skills. After their annotation, we calculate a raw agreement of 0.85, a Cohen Kappa score of 0.78 and only keep the data where both annotators agree. After the two stages, we end up with a total of 1007 data.

Label	No. of Data	Percentage
Positive	420	41.71%
Neutral	234	23.24%
Negative	353	35.05%
Total	1,007	100%

Table 1: Label distribution in SentMix-3L.

Dataset Statistics A detailed description of the dataset statistics is provided in Table 2. Since the dataset was generated by people whose first language is Bangla, we observe that the majority portion of the tokens in the dataset is in Bangla. It is also observed that all the data instances contain tokens from all three languages. There are several *Other* tokens in the dataset that are not from Bangla, English, or Hindi language. These tokens contain transliterated words and misspelled words as well as emojis and hashtags. We have Positive, Neutral, and Negative labels for the 1007 data. The label distribution is shown in table 1.

	All	Bangla	English	Hindi	Other
Tokens	89494	32133	5998	15131	36232
Types	19686	8167	1073	1474	9092
Avg	88.87	31.91	5.96	15.03	35.98
Std Dev	19.19	8.39	2.94	5.81	9.70

Table 2: SentMix-3L Data Card. The row *Avg* represents the average number of tokens with its standard deviation in row *Std Dev*.

Synthetic Train and Development Set We present SentMix-3L as a test dataset, hence for experimental purposes, we build a synthetic train and development set that contains Code-mixing for Bangla, English, and Hindi. We originally take the Amazon Review Dataset (Ni et al., 2019) as seed data and pick 100K data instances randomly. The dataset labels are ratings on a 1 to 5 scale. We convert them into Positive (rating > 3), Neutral (rating = 3), and Negative (rating < 3) for our task. We carefully choose an equal number of instances for Positive, Neutral, and Negative labels. We then use two separate methodologies called *Random Code-mixing Algorithm* by Krishnan et al. (2021) and *r-CM* by Santy et al. (2021) to generate the synthetic Code-mixed dataset.

4 Experiments

Monolingual Models We use 5 monolingual models DistilBERT (Sanh et al., 2019), BERT (Devlin et al., 2019), BanglaBERT (Kowsher et al., 2022), roBERTa (Liu et al., 2019), HindiBERT (Nick Doiron, 2023) for this experiment. Here BanglaBERT is specifically trained on only Bangla and HindiBERT on only Hindi language. The rest of the models are trained in the English language only.

Bilingual Models BanglishBERT (Bhattacharjee et al., 2022) and HingBERT (Nayak and Joshi, 2022) is used as bilingual models which are trained on both Bangla-English and Hindi-English respectively thus effective for the purpose of code mixing tasks including where any two of these languages are involved.

Multilingual Models We use mBERT (Devlin et al., 2019) and XLM-R (Conneau et al., 2020) as multilingual models which are respectively trained on 104 and 100 languages. These two models are very effective while we are working in a trilingual Bangla, Hindi and English domain. Moreover, we use IndicBERT (Kakwani et al., 2020) and MuRIL (Khanuja et al., 2021) which covers 12 and 17 Indian languages respectively including Bangla-English-Hindi. Thus these two models and the respective list of languages justify the inclusion of them for our targeted tri-lingual code-mixing task. We also perform hyper-parameter tuning while using all the models to prevent overfitting and ensure optimal F1 score.

Prompting We use prompting with GPT-3.5-turbo model (OpenAI, 2023) from OpenAI for this task. We use the API for zero-shot prompting (see Figure 1) and ask the model to label the test set.

Role: "You are a helpful AI assistant. You are given the task of sentiment analysis.

Definition: Sentiment Analysis is the process of identifying and categorizing opinions expressed in a piece of text. You will be given a text to label either 'Positive' or 'Negative' or 'Neutral'.

Task: Generate the label for this **"text"** in the following format: *<label> Your_Predicted_Label <\label>*. Thanks."

Figure 1: Sample GPT-3.5 prompt.

Additionally, we run the same experiments separately on synthetic and natural datasets splitting both in a 60-20-20 way for training, evaluating, and testing purposes.

5 Results

In this experiment, synthetic data is used as train set, and natural data is used as test set. The F1 scores of monolingual models range from 0.47 to 0.55 where BERT performs the best. Among the two bilingual models BanglishBERT scores 0.56 which is better than HingBERT. XLM-R is the best multilingual model with an F1 score of 0.59. On the other hand, a zero shot prompting technique on GPT 3.5 turbo performs the best with a 0.62 weighted F1 score. These results are available in Table 3.

Models	Weighted F1 Score
GPT 3.5 Turbo	**0.62**
XLM-R	0.59
BanglishBERT	0.56
mBERT	0.56
BERT	0.55
roBERTa	0.54
MuRIL	0.54
IndicBERT	0.53
DistilBERT	0.53
HindiBERT	0.48
HingBERT	0.47
BanglaBERT	0.47

Table 3: Weighted F-1 score for different models: training on synthetic, testing on natural data.

We perform the same procedure by using synthetic data for both the training and testing where MuRIL and XLM-R with 0.77 F1 score are the best-performing models. These results are available in Table 4.

Models	Weighted F1 Score
MuRIL	**0.77**
XLM-R	**0.77**
mBERT	0.74
BanglishBERT	0.72
BERT	0.68
HingBERT	0.67
DistilBERT	0.66
roBERTa	0.66
IndicBERT	0.66
BanglaBERT	0.60
HindiBERT	0.59

Table 4: Weighted F-1 score for different models: training and testing on synthetic data.

5.1 Error Analysis

We observe *Other* tokens in almost 40% of the whole dataset, as shown in Table 2. These tokens occur due to transliteration which poses a challenge for most of the models since not all of the models are pre-trained on transliterated tokens. BanglishBERT did better than HingBERT since it recognizes both Bangla and English tokens and the total number of tokens for Hindi-English is less than Bangla-English tokens (see Table 3). Also, misspelled words and typos are also observed in the datasets, making the task even more difficult. Some examples are available in Appendix A which are classified wrongly by all the models.

6 Conclusion and Future Work

In this paper, we presented SentMix-3L, a Bangla-English-Hindi code-mixed offensive language identification dataset containing 1,007 instances. We also created 100,000 synthetic data in the same three languages for training. We evaluated various monolingual models on these two datasets. Our results show that prompting GPT3.5 generates the best result on SentMix-3L. When using synthetic data for both training and testing, multilingual models such as mBERT and XLM-R perform well. In the future, we would like to expand SentMix-3L so that it can serve as both training and testing data. Additionally, we are working on pre-training Bangla-English-Hindi trilingual code-mixing models for offensive language identification.

Acknowledgements

We thank the annotators who helped us with the annotation of SentMix-3L. We further thank the anonymous workshop reviewers for their insightful feedback. Antonios Anastasopoulos is generously supported by NSF award IIS-2125466.

Limitations

Although most datasets for the downstream tasks are scraped from social media posts in the real world, in our case these data instances are generated in a semi-natural manner, meaning that they were generated by people but not scraped from social media directly. This was done due to the complexity of extracting contents that contain a specific 3 language code-mixing in them. Also, the dataset is comparatively smaller in size, since it is costly to generate data by a specific set of people who are fluent in all 3 target languages.

Ethics Statement

The dataset introduced in this paper, which centers on the analysis of offensive language in Bangla-English-Hindi code-mixed text, adheres to the ACL Ethics Policy and seeks to make a valuable contribution to the realm of online safety. SentMix-3L serves as an important resource for opinion analysis of online content. Moreover, the contributors and annotators of the dataset are paid respectable remuneration for their efforts towards this dataset.

References

Suraiya Alam. 2006. Code-mixing in bangladesh: A case study of non-government white-collar service holders and professionals. *Asian affairs*, 28(4):52–70.

Muhammad Mooneeb Ali, Mazhar Iqbal Ranjha, and Sartaj Fakhar Jillani. 2019. Effects of code mixing in indian film songs. *Journal of Media Studies*, 31(2).

Fotini Anastassiou. 2017. Factors associated with the code mixing and code-switching of multilingual children: An overview. *International Journal of Linguistics, Literature and Culture*, 4(3):13–26.

Kalika Bali, Jatin Sharma, Monojit Choudhury, and Yogarshi Vyas. 2014. i am borrowing ya mixing?" an analysis of english-hindi code mixing in facebook. In *Proceedings of CodeSwitch*.

Most Tasnim Begum and Md Mahmudul Haque. 2013. Code mixing in the ksa: A case study of expatriate bangladeshi and indian esl teachers. *Arab World English Journal*, 4(4).

Abhik Bhattacharjee, Tahmid Hasan, Wasi Ahmad, Kazi Samin Mubasshir, Md Saiful Islam, Anindya Iqbal, M. Sohel Rahman, and Rifat Shahriyar. 2022. BanglaBERT: Language model pretraining and benchmarks for low-resource language understanding evaluation in Bangla. In *Findings of the ACL*.

Krista Byers-Heinlein and Casey Lew-Williams. 2013. Bilingualism in the early years: What the science says. *LEARNing landscapes*, 7(1):95.

Alexis Conneau, Kartikay Khandelwal, Naman Goyal, Vishrav Chaudhary, Guillaume Wenzek, Francisco Guzmán, Edouard Grave, Myle Ott, Luke Zettlemoyer, and Veselin Stoyanov. 2020. Unsupervised cross-lingual representation learning at scale. In *Proceedings of ACL*.

Databricks. 2023. Dolly 2.0: An open source, instruction-following large language model. Accessed: 2023-09-10.

Jacob Devlin, Ming-Wei Chang, Kenton Lee, and Kristina Toutanova. 2019. BERT: Pre-training of Deep Bidirectional Transformers for Language Understanding. In *Proceedings of NAACL*.

Md Kamrul Hasan, Mohd Akhand, et al. 2015. Reviewing the challenges and opportunities presented by code switching and mixing in bangla. *Journal of Education and Practice*, 6(1):103–109.

Didar Hossain and Kapil Bar. 2015. A case study in code-mixing among jahangirnagar university students. *International Journal of English and Literature*, 6(7):123–139.

Jill V Jeffery and Catherine van Beuningen. 2020. Language education in the eu and the us: Paradoxes and parallels. *Prospects*, 48(3-4):175–191.

Navya Jose, Bharathi Raja Chakravarthi, Shardul Suryawanshi, Elizabeth Sherly, and John P McCrae. 2020. A survey of current datasets for code-switching research. In *Proceedings of ICACCS*.

Aditya Joshi, Ameya Prabhu, Manish Shrivastava, and Vasudeva Varma. 2016. Towards sub-word level compositions for sentiment analysis of hindi-english code mixed text. In *Proceedings of COLING*.

Divyanshu Kakwani, Anoop Kunchukuttan, Satish Golla, NC Gokul, Avik Bhattacharyya, Mitesh M Khapra, and Pratyush Kumar. 2020. Indicnlpsuite: Monolingual corpora, evaluation benchmarks and pre-trained multilingual language models for indian languages. In *Findings of the ACL*.

Mahamudur Rahaman Khan, SM Nawsad Rahmatullah, Md Fuadul Islam, Abu Raihan Mostofa Kamal, and Md Azam Hossain. 2022. Sentiment analysis of covid-19 vaccination in bangla language with code-mixed text from social media. In *Proceedings of ICECE*.

Simran Khanuja, Diksha Bansal, Sarvesh Mehtani, Savya Khosla, Atreyee Dey, Balaji Gopalan, Dilip Kumar Margam, Pooja Aggarwal, Rajiv Teja Nagipogu, Shachi Dave, Shruti Gupta, Subhash Chandra Bose Gali, Vish Subramanian, and Partha Talukdar. 2021. Muril: Multilingual representations for indian languages.

M Kowsher, Abdullah As Sami, Nusrat Jahan Prottasha, Mohammad Shamsul Arefin, Pranab Kumar Dhar, and Takeshi Koshiba. 2022. Bangla-bert: transformer-based efficient model for transfer learning and language understanding. *IEEE Access*, 10:91855–91870.

Jitin Krishnan, Antonios Anastasopoulos, Hemant Purohit, and Huzefa Rangwala. 2021. Multilingual code-switching for zero-shot cross-lingual intent prediction and slot filling. In *Proceedings of the 1st Workshop on Multilingual Representation Learning*.

Yinhan Liu, Myle Ott, Naman Goyal, Jingfei Du, Mandar Joshi, Danqi Chen, Omer Levy, Mike Lewis, Luke Zettlemoyer, and Veselin Stoyanov. 2019. Roberta: A robustly optimized BERT pretraining approach. *CoRR*, abs/1907.11692.

Ahmad Mahbub-ul Alam and Shaima Quyyum. 2016. A sociolinguistic survey on code switching & code mixing by the native speakers of bangladesh. *Journal of Manarat International University*, 6(1):8–9.

Daniele Mazzocchi. 2012. langdetect: Language detection library. Python library.

Ravindra Nayak and Raviraj Joshi. 2022. L3Cube-HingCorpus and HingBERT: A code mixed Hindi-English dataset and BERT language models. In *Proceedings WILDRE*.

Jianmo Ni, Jiacheng Li, and Julian McAuley. 2019. Justifying recommendations using distantly-labeled reviews and fine-grained aspects. In *Proceedings of EMNLP*.

Nick Doiron. 2023. hindi-bert (revision aefac8e).

Jianzhi Nie. 2023. Awesome instruction datasets. Accessed: 2023-09-10.

OpenAI. 2023. Gpt-3.5 turbo fine-tuning and api updates. Accessed: 2023-08-28.

Victor Sanh, Lysandre Debut, Julien Chaumond, and Thomas Wolf. 2019. Distilbert, a distilled version of BERT: smaller, faster, cheaper and lighter. *CoRR*, abs/1910.01108.

Sebastin Santy, Anirudh Srinivasan, and Monojit Choudhury. 2021. Bertologicomix: How does code-mixing interact with multilingual bert? In *Proceedings of AdaptNLP*.

Rajendra Singh. 1985. Grammatical constraints on code-mixing: Evidence from hindi-english. *Canadian Journal of Linguistics/Revue canadienne de linguistique*, 30(1):33–45.

Dinkar Sitaram, Savitha Murthy, Debraj Ray, Devansh Sharma, and Kashyap Dhar. 2015. Sentiment analysis of mixed language employing hindi-english code switching. In *Proceedings of ICMLC*.

Mohammad Tareq, Md Fokhrul Islam, Swakshar Deb, Sejuti Rahman, and Abdullah Al Mahmud. 2023. Data-augmentation for bangla-english code-mixed sentiment analysis: Enhancing cross linguistic contextual understanding. *IEEE Access*.

S Thara and Prabaharan Poornachandran. 2018. Code-mixing: A brief survey. In *Proceedings of ICACCI*.

Konark Yadav, Aashish Lamba, Dhruv Gupta, Ansh Gupta, Purnendu Karmakar, and Sandeep Saini. 2020. Bi-lstm and ensemble based bilingual sentiment analysis for a code-mixed hindi-english social media text. In *Proceedings of INDICON*.

A Examples of Misclassified Instances

Positive: জাস্ট গিভ এ পাবলিক স্পিচ এন্ড আই এম ওভার দ্যা মুন। এইটা আমার জন্য খুবই বড় একটা ব্যাপার কারণ আমি always been terrified of public speaking But I pushed through the fear and delivered a speech and দর্শকরা খুব ভালাভোবে গ্রহণ করেছে। उपलब्धि की भावना अद्भुत है और मुझे खुद पर बहुत गर्व है। yadi mujhase yah ho sakata hai, to tumase bhee ho sakata hai #publicspeaking #overcomingfears

Neutral: পিছলে 30 মিনাত বিনা কিসি পষ্ট ইয়া বাতাছেতে মে উলঝে মেরে সাশোল মেডিয়া ফেড কে মধ্যম সে স্ক্রোল করানে মে বিতাযে, অর ইমানদারি সে কাহুন ত ইয়া বহুত ভাল লাগা। কখনও কখনও আমাদের পৃথিবী থেকে বিচ্ছিন্ন এবং সংযাগে বিচ্ছিন্ন করার জন্য কিছুটা mindless scrolling প্রয়োজন। Of course, it's important to find balance and not let সাশ্যোল মিডিয়া consume too much of our time and energy. आप अपने दैनिक जीवन में सोशल मीडिया के उपयोग को कैसे नेविगेट करते हैं? Nicera mantabya apanara cinta seyara karuna! #Digitaldetox #mindfulness #socialmedia

Negative: ভারাক্রান্ত হৃদয়ে আমি শেয়ার করছি I loss of my beloved mini. দিস বরট সাে মাচ জয়, লাভ, এন্ড হ্যাপিনেস ইনটু মাই লাইফ, এন্ড ইটস অবসেন্স লিভস আ ভয়েড, কান্নত বে ফিলড उन्हें खोना अविश्वसनीय रूप से दर्दनाक रहा है, और मैं खुद को दुख से उबरता हुआ पाता हूं। They were more than just a pet; তারা ছিল একটি লালিত সঙ্গী এবং নিঃশর্ত ভালবাসার উৎস। aaie yaadon ko sanjoen, unakee viraasat ka sammaan karen aur hamaare dvaara saajha kie gae pyaar mein taakat paen.

IndoToD: A Multi-Domain Indonesian Benchmark For End-to-End Task-Oriented Dialogue Systems

Muhammad Dehan Al Kautsar[1], **Rahmah Khoirussyifa' Nurdini**[1], **Samuel Cahyawijaya**[3], **Genta Indra Winata**[2], **Ayu Purwarianti**[1]

[1]Institut Teknologi Bandung [2]Bloomberg

[3]The Hong Kong University of Science and Technology

dehanalkautsar3@gmail.com

Abstract

Task-oriented dialogue (ToD) systems have been mostly created for high-resource languages, such as English and Chinese. However, there is a need to develop ToD systems for other regional or local languages to broaden their ability to comprehend the dialogue contexts in various languages. This paper introduces IndoToD, an end-to-end multi-domain ToD benchmark in Indonesian. We extend two English ToD datasets to Indonesian, comprising four different domains by delexicalization to efficiently reduce the size of annotations. To ensure a high-quality data collection, we hire native speakers to manually translate the dialogues. Along with the original English datasets, these new Indonesian datasets serve as an effective benchmark for evaluating Indonesian and English ToD systems as well as exploring the potential benefits of cross-lingual and bilingual transfer learning approaches.

1 Introduction

Task-oriented dialogue (ToD) systems are conversational agents designed to interact with users and assist them in various domains, such as restaurant (Bordes et al., 2016; Wen et al., 2017), public transport (Budzianowski et al., 2018; Lin et al., 2021b), and in-car assistance (Eric et al., 2017). This system also serves as the base for many commercial products that operate using the dialogue systems approach because of its ability to operate and understand the dialogue context without using hand-crafted rules (Lin et al., 2021b). Despite the recent growing interest in developing end-to-end ToD systems due to their simplicity, ToD systems are mostly created using monolingual datasets in high-resource languages such as English and Chinese. Moreover, building a ToD system can be challenging due to the limited availability of datasets for training and evaluating the system, which has been identified as the most critical factor in preventing the creation of bilingual/multilingual ToD systems (Wen et al., 2017; Razumovskaia et al., 2021).

Developing ToD systems in additional underrepresented languages is essential to expand their capabilities to understand dialogue contexts in diverse languages (Kanakagiri and Radhakrishnan, 2021). One of them is Indonesian, a language spoken by many people worldwide yet still considered an underrepresented language in the end-to-end ToD system. Indonesian is ranked as the fourth most internet users in the world based on the latest data per country (Aji et al., 2022), with around 212 million internet users.[1] However, the language itself is still categorized as an underrepresented language in the natural language processing (NLP) community because of problems such as scattered datasets and minimum community engagement (Wilie et al., 2020; Cahyawijaya et al., 2021, 2022). To the best of our knowledge, there is only one publicly available end-to-end Indonesian ToD dataset[2] which is COD (Majewska et al., 2023), a multilingual ToD dataset that is solely used for evaluation – only test set available. It has a very limited number of samples for Indonesian with 194 dialogues across 11 domains (~18 dialogues per domain) and no training data provided. This emphasizes the need to create larger end-to-end Indonesian ToD datasets to expand the capabilities to build and evaluate localized Indonesian ToD systems.

To address the aforementioned issues, we propose **IndoToD**, an end-to-end multi-domain ToD benchmark in Indonesian. IndoToD comprises the collection of two parallel Indonesian end-to-end ToD datasets covering four different domains by manually translating two existing English datasets: CamRest676 (Wen et al., 2017) and SMD (Eric et al., 2017) using delexicalization and lexicalization processes, as well as the evaluation of existing end-to-end ToD frameworks in various settings

[1]https://www.internetworldstats.com/stats3.htm

[2]https://indonlp.github.io/nusa-catalogue/

Proceedings of the First Workshop in South East Asian Language Processing, pages 85–99
November 1, 2023. ©2023 Association for Computational Linguistics

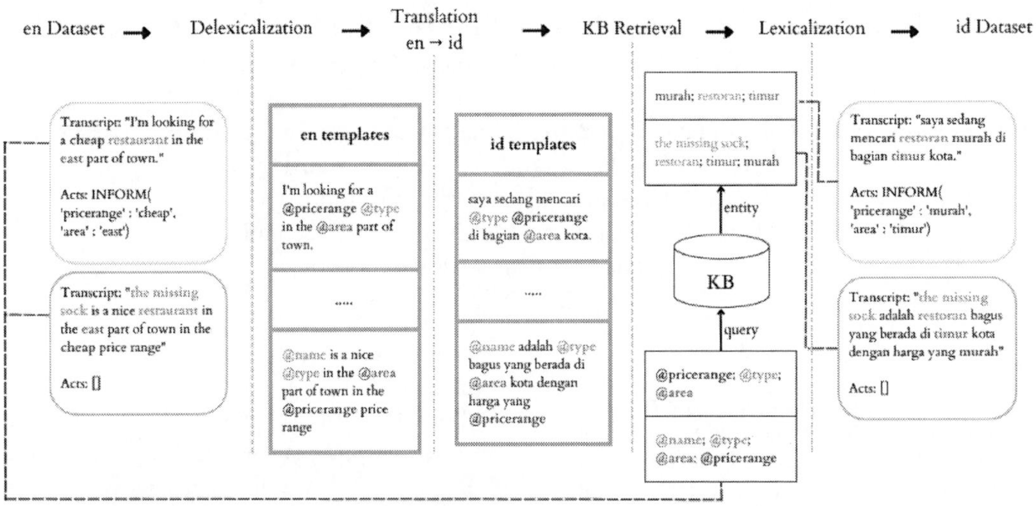

Figure 1: Illustration of the dialogues collection pipeline: a) Delexicalize dialogue conversations to create English templates; b) Translate English conversation templates to Indonesian; c) Retrieve KB to retrieve corresponding entities; d) Lexicalize the dialogue conversations to collect Indonesian dialogues.

such as monolingual, cross-lingual, and bilingual. IndoToD provides more dialogue samples compared to (Majewska et al., 2023) that can be utilized for training and evaluation.

This paper's contributions are summarized threefold as follows:

- We introduce IndoToD, the multi-domain benchmark for Indonesian ToD systems. The benchmark comprises two datasets: IndoCamRest and IndoSMD, with four different domains that serve as resources for training and evaluation.
- We establish baselines on monolingual, bilingual, and cross-lingual settings on existing end-to-end ToD frameworks.
- We analyze the effectiveness of training bilingual datasets to leverage more training data and handle tasks in both languages in building ToD systems.

2 IndoToD Benchmark

IndoToD benchmark[3] is created to develop the Indonesian ToD system. The benchmark covers four different domains, i.e., `restaurant search`, `point-of-interest (POI) navigation`, `calendar scheduling`, and `weather information`. IndoToD extends the existing English datasets, and we follow a streamlined process to conduct dialogue collection. The dialogues are multi-turn conversations that involve two speakers (i.e., user U and system S). For each conversation, there is a knowledge base (KB) for the system to generate the correct entity for the user.

[3] `https://github.com/dehanalkautsar/IndoToD`

2.1 Dataset Collection

We use CamRest676 (Wen et al., 2017) and SMD (Eric et al., 2017) as the original English datasets that will go through several stages before becoming datasets that can be used in various Indonesian Task-oriented Dialogue (ToD) system experiments. CamRest676 is a ToD dataset that focuses on restaurant search queries collected via Wizard-of-Oz (WoZ) framework (Kelley, 1984). It consists of a collection of dialogues between the user and the system, where each dialogue has a task-specific goal (e.g., finding a restaurant). In this dataset, the user acts as a client who requests restaurant information and the system acts as an information provider that guides and answers the user's request.

Meanwhile, SMD is an in-car assistant multi-domain ToD dataset. It covers several domains such as POI navigation, calendar scheduling, and weather information. This dataset was also created by using the same WoZ framework to get a high-quality dataset that imitates a conversation between two individuals in a way that resembles a

Statistics	COD-id	IndoCamRest (ours)	IndoSMD (ours)
# domains	11: Flights, Weather, Alarm, Ride Sharing, Movies, Music, Media, Homes, Banks, Travel, Payment	1: Restaurant Search	3: POI navigation, Calendar Scheduling, Weather Information
# dialogues	194	676	323
# dialogues/domain	17.64	676	107.67
# distinct entities	N/A	110	325
# turns/dialogue	12.83	4.06	2.63
# tokens/utterance	N/A	9.54	8.14
# vocab (lexicalized)	N/A	1,103	883
# vocab (delexicalized)	N/A	829	577

Table 1: Comparison of our IndoToD benchmark with the Indonesian subset of COD (Majewska et al., 2023).

real-life interaction between a driver and an in-car assistant. In the WoZ framework, the source of conversation is created through a human-to-human dialogue conversation which is collected through crowd-sourcing. Because of that, the conversations between the user and the system are more natural.

These datasets then will be used as a reference for generating a ToD dataset that mimics natural conversation between two speakers and includes relevant knowledge base information for generating accurate responses. Both two datasets provide a diverse variety of dialogues since they have a different set of domains that complement the IndoToD benchmark.

2.2 Dataset Construction

The datasets have been created through several steps, as shown in Figure 1. First, existing English datasets are delexicalized into several user and system template sentences using Madotto et al. (2020) approach. Then, these template sentences are translated by native Indonesian annotators into Indonesian sentences. Lastly, new Indonesian datasets are built through the KB retrieval and lexicalization process.

Delexicalization Initially, the datasets are preprocessed by delexicalizing the entities. The process is carried out using the source code implemented by Madotto et al. (2020) to remove the entities in the dataset's dialogue. The aim of this step is to reduce the number of dialogues that require annotation (translation) by replacing all entities with a common, pre-defined value based on the type of entity. This pre-processing method is effective because the number of sentences that need to be translated is reduced by 30% and 34% for CamRest676 and SMD, respectively. The output of this step is a list of pre-processed, entity-less sentences for each dataset.

Translation The list of pre-processed sentences is translated into Indonesian by annotators. In total, there are 3,834 and 1,126 sentences translated from CamRest676 and SMD, respectively. This process is followed by a cross-validation process where an annotator has to check the work of other annotators to maintain the dataset's quality. Note that for the SMD dataset, we only use 11% (323 dialogues) of its original dialogues due to the limitations on the annotator side.

KB Retrieval and Lexicalization After the translation process, to build each dialogue, a collection of Indonesian sentences and their corresponding entities are needed to begin the lexicalization process. We retrieve the Indonesian entities by querying the KB for the required slots to construct the dialogue. The lexicalization process is conducted by using Indonesian entities and sentences that have been retrieved earlier. This process ends with an evaluation of 100 randomly selected newly created Indonesian dialogues by human evaluators to detect any errors to ensure the quality of the resulting dialogues. If there are any errors, we ask them to manually edit that utterance. The sample of corrected Indonesian utterances is presented in Appendix Table 1.

2.3 Dataset Statistics

We collect a total of 999 dialogues with 6,338 utterances from two datasets, named as IndoCamRest and IndoSMD, which are derived from CamRest676 and SMD datasets, respectively. We com-

Statistics	IndoCamRest	IndoSMD		
	Restaurant Search	POI Navigation	Calendar Scheduling	Weather Information
# dialogues	676	100	114	109
# slot types	6 (area, food, price range, postcode, phone, address)	5 (POI name, traffic info, POI category, address, distance)	6 (event, time, date, party, room, agenda)	4 (location, weekly time, temperature, weather attr.)
# distinct slot values	88	131	79	78

Table 2: Per-domain statistics of IndoCamRest and IndoSMD.

pare several statistic attributes between our datasets (IndoCamRest and IndoSMD) and COD that are shown in Table 1. Furthermore, the per-domain statistics of IndoCamRest and IndoSMD are presented in Table 2. IndoCamRest and IndoSMD share some of the same statistical characteristics as the previous datasets, including the number of domains, intents, and slot types. It is worth noting that both of our datasets have a substantially larger number of dialogues per domain compared to COD. In addition, IndoCamRest and IndoSMD comprise both the lexicalized and delexicalized forms in the dialogue. The inclusion of the delexicalized form is intended to facilitate the generation of dialogues by lexicalizing the delexicalized sentences.

3 Experimental Setup

3.1 Experiment Settings

We set up a benchmark for both Indonesian and English ToD to evaluate the performance of the current ToD systems. We explore three different training and evaluation settings:

- **Monolingual – id/en**. We train the end-to-end ToD systems using monolingual corpus in each language independently.
- **Cross-lingual**. We train the systems using the English end-to-end ToD dataset before testing it using an Indonesian test set to analyze the effectiveness of the cross-lingual approach in understanding the context of the dialogue.
- **Bilingual – id+en**. We train the systems by combining English and Indonesian datasets, utilizing parallel corpora from CamRest and SMD. This allows us to examine how the system's performance is affected by exposure to bilingual languages.

For monolingual and bilingual settings, we test each ToD framework in English and Indonesian test sets separately to analyze the impact of monolingual and bilingual training in each language. We also split the data into 3:1:1 and 8:1:1 for the CamRest and SMD, respectively.

3.2 ToD Baselines

As baselines, We evaluate four ToD frameworks: Sequicity (Lei et al., 2018), LABES (Zhang et al., 2020a), MinTL (Lin et al., 2020), and GALAXY (He et al., 2022). Since the four ToD system frameworks are designed for English, we have made adjustments to the frameworks to suit the requirements of our experiments. We largely adopt the configuration settings used in the original paper, including batch size, decoding method, early stop count, and learning rate.

To adapt the Sequicity and LABES frameworks for our experiments, we utilize fastText (Bojanowski et al., 2017) instead of GloVe (Pennington et al., 2014). This was necessary because fastText can accommodate English, Indonesian, and bilingual Indonesian-English word vectors (Conneau et al., 2017). Specifically, we incorporate common crawl[4] English and Indonesian fastText word vectors for monolingual English and Indonesian experiment settings respectively. Meanwhile, we use bilingual English-Indonesian word vectors (Conneau et al., 2017) for other settings.

Unlike the other frameworks, MinTL utilizes T5 (Raffel et al., 2020) and BART (Lewis et al., 2020) as its backbone, which sets it apart regarding approach and potential performance. Note that for this experiment, we only use T5 (Raffel et al., 2020) and mT5 (Xue et al., 2021) as the backbone models, and use this framework without utilizing

[4] https://fasttext.cc/docs/en/crawl-vectors.html

Baselines	IndoCamRest				IndoSMD			
	BLEU	Match	Success	Combined	BLEU	Match	Success	Combined
monolingual								
Sequicity (Lei et al., 2018)	16.74	92.31	81.29	103.54	**8.75**	**44.83**	**61.04**	**61.69**
LABES (Zhang et al., 2020a)	17.59	70.00	78.49	91.83	1.01	0.00	34.82	18.42
MinTL (Lin et al., 2020)	14.61	80.33	80.31	94.93	0.45	24.14	23.70	24.37
GALAXY (He et al., 2022)	**17.89**	**96.24**	**84.62**	**108.32**	-	-	-	-
cross-lingual								
Sequicity (Lei et al., 2018)	0.08	8.46	31.58	20.10	0.00	15.52	29.46	22.50
LABES (Zhang et al., 2020a)	0.02	0.00	60.96	30.50	0.00	**15.79**	55.84	**35.82**
MinTL (Lin et al., 2020)	**1.61**	**16.67**	**68.81**	**44.35**	0.00	13.33	**56.75**	35.04
GALAXY (He et al., 2022)	0.05	0.00	47.24	23.67	0.00	0.00	37.11	18.56
bilingual								
Sequicity (Lei et al., 2018)	15.84	89.23	**84.01**	102.46	10.95	**58.33**	75.66	**77.94**
LABES (Zhang et al., 2020a)	**18.77**	**96.36**	81.68	**107.79**	8.78	47.37	71.11	68.02
MinTL (Lin et al., 2020)	18.65	87.30	79.63	102.12	**11.59**	48.33	**77.86**	74.68
GALAXY (He et al., 2022)	17.09	94.74	83.60	106.26	0.08	45.00	9.17	27.17

Table 3: Experiment settings result on Indonesian test set. **bold** denotes the best score per metric.

Levenshtein Belief Spans (Lev) resulting in an inference process similar to Sequicity. In all of the experiment settings, mT5-small is implemented in the framework and used as the backbone of the framework. We also try to use T5 for monolingual and bilingual settings to analyze the impact of using two different kinds of pre-trained language models (LMs) that will be discussed later in the Subsection 4.2. We implement reader and evaluator modules for both CamRest and SMD datasets in MinTL, as their paper only included the reader and evaluator for the MultiWOZ (Budzianowski et al., 2018) dataset.

3.3 Hyper-parameters

We conduct the learning rate search [1e-4, 6e-4, 1e-5] to optimize the performance of MinTL on the new datasets, and the best learning rate is 6e-4. For other ToD frameworks, we adopt their proposed learning rate in our experiments. We use a learning rate of 3e-3 for Sequicity, 1e-4 for GALAXY, and, for LABES, we set the learning rate to 3e-4 and 1e-4 in the CamRest and SMD experiments, respectively. We follow the inference sampling strategies recommended by the original papers that introduce the frameworks. We use a beam size of 5 for generating inference responses in GALAXY, while in the other frameworks, we employ greedy search. We run each experiment once per experiment setting for uniformity with an A100 40GB GPU.

3.4 Evaluation Metrics

We use four evaluation metrics for end-to-end ToD tasks to evaluate the quality of responses. There are 1) **BLEU** score (Papineni et al., 2002) to assess how fluent the generated response is, 2) **Match** rate (Lin et al., 2020), checks whether the ToD system can produce the entity constraints specified by the user, thereby measuring task completion, 3) **Success** F1 score (Lei et al., 2018), which determines whether the system has successfully provided all of the information that the user has requested, such as the address or phone number, and 4) **Combined** score (Lin et al., 2020; Mehri et al., 2019) using the equation **Combined** = (Match + Success) $\times$ 0.5 + BLEU. We assess the performance of all frameworks using the CamRest and SMD datasets, along with the designated experiment settings.

4 Results & Analysis

4.1 Results

Tables 3 and 4 show the experiment results for Indonesian and English test sets, respectively. We conclude that GALAXY has a decent score in both monolingual settings for CamRest, and Sequicity with fastText word vector has the best model in monolingual settings for SMD. Furthermore, MinTL outperforms other frameworks in zero-shot cross-lingual settings for both datasets. The non-contextual word-embedding frameworks, such as Sequicity and LABES achieve the highest combined scores for bilingual settings. Furthermore, it was observed that GALAXY does not perform

Baselines	CamRest				SMD			
	BLEU	**Match**	**Success**	**Combined**	**BLEU**	**Match**	**Success**	**Combined**
monolingual								
Sequicity (Lei et al., 2018)	**21.17**	90.30	80.99	106.81	**21.04**	82.12	78.21	**101.20**
LABES (Zhang et al., 2020a)	19.98	93.64	72.93	103.26	1.94	80.81	60.07	72.39
MinTL (Lin et al., 2020)	20.34	83.21	83.64	103.77	18.53	**83.90**	**78.60**	99.78
GALAXY (He et al., 2022)	20.53	**96.24**	**84.62**	**110.96**	18.25	80.00	77.32	96.91
bilingual								
Sequicity (Lei et al., 2018)	22.53	91.04	82.06	109.08	21.04	75.56	**83.48**	100.56
LABES (Zhang et al., 2020a)	22.58	**97.27**	79.33	**110.88**	**22.35**	**83.83**	74.02	**101.28**
MinTL (Lin et al., 2020)	**22.88**	86.26	82.26	107.14	18.39	80.23	79.10	98.05
GALAXY (He et al., 2022)	20.31	95.49	**84.67**	110.39	16.58	77.37	76.84	93.68

Table 4: Experiment settings result on English test set. **bold** denotes the best score per metric.

as well as other frameworks when dealing with Indonesian, as we denote its results by using '-' in Table 3.

Additionally, we present the combined metric results of the ToD frameworks on the IndoSMD test set, categorized by domain, in Figure 2. We discover that `POI navigation` is relatively easier than other domains to learn, while `calendar scheduling` is the hardest domain for ToD frameworks on SMD dataset. Fine-grained results can be found in Appendix Table 2.

4.2 Analysis

Monolingual English vs. Indonesian Performance. In general, the monolingual model trained and tested in English performs better than in Indonesian across different frameworks and datasets. We hypothesize that the pre-trained LMs used in the experiments are better trained to handle English data. GALAXY outperforms the monolingual setting on both Indonesian and English CamRest datasets. However, we find that the GALAXY framework fails to adapt to the IndoSMD dataset and the model is not converged. We further observe that the experiments using GALAXY in Indonesian are not as effective as English, as evidenced by the superior performance on the English CamRest dataset, despite having the same amount of dialogue and utterance as IndoCamRest. Furthermore, it is worth noting on the IndoToD benchmark that we are not using Indonesian T5 models. This is because there is no paper working on releasing the Indonesian T5 models that are comparable to the English T5 models we use in the experiment.

Transferability from English to Indonesian. Based on the cross-lingual results, it can be concluded that existing ToD frameworks are unable to handle the task when trained in a different language. While not all training data needs to be in the same language as the test set, it is still essential for the framework to have some knowledge of the target language in order to understand the task at hand. Based on the inference results, we observe that all of the ToD frameworks generate responses in English despite Indonesian user inputs. This can be correlated to the fact that the training data used in the cross-lingual setting is in English. Among all the ToD frameworks that are evaluated in this setting, MinTL performs the best in the cross-lingual setting (due to mT5 as its pre-trained model, trained on multilingual datasets), while GALAXY and Sequicity do not perform well.

Monolingual vs. Bilingual. The results demonstrate that, in most cases, the bilingual setting yields higher scores than the monolingual (i.e., Indonesian and English monolingual setting), especially in the Indonesian test set. The bilingual setting has the advantage of using a larger amount of training data and performing tasks in both languages (Lin et al., 2021b), increasing both the overall metric scores and the individual metric components. We also compare and analyze the framework's performance closely based on the test set we used. The results show that most of the bilingual settings scores are higher than monolingual settings in both the Indonesian and English test sets showing the effective usage of language data counterpart for domain adaptation.

However, based on the inference result in Table 5, we observe that the responses generated between bilingual and monolingual settings are not substantially different in terms of the semantics, confirmed by the fact that the difference in

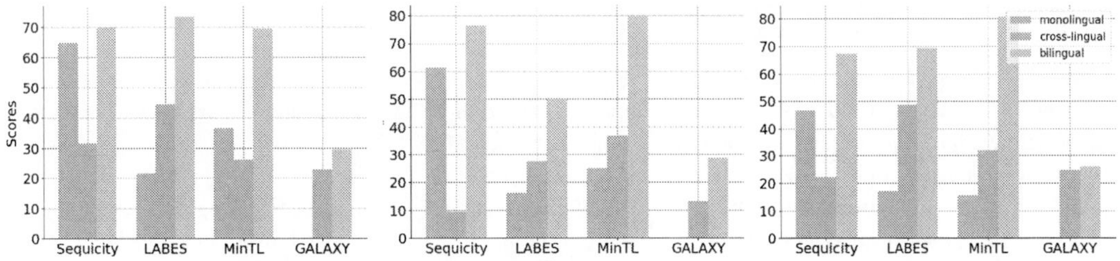

Figure 2: ToD framework results on IndoSMD per domain. **Left**: `POI navigation` domain, **Center**: `Calendar scheduling` domain, and **Right**: `Weather information` domain.

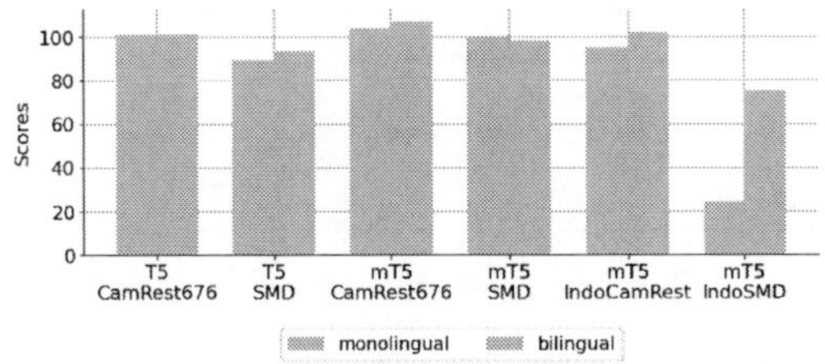

Figure 3: Monolingual and bilingual MinTL combined score using T5 and mT5 models on CamRest676, SMD, IndoCamRest, and IndoSMD as test sets.

BLEU scores between these two settings is not significant. However, we see some improvements in belief spans generation in the bilingual setting. ToD frameworks can understand the context from the user better when they are trained with a larger amount of training data, although the training data are a mixture of English and Indonesian. This highlights the significance of leveraging cross-lingual data, in this case, using English data on top of Indonesian data, in the training process of the ToD system to enhance the model performance and achieve better metric scores in the target language.

Furthermore, we delve deeper into analyzing the potential of bilingual training using the MinTL framework. Interestingly, this framework is flexible since we can modify the pre-trained transformer LM unlike other frameworks. We explore not only English T5, but also multilingual version of T5. We compare the performance of T5-small and mT5-small as the backbone of the MinTL framework, shown in Figure 3 and Appendix Table 3 for per metric details. Based on our findings, we observe that bilingual training positively impacts the BLEU score, match rate, and combined metrics for the MinTL framework, either using T5 or mT5. The results indicate that the bilingual setting can yield benefits on the efficient training process of T5 and mT5, especially in Indonesian, that is considered as underrepresented language. Moreover, we notice that mT5-small is more effective than T5-small in end-to-end ToD tasks. Overall, the bilingual training is beneficial for training end-to-end ToD, especially to improve the performance on non-English languages.

Error Analysis. We conduct an error analysis to investigate the limitations of existing frameworks. In general, most issues occur in the form of a "template response". The end-to-end ToD systems sometimes generate responses that appear to be template-like despite varying user inputs which might be because of the limited trainable parameters and dataset used in the training process. Despite its goal to complete the user's task, the ToD must also be able to maintain the user's satisfaction whenever using the ToD as a product. Users may become disinterested if they receive repeated responses, potentially leading to reduced usage. Another issue we notice is the occurrence of repeated tokens in the generated output by the framework during the inference phase. Specifically, we find that the Sequicity and MinTL frameworks tend to produce responses with repeated tokens more than the other ToD frameworks. This could be due to the decoding method applied by these frameworks in our research which relied on a greedy search approach. The other issue that is worth mentioning in inference examples is the hallucination in the generated outputs. Some of the outputs do not have the correct combination of slots that are found in the training set.

5 Related Work

ToD Datasets. Multiple studies have contributed to creating datasets for ToD using various approaches. bAbI (Bordes et al., 2016) is an English synthetic dataset combining five subtasks into ToD system datasets. SMD (Eric et al., 2017)

Input	Belief spans	Response
"carikan saya restoran mahal yang menyediakan makanan internasional." *(find me an expensive restaurant that serves international food)*	**gold:** "restaurant-food": "internasional", "restaurant-pricerange": "mahal" **monolingual:** "restaurant-food": "internasional", "restaurant-pricerange": "menengah" **bilingual:** "restaurant-food": "internasional", "restaurant-pricerange": "mahal"	**gold:** "maafkan saya. saya tidak bisa menemukan restoran apapun yang menyediakan makanan internasional di kisaran harga yang mahal" *(I am sorry. I couldn't find any restaurant that provides international food at such an expensive price range)* **monolingual:** "value_name adalah restoran mahal yang menyediakan makanan internasional. apakah kamu ingin tahu lokasinya?" *(value_name is an expensive restaurant that serves international food. Would you like to know its location?)* **bilingual:** "value_name menyediakan makanan internasional. apakah kamu ingin informasi lebih lanjut?" *(value_name serves international foods. Would you like other further information?)*

Table 5: Example of the LABES response on IndoCamRest using monolingual and bilingual settings. The English translation is in *italic*.

uses the WoZ scheme to build an English car assistant dialogue system that has knowledge of weather and places. Other English datasets using the WoZ scheme are CamRest (Wen et al., 2017), a dataset for a restaurant reservation, MultiWoZ (Budzianowski et al., 2018), a multi-domain WoZ dataset containing five domains collected using the human-to-human scheme, and OpenDialKG (Moon et al., 2019), a synthetic dataset containing four domains. On non-English datasets. such as Chinese, there are CrossWoZ (Zhu et al., 2020), a large-scale Chinese WoZ dataset with five domains, and RiSAWoZ (Quan et al., 2020), a large-scale multidomain Chinese WoZ dataset with rich semantic annotations up to 12 domains. MetaLWOz (Lee et al., 2019) is a goal-oriented dialogue corpus containing 51 domains and collected using WoZ. Other datasets include bilingual languages, such as BiToD (Lin et al., 2021b), a dataset for tourism assistants focusing on English and Chinese languages, and COD (Majewska et al., 2023), a dataset containing Russian, Arabic, Indonesian, and Swahili. Based on the aforementioned datasets, we conclude that the ToD dataset with contextual knowledge focusing on Indonesian is not yet available.

Indonesian Dialogue Systems Datasets. Research for the ToD system in the Indonesian language is still underway. IndoNLG (Cahyawijaya et al., 2021), a benchmark for natural language generation in low-resource languages, focuses on summarization, question answering, chit-chat, and machine translation for Indonesian, Javanese, and Sundanese languages. An Indonesian language subset of the XPersona (Lin et al., 2021a) dataset, which consists of approximately 17 thousand dialogues, is used for the chit-chat task. It is worth noting that although IndoNLG is making significant progress, it has not yet explored the ToD system. Furthermore, NusaCrowd (Cahyawijaya et al., 2022), a large pool of hundreds of Indonesian NLP data, only listed one Indonesian ToD dataset, i.e., COD (Majewska et al., 2023), which is a multilingual ToD dataset that is solely used for evaluation with only 194 dialogues spanning across 11 domains. Therefore, the Indonesian ToD dataset is still very limited, and urgent action is required to increase the coverage of Indonesian ToD datasets.

Frameworks for End-to-End ToD. GALAXY (He et al., 2022) is a pre-trained dialogue model that uses semi-supervised learning to learn dialogue policy from limited labeled dialogues and large-scale unlabeled dialogue corpora. LABES (Zhang et al., 2020a), conversely, represents belief states as discrete latent variables and models them jointly with system responses given user inputs. MinTL (Lin et al., 2020) efficiently uses pretrained LMs in developing task-oriented dialogue systems, eliminating the need for ad hoc modules in studies that use this framework. DAMD (Zhang et al., 2020b) is a network that accommodates state-action pair structure in generation and can leverage the proposed multi-action data augmentation framework to address the multidomain response generation problem. Sequicity (Lei et al., 2018) uses the Seq2Seq model for dialogue state tracking and generating a response to the user. Some other recent works (Bang et al., 2023; Hudeček and Dušek, 2023) explore the potential of using large LMs for performing zero-shot ToD. In this paper, we utilize GALAXY, LABES, MinTL, and Sequicity to evaluate the performance of various end-to-end ToD frameworks.

6 Conclusion

We introduce IndoToD, an end-to-end multi-domain Indonesian ToD benchmark. We extend the existing two English ToD datasets using an efficient framework by delexicalizing the conversation into templates and reconstruction using KB. We evaluate our benchmark in monolingual, cross-lingual, and bilingual settings. We also show the benefits of having English data to improve Indonesian performance. Furthermore, we conduct some analysis from multiple viewpoints that shows the existing ToD system's inability to understand dialogue context from unseen language and the current ToD system's behavior in handling underrepresented language such as Indonesian using our datasets. We also investigate some errors that usually occur in ToD system responses to explore its limitation.

7 Limitations

There are several limitations that hinder our progress in creating the first Indonesian end-to-end ToD benchmark. Firstly, we encountered a limitation in translating the English dataset. Due to the constraints of our resources, specifically having only three annotators, we could only translate the CamRest dataset and a mere 10% of the SMD dataset. Expanding the dataset size would significantly contribute to advancing the Indonesian ToD system. Second, we only use publicly available end-to-end ToD system framework repositories as our baselines. Based on MultiWoZ benchmark[5], there are several end-to-end ToD frameworks with slightly superior metric scores compared to our baselines (Budzianowski et al., 2018). But because of their unavailability, we could not evaluate them and only focused on evaluating the best available ToD frameworks possible.

[5]https://github.com/budzianowski/multiwoz

8 Ethics Statement

Our work spotlights a need to develop ToD systems for underrepresented languages such as Indonesian through our new ToD datasets: IndoCamRest and IndoSMD. During our study, we commit to the ethical principles of NLP research and are well aware of its impact on the language community. We strongly believe that there is no ethical issue within this work, including the data collection process, annotation, existing dataset usage, and experiments. Within our work, annotators are well-rewarded and give us informed consent as they understand and agree to provide their annotations to build new ToD datasets. We uphold our annotator's privacy and follow the data protection and privacy regulation for releasing the datasets. The dataset itself is free from abusive language and personal information as our ultimate goal in this work is to contribute and make an impact on society with provide useful NLP task resources and more linguistic diversity in the NLP field.

References

Alham Fikri Aji, Genta Indra Winata, Fajri Koto, Samuel Cahyawijaya, Ade Romadhony, Rahmad Mahendra, Kemal Kurniawan, David Moeljadi, Radityo Eko Prasojo, Timothy Baldwin, Jey Han Lau, and Sebastian Ruder. 2022. One country, 700+ languages: NLP challenges for underrepresented languages and dialects in Indonesia. In *Proceedings of the 60th Annual Meeting of the Association for Computational Linguistics (Volume 1: Long Papers)*, pages 7226–7249, Dublin, Ireland. Association for Computational Linguistics.

Yejin Bang, Samuel Cahyawijaya, Nayeon Lee, Wenliang Dai, Dan Su, Bryan Wilie, Holy Lovenia, Ziwei Ji, Tiezheng Yu, Willy Chung, Quyet V. Do, Yan Xu, and Pascale Fung. 2023. A multitask, multilingual, multimodal evaluation of chatgpt on reasoning, hallucination, and interactivity.

Piotr Bojanowski, Edouard Grave, Armand Joulin, and Tomas Mikolov. 2017. Enriching word vectors with subword information. *Transactions of the association for computational linguistics*, pages 135–146.

Antoine Bordes, Y-Lan Boureau, and Jason Weston. 2016. Learning end-to-end goal-oriented dialog. *arXiv preprint arXiv:1605.07683*.

Paweł Budzianowski, Tsung-Hsien Wen, Bo-Hsiang Tseng, Iñigo Casanueva, Stefan Ultes, Osman Ramadan, and Milica Gasic. 2018. Multiwoz-a large-scale multi-domain wizard-of-oz dataset for task-oriented dialogue modelling. In *Proceedings of the 2018 Conference on Empirical Methods in Natural Language Processing*, pages 5016–5026.

Samuel Cahyawijaya, Holy Lovenia, Alham Fikri Aji, Genta Indra Winata, Bryan Wilie, Rahmad Mahendra, Christian Wibisono, Ade Romadhony, Karissa Vincentio, Fajri Koto, Jennifer Santoso, David Moeljadi, Cahya Wirawan, Frederikus Hudi, Ivan Halim Parmonangan, Ika Alfina, Muhammad Satrio Wicaksono, Ilham Firdausi Putra, Samsul Rahmadani, Yulianti Oenang, Ali Akbar Septiandri, James Jaya, Kaustubh D. Dhole, Arie Ardiyanti Suryani, Rifki Afina Putri, Dan Su, Keith Stevens, Made Nindyatama Nityasya, Muhammad Farid Adilazuarda, Ryan Ignatius, Ryandito Diandaru, Tiezheng Yu, Vito Ghifari, Wenliang Dai, Yan Xu, Dyah Damapuspita, Cuk Tho, Ichwanul Muslim Karo Karo, Tirana Noor Fatyanosa, Ziwei Ji, Pascale Fung, Graham Neubig, Timothy Baldwin, Sebastian Ruder, Herry Sujaini, Sakriani Sakti, and Ayu Purwarianti. 2022. Nusacrowd: Open source initiative for indonesian nlp resources.

Samuel Cahyawijaya, Genta Indra Winata, Bryan Wilie, Karissa Vincentio, Xiaohong Li, Adhiguna Kuncoro, Sebastian Ruder, Zhi Yuan Lim, Syafri Bahar, Masayu Khodra, et al. 2021. Indonlg: Benchmark and resources for evaluating indonesian natural language generation. In *Proceedings of the 2021 Conference on Empirical Methods in Natural Language Processing*, pages 8875–8898.

Alexis Conneau, Guillaume Lample, Marc'Aurelio Ranzato, Ludovic Denoyer, and Hervé Jégou. 2017. Word translation without parallel data. *CoRR*, abs/1710.04087.

Mihail Eric, Lakshmi Krishnan, Francois Charette, and Christopher D Manning. 2017. Key-value retrieval networks for task-oriented dialogue. In *Proceedings of the 18th Annual SIGdial Meeting on Discourse and Dialogue*, pages 37–49.

Wanwei He, Yinpei Dai, Yinhe Zheng, Yuchuan Wu, Zheng Cao, Dermot Liu, Peng Jiang, Min Yang, Fei Huang, Luo Si, Jian Sun, and Yongbin Li. 2022. Galaxy: A generative pre-trained model for task-oriented dialog with semi-supervised learning and explicit policy injection. *Proceedings of the AAAI Conference on Artificial Intelligence*, 36(10):10749–10757.

Vojtěch Hudeček and Ondřej Dušek. 2023. Are llms all you need for task-oriented dialogue?

Tushar Kanakagiri and Karthik Radhakrishnan. 2021. Task-oriented dialog systems for dravidian languages. In *Proceedings of the First Workshop on Speech and Language Technologies for Dravidian Languages*, pages 85–93.

J. F. Kelley. 1984. An iterative design methodology for user-friendly natural language office information applications. *ACM Trans. Inf. Syst.*, 2:26–41.

Sungjin Lee, Hannes Schulz, Adam Atkinson, Jianfeng Gao, Kaheer Suleman, Layla El Asri, Mahmoud Adada, Minlie Huang, Shikhar Sharma, Wendy Tay, and Xiujun Li. 2019. Multi-domain task-completion dialog challenge. In *Dialog System Technology Challenges 8*.

Wenqiang Lei, Xisen Jin, Min-Yen Kan, Zhaochun Ren, Xiangnan He, and Dawei Yin. 2018. Sequicity: Simplifying task-oriented dialogue systems with single sequence-to-sequence architectures. In *Proceedings of the 56th Annual Meeting of the Association for Computational Linguistics (Volume 1: Long Papers)*, pages 1437–1447.

Mike Lewis, Yinhan Liu, Naman Goyal, Marjan Ghazvininejad, Abdelrahman Mohamed, Omer Levy, Veselin Stoyanov, and Luke Zettlemoyer. 2020. Bart: Denoising sequence-to-sequence pre-training for natural language generation, translation, and comprehension. In *Proceedings of the 58th Annual Meeting of the Association for Computational Linguistics*, pages 7871–7880.

Zhaojiang Lin, Zihan Liu, Genta Indra Winata, Samuel Cahyawijaya, Andrea Madotto, Yejin Bang, Etsuko Ishii, and Pascale Fung. 2021a. Xpersona: Evaluating multilingual personalized chatbot. In *Proceedings of the 3rd Workshop on Natural Language Processing for Conversational AI*, pages 102–112.

Zhaojiang Lin, Andrea Madotto, Genta Indra Winata, and Pascale Fung. 2020. Mintl: Minimalist transfer learning for task-oriented dialogue systems. In *Proceedings of the 2020 Conference on Empirical Methods in Natural Language Processing (EMNLP)*, pages 3391–3405.

Zhaojiang Lin, Andrea Madotto, Genta Indra Winata, Peng Xu, Feijun Jiang, Yuxiang Hu, Chen Shi, and Pascale Fung. 2021b. Bitod: A bilingual multi-domain dataset for task-oriented dialogue modeling. *arXiv preprint arXiv:2106.02787*.

Andrea Madotto, Samuel Cahyawijaya, Genta Indra Winata, Yan Xu, Zihan Liu, Zhaojiang Lin, and Pascale Fung. 2020. Learning knowledge bases with parameters for task-oriented dialogue systems. In *Findings of the Association for Computational Linguistics: EMNLP 2020*, pages 2372–2394.

Olga Majewska, Evgeniia Razumovskaia, Edoardo M Ponti, Ivan Vulić, and Anna Korhonen. 2023. Cross-lingual dialogue dataset creation via outline-based generation. *Transactions of the Association for Computational Linguistics*, 11:139–156.

Shikib Mehri, Tejas Srinivasan, and Maxine Eskenazi. 2019. Structured fusion networks for dialog. In *Proceedings of the 20th Annual SIGdial Meeting on Discourse and Dialogue*, pages 165–177.

Seungwhan Moon, Pararth Shah, Anuj Kumar, and Rajen Subba. 2019. Opendialkg: Explainable conversational reasoning with attention-based walks over knowledge graphs. In *Proceedings of the 57th Annual Meeting of the Association for Computational Linguistics*, pages 845–854.

Kishore Papineni, Salim Roukos, Todd Ward, and Wei-Jing Zhu. 2002. Bleu: a method for automatic evaluation of machine translation. In *Proceedings of the 40th annual meeting of the Association for Computational Linguistics*, pages 311–318.

Jeffrey Pennington, Richard Socher, and Christopher Manning. 2014. GloVe: Global vectors for word representation. In *Proceedings of the 2014 Conference on Empirical Methods in Natural Language Processing (EMNLP)*, pages 1532–1543, Doha, Qatar. Association for Computational Linguistics.

Jun Quan, Shian Zhang, Qian Cao, Zizhong Li, and Deyi Xiong. 2020. Risawoz: A large-scale multi-domain wizard-of-oz dataset with rich semantic annotations for task-oriented dialogue modeling. In *Proceedings of the 2020 Conference on Empirical Methods in Natural Language Processing (EMNLP)*, pages 930–940.

Colin Raffel, Noam Shazeer, Adam Roberts, Katherine Lee, Sharan Narang, Michael Matena, Yanqi Zhou, Wei Li, and Peter J Liu. 2020. Exploring the limits of transfer learning with a unified text-to-text transformer. *The Journal of Machine Learning Research*, 21(1):5485–5551.

Evgeniia Razumovskaia, Goran Glavavs, Olga Majewska, E. Ponti, Anna Korhonen, and Ivan Vulic. 2021. Crossing the conversational chasm: A primer on natural language processing for multilingual task-oriented dialogue systems. *J. Artif. Intell. Res.*, 74:1351–1402.

Tsung-Hsien Wen, David Vandyke, Nikola Mrkšić, Milica Gasic, Lina M Rojas Barahona, Pei-Hao Su, Stefan Ultes, and Steve Young. 2017. A network-based end-to-end trainable task-oriented dialogue system. In *Proceedings of the 15th Conference of the European Chapter of the Association for Computational Linguistics: Volume 1, Long Papers*, pages 438–449.

Bryan Wilie, Karissa Vincentio, Genta Indra Winata, Samuel Cahyawijaya, Xiaohong Li, Zhi Yuan Lim, Sidik Soleman, Rahmad Mahendra, Pascale Fung, Syafri Bahar, et al. 2020. Indonlu: Benchmark and resources for evaluating indonesian natural language understanding. In *Proceedings of the 1st Conference of the Asia-Pacific Chapter of the Association for Computational Linguistics and the 10th International Joint Conference on Natural Language Processing*, pages 843–857.

Linting Xue, Noah Constant, Adam Roberts, Mihir Kale, Rami Al-Rfou, Aditya Siddhant, Aditya Barua, and Colin Raffel. 2021. mt5: A massively multilingual pre-trained text-to-text transformer. In *Proceedings of the 2021 Conference of the North American Chapter of the Association for Computational Linguistics: Human Language Technologies*, pages 483–498.

Yichi Zhang, Zhijian Ou, Min Hu, and Junlan Feng. 2020a. A probabilistic end-to-end task-oriented dialog model with latent belief states towards semi-supervised learning. In *Proceedings of the 2020 Conference on Empirical Methods in Natural Language Processing (EMNLP)*, pages 9207–9219.

Yichi Zhang, Zhijian Ou, and Zhou Yu. 2020b. Task-oriented dialog systems that consider multiple appropriate responses under the same context. In *Proceedings of the AAAI Conference on Artificial Intelligence*, volume 34, pages 9604–9611.

Qi Zhu, Kaili Huang, Zheng Zhang, Xiaoyan Zhu, and Minlie Huang. 2020. Crosswoz: A large-scale chinese cross-domain task-oriented dialogue dataset. *Transactions of the Association for Computational Linguistics*, 8:281–295.

A Annotator Recruitment

We recruit two Indonesian native speakers that can speak English to translate the delexicalized English utterance template to Indonesian. The age of the annotators ranged from 19 to 25, and they were college students by profession. They work around 18 hours in total, and they are compensated approximately 22,583 IDR per hour for their work, 18,62% bigger than the worker minimum wage in West Java (19,038 IDR per hour)[6].

B Sample Evaluation Correction by Annotators

Appendix Table 1 shows several examples of evaluation by annotators. The evaluation process is intended to maintain high-quality translation from the annotator. We report five sampled English utterances, incorrect Indonesian utterances, and corrected Indonesian utterances by annotators.

C Per Domain Experiment Settings Result on IndoSMD Test Set

We report per domain results for all of the baselines on IndoSMD dataset on Appendix Table 2. We can conclude that Sequicity has the best score on monolingual Indonesian setting, meanwhile MinTL outperforms other frameworks on cross-lingual and bilingual settings by having the most biggest metric score compared to others when handling Indonesian test set.

D MinTL Result Comparisons

We present MinTL result comparisons by using two pre-trained LM: T5 and mT5 on Appendix Table 3.

[6]https://www.bps.go.id/indicator/19/1172/1/upah-rata---rata-per-jam-pekerja-menurut-provinsi.html

The table compares monolingual and bilingual approach on English test set. The result shows that bilingual setting have a beneficial impact on MinTL to learn the task well compares to monolingual setting.

E Annotator Instruction and Consent

We report instructions for annotators to translate several English CamRest and SMD utterance templates, as well as annotator informed consent templates on Appendix Figure 1, Appendix Figure 2, and Appendix Figure 3. The instructions are in Indonesian as all of the annotators are Indonesian native speakers.

English Utterance	Incorrect Indonesian utterance	Corrected Indonesian utterance
"remind me that i have a doctors appointment at 5 pm"	"ingatkan saya bahwa saya akan janji temu dengan dokter pada pukul 5 sore"	"ingatkan saya bahwa saya **memiliki** janji temu dengan dokter pada pukul 5 sore"
"that you, that's all I need to know."	"itu kamu, hanya itu saja yang perlu saya ketahui"	"**terimakasih**, hanya itu saja yang perlu saya ketahui" (there is a typo on the English utterance. It suppose to be 'thank you', not 'that you')
"are there ant jamaican restaurants in any part of town?"	"apakah ada restoran semut jamaika di bagian manapun dari kota ini?"	"apakah ada restoran jamaika di bagian manapun dari kota ini?" (there is a typo on the English utterance. It suppose to be 'any', not 'ant')
"la tasca is located at 14-16 Bridge Street and the postcode is C.B 2, 1 U.F. Their phone number is 1223 464630. May I help you with anything else?"	"la tasca berlokasi di 14 -16 bridge street dan kode pos nya adalah c.b 2, 1 u.f. nomornya adalah 1223 464630. bisakah saya membantu kamu dengan hal yang lain?"	"la tasca berlokasi di 14 -16 bridge street dan kode pos nya adalah c.b 2, 1 u.f. nomornya adalah **01223 464630**. bisakah saya membantu kamu dengan hal yang lain?" (we check in to the KB and we find out the correct entity for its phone number is '01223 464630')
"it is located at Quayside Off Bridge street. The phone number is is 01223 301030."	"alamatnya adalah quayside off bridge street. nomor teleponnya adalah 01223 301030."	"alamatnya adalah quayside off bridge street. nomor teleponnya adalah **01223 307030**." (we check in to the KB and find out that the correct entity is 01223 307030)

Table 1: Sample evaluation correction by annotators.

Baselines	POI Navigation				Calendar Scheduling				Weather Information			
	BL	Ma	Su	Co	BL	Ma	Su	Co	BL	Ma	Su	Co
monolingual												
Sequicity	**7.90**	25.00	**89.05**	**64.93**	**6.85**	**61.90**	**46.91**	**61.26**	**10.57**	**33.33**	**38.71**	**46.59**
LABES	1.30	0.00	40.50	21.55	0.00	0.00	32.30	16.15	0.00	14.30	20.00	17.15
MinTL	0.02	**50.00**	22.92	36.48	0.34	19.05	30.30	25.02	0.004	4.76	26.51	15.64
GALAXY	-	-	-	-	-	-	-	-	-	-	-	-
cross-lingual												
Sequicity	0.00	12.50	50.53	31.52	0.00	14.29	4.82	9.56	0.00	19.05	25.45	22.25
LABES	0.00	13.30	**75.50**	**44.40**	0.00	**16.70**	38.30	27.50	0.00	**42.90**	54.50	**48.70**
MinTL	0.00	**16.67**	35.29	25.98	**0.004**	14.29	**59.54**	**36.92**	0.00	4.76	**59.41**	32.09
GALAXY	**0.01**	11.76	33.66	22.72	0.00	0.00	26.17	13.09	0.00	0.00	49.54	24.77
bilingual												
Sequicity	**8.92**	44.44	77.47	69.88	11.73	**61.90**	67.37	76.37	11.72	**57.14**	54.05	67.32
LABES	4.50	**60.00**	**77.90**	**73.45**	6.90	33.30	53.70	50.40	9.70	42.90	76.30	69.30
MinTL	4.75	55.56	74.24	69.65	**15.94**	47.62	**80.00**	**79.75**	**13.85**	52.38	**81.54**	**80.81**
GALAXY	0.06	47.06	11.76	29.47	0.06	50.00	7.23	28.68	0.12	42.86	8.96	26.03

Table 2: Per domain experiment settings result on Indonesian test set using SMD dataset. **bold** denotes the best score per metric. BL, Ma, Su, and Co denote the **BL**EU score, **Ma**tch rate, **Su**ccess F1, and **Co**mbined score respectively.

Experiment Setting	CamRest				SMD			
	BLEU	Match	Success	Combined	BLEU	Match	Success	Combined
T5-small								
Monolingual	17.57	83.21	**83.25**	100.80	15.31	71.54	76.22	89.19
Bilingual	**18.50**	**85.50**	80.35	**101.42**	**16.23**	**75.29**	**79.52**	**93.63**
mT5-small								
Monolingual	20.34	83.21	**83.64**	103.77	**18.53**	**83.90**	78.60	**99.78**
Bilingual	**22.88**	**86.26**	82.26	**107.14**	18.39	80.23	**79.10**	98.05

Table 3: MinTL (Lin et al., 2020) result comparisons using pre-trained LM: T5 and mT5 as backbone model on English test set. **bold** denotes the best score per metric.

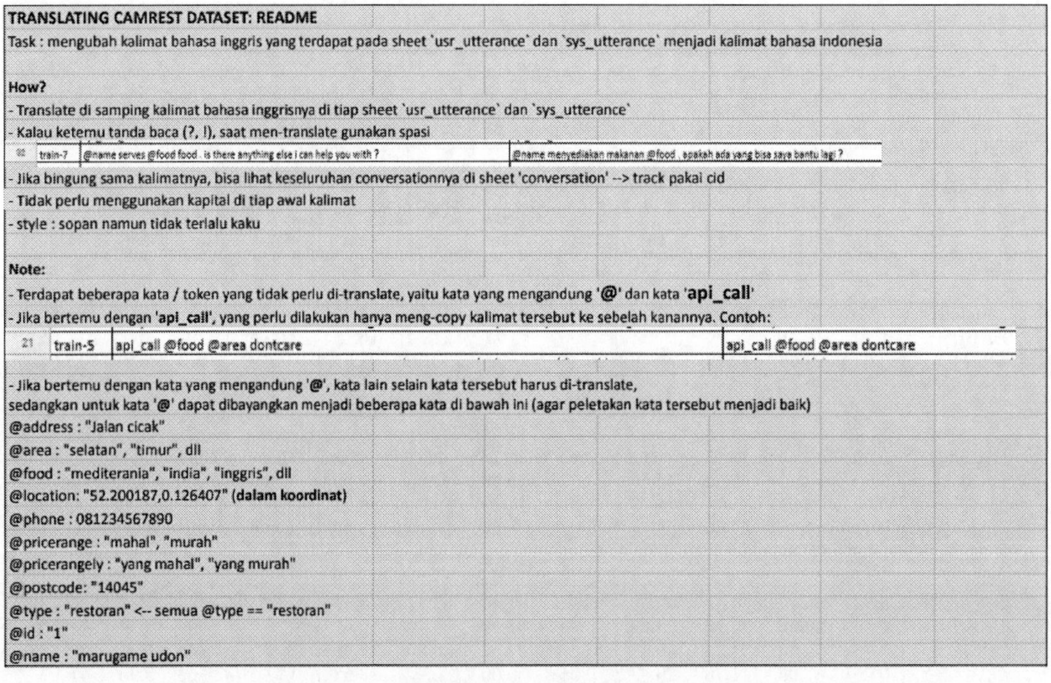
TRANSLATING CAMREST DATASET: README

Task : mengubah kalimat bahasa inggris yang terdapat pada sheet `usr_utterance` dan `sys_utterance` menjadi kalimat bahasa indonesia

How?

- Translate di samping kalimat bahasa inggrisnya di tiap sheet `usr_utterance` dan `sys_utterance`
- Kalau ketemu tanda baca (?, !), saat men-translate gunakan spasi

92	train-7	@name serves @food food . is there anything else i can help you with ?	@name menyediakan makanan @food . apakah ada yang bisa saya bantu lagi ?

- Jika bingung sama kalimatnya, bisa lihat keseluruhan conversationnya di sheet 'conversation' --> track pakai cid
- Tidak perlu menggunakan kapital di tiap awal kalimat
- style : sopan namun tidak terlalu kaku

Note:

- Terdapat beberapa kata / token yang tidak perlu di-translate, yaitu kata yang mengandung '@' dan kata 'api_call'
- Jika bertemu dengan 'api_call', yang perlu dilakukan hanya meng-copy kalimat tersebut ke sebelah kanannya. Contoh:

21	train-5	api_call @food @area dontcare	api_call @food @area dontcare

- Jika bertemu dengan kata yang mengandung '@', kata lain selain kata tersebut harus di-translate,
sedangkan untuk kata '@' dapat dibayangkan menjadi beberapa kata di bawah ini (agar peletakan kata tersebut menjadi baik)

@address : "Jalan cicak"
@area : "selatan", "timur", dll
@food : "mediterania", "india", "inggris", dll
@location: "52.200187,0.126407" (dalam koordinat)
@phone : 081234567890
@pricerange : "mahal", "murah"
@pricerangely : "yang mahal", "yang murah"
@postcode: "14045"
@type : "restoran" <-- semua @type == "restoran"
@id : "1"
@name : "marugame udon"

Figure 1: Instruction for annotators to translating English CamRest templates.

TRANSLATING SMD DATASET: README
Task : mengubah kalimat bahasa inggris yang terdapat pada sheet `usr_utterance` dan `sys_utterance` menjadi kalimat bahasa indonesia

How?
- Translate di samping kalimat bahasa inggrisnya di tiap sheet `usr_utterance` dan `sys_utterance` :D

- Kalau bingung sama kalimatnya, bisa lihat keseluruhan conversationnya di sheet 'conversation' --> track pakai cid
- Gausah pakai kapital
- style : sopan tapi ngga terlalu kaku

Note:
- Terdapat beberapa kata / token yang tidak perlu di-translate, yaitu kata yang mengandung '@'

- Jika bertemu dengan kata yang mengandung '@', kata lain selain kata tersebut harus di-translate,
sedangkan untuk kata '@' dapat dibayangkan menjadi beberapa kata di bawah ini (agar peletakan kata tersebut menjadi baik)
@event : jadwal berobat / makan malam
@time : jam 1 siang / 8 malam
@date : senin / tanggal 1
@party : tim eksekutif / HR / ibu / kakak
@room : ruangan konferensi 102
@agenda : membahas liburan perusahaan / penerimaan karyawan baru / membahas dresscode (aturan berbusana)
@location : oakland / san fransisco
@weekly_time : hari ini / besok / lusa
@temperature : 20 derajat / 30 derajat
@weather_attribute : berawan / badai / berembun
@traffic_info : tabrakan mobil / kemacetan / lancar
@poi_type : rumah teman / rumah / kafe / rumah sakit
@poi : Pizza hut / McDonalds / Taman bermain
@poi_address : jalan kacang panjang
@distance : 1 km / 1 mil

Figure 2: Instruction for annotators to translating English SMD templates.

Data Collection Informed Consent

Name :
Age :
E-mail :

I agree to participate as an annotator in the research project conducted by:

Name :
E-mail :
Research title :

As an annotator, I understand that I will be asked to translate 748 English sentences into Indonesian and validate the translated samples from November 1st to November 9th. I will also be required to follow specific guidelines and instructions the research team provides. The fee that I will receive is Rp

I agree to allow the research team to use and publish the annotations I provide to create an open-source dataset. I also understand that the translation results will be published as part of the research, and my personal information may be included in the publication (i.e. ethnicity, age, profession).

I have read and understood the information provided in this consent form, and I have had the opportunity to ask any questions about the research project and my participation in it.

Annotator,

Figure 3: Annotator informed consent template.

Replicable Benchmarking of Neural Machine Translation (NMT) on Low-Resource Local Languages in Indonesia

Lucky Susanto[§,♠]
lucky.susanto@ui.ac.id

Ryandito Diandaru[§,♢]
13519157@std.stei.itb.ac.id

Adila Krisnadhi[♠]
adila@cs.ui.ac.id

Ayu Purwarianti[♢]
ayu@itb.ac.id

Derry Wijaya[♣,♡]
derry.wijaya@monash.edu

[♠]University of Indonesia [♢]Bandung Institute of Technology [♣]Boston University

[♡]Monash University Indonesia

Abstract

Neural machine translation (NMT) for low-resource local languages in Indonesia faces significant challenges, including the need for a representative benchmark and limited data availability. This work addresses these challenges by comprehensively analyzing training NMT systems for four low-resource local languages in Indonesia: Javanese, Sundanese, Minangkabau, and Balinese. Our study encompasses various training approaches, paradigms, data sizes, and a preliminary study into using large language models for synthetic low-resource languages parallel data generation. We reveal specific trends and insights into practical strategies for low-resource language translation. Our research demonstrates that despite limited computational resources and textual data, several of our NMT systems achieve competitive performances, rivaling the translation quality of zero-shot gpt-3.5-turbo. These findings significantly advance NMT for low-resource languages, offering valuable guidance for researchers in similar contexts.

1 Introduction

Neural Machine Translation (NMT) holds a crucial role for local languages in Indonesia, supporting language documentation (Abney and Bird, 2010), native language preservation (Bird and Chiang, 2012; Costa-jussà et al., 2022), and bridging socioeconomic gaps (Azzizah, 2015). However, challenges unique to low-resource languages have hindered progress in this field (Aji et al., 2022). Our work addresses these challenges for four prominent local languages in Indonesia: Javanese, Sundanese, Minangkabau, and Balinese.

Impressive NMT advancements often come from well-resourced entities (i.e., Google's PaLM2 (Anil et al., 2023), OpenAI's gpt-3.5-turbo (Brown et al., 2020), Facebook's NLLB-200 (Costa-jussà et al., 2022)), focusing primarily on high-resource languages like English. This phenomenon highlights a research gap for languages with limited resources in data availability and computing power. For instance, benchmark NMT systems like NLLB-200 (Costa-jussà et al., 2022) rely on substantial computing power, a luxury many researchers lack, especially those working with local Indonesian languages (Cahyawijaya et al., 2022). This hampers progress due to the difficulty of gauging whether a new approach, method, architecture, or data augmentation would help improve model performance.

In this work, our contribution is a replicable benchmark of NMT systems for these local Indonesian languages trained on publicly available data and tested on the publicly available FLORES-200 dataset. We prioritize accessible computing resources. Our base cross-lingual (Conneau and Lample, 2019) XLM model uses only a modest compute setup. It is trained with only two languages at a time and on a single GPU with at most 48GB of memory, which we believe is within the reach of most researchers in this domain. We also only use publicly available data sources to train, including the NusaCrowd repository of Indonesian languages (Cahyawijaya et al., 2022) and parsed wikidumps results [1]. Extending prior work, such as (Winata et al., 2023), we benchmark NMT models on multiple domains.

In addition, in a preliminary study, we explore the impact of using gpt-3.5 (Brown et al., 2020) for synthetic low-resource language data generation to augment training. We also investigate code-switching's potential (Kuwanto et al., 2021) for improving low-resource language NMT that was

[§]Equal contributions.

[1]Wikidumps Page

Proceedings of the First Workshop in South East Asian Language Processing, pages 100–115
November 1, 2023. ©2023 Association for Computational Linguistics

previously unexplored for Indonesian languages.

2 Related Work

2.1 NMT Benchmarks for Low-resource Local Languages in Indonesia

Neural Machine Translation (NMT) benchmarks are pivotal in documenting and preserving low-resource local languages like those in Indonesia. Prior works (Costa-jussà et al., 2022; Cahyawijaya et al., 2022; Winata et al., 2023) have contributed to the creation of these NMT Benchmarks in two significant ways: (1) the creation and compilation of datasets accompanied by (2) exploration and evaluation of different methodologies.

Costa-jussà et al. (2022) focused on developing NMT Benchmarks for low-resource languages. Their NLLB-200 model supports 200+ languages with more than 40K translation directions. Among these 200+ languages, some are local languages in Indonesia. They obtain state-of-the-art results for many translation directions through massive data collection efforts and computing resources.

Similarly, Winata et al. (2023) also collects a multilingual dataset for both machine translation and sentiment analysis for ten local languages in Indonesia. They use the collected dataset to create a benchmark for both tasks, obtaining impressive results in the machine translation tasks for the review domain by fine-tuning pre-trained models. Winata et al. (2023) also shows that fine-tuning a non-English-centric pre-trained model on local Indonesian languages outperforms its English-centric counterpart for the machine translation task.

However, it is essential to recognize that the NMT benchmark created by Costa-jussà et al. (2022) is challenging to replicate. Many researchers and institutions, including top Indonesian universities (Cahyawijaya et al., 2022), do not have access to massive compute resources or extensive and proprietary training data required to train the NLLB-200 models. Meanwhile, the NMT benchmark created by Winata et al. (2023) is limited only to the review domain. These leave a research gap that needs to be filled by benchmark NMT models that are replicable and cover more general domains.

2.2 High-resource vs Low-resource NMT

Unlike low-resource NMT systems (where either the source or target language is a low-resource language), NMT systems for high-resource languages have achieved impressive results (Costa-jussà et al., 2022). Even with the progress achieved by the grassroots movement mentioned in the previous section, the performance gaps are wide. This phenomenon is due to research in the field of NMT and NLP being dominated by English and other major languages, which means that more efforts have significantly been put into developing language technologies for these significant languages, and more data have been collected and made available for these languages (Akhbardeh et al., 2021; Kocmi et al., 2022). This means that while low-resource NMTs face problems no longer found in high-resource NMTs, insufficient resources and attention are being allocated.

One significant issue NMT systems face is the pivotal role parallel data plays in model performance (Koehn and Knowles, 2017). By definition, low-resource languages have little to no parallel data. One problem that negatively impacts the model performance is out-of-vocabulary (OOV) occurrences (Aji et al., 2022; Wibowo et al., 2021), where the model needs to see a token more to learn what it means. While this issue exists even in high-resource languages, the rate of occurrence for low-resource languages is substantially higher. However, usage of byte pair encoding (BPE) (Sennrich et al., 2016b) is capable of alleviating this issue to some degree (Lample et al., 2018b; Yang et al., 2020).

While previous research has made noteworthy strides in addressing out-of-vocabulary (OOV) occurrences, the most effective solution continues to be expanding available training data. However, building textual resources for translation tasks necessitates a significant investment of money, time, and expertise. Because of this, current research increasingly centers on finding innovative ways to augment the training of NMT models.

2.3 Augmenting Training for NMT

To combat the issue of data starvation, many researchers aim to utilize monolingual data to train NMT systems (Lample et al., 2018a; Artetxe et al., 2018; Conneau and Lample, 2019) and find ways to generate more training data, either comparable or synthetic data. Comparable data are extracted using various bitext retrieval methods (Zhao and Vogel, 2002; Fan et al., 2021; Jones and Wijaya, 2021; Kocyigit et al., 2022), multimodal signals (Hewitt et al., 2018; Rasooli et al., 2021), dictionary- or knowledge-based approaches (Wijaya and Mitchell,

2016; Wijaya et al., 2017; Tang and Wijaya, 2022); while synthetic data are created and utilized either through innovative training data augmentation (Kuwanto et al., 2021), utilizing automatic back-translation (Sennrich et al., 2016a; Wang et al., 2019), or even outright generating synthetic data using generative models (Lu et al., 2023), which has gained increasing attention by the community lately due to the advancement of large language models (LLMs).

Both Artetxe et al. (2018) and Lample et al. (2018a) show that NMT systems can be trained using only monolingual data while achieving impressive results. Conneau and Lample (2019) then create the XLM architecture, which allows NMT systems to be traine using monolingual and parallel data. Afterward, (Kuwanto et al., 2021) exploits the cross-lingual nature of the XLM models by corrupting the monolingual data using code-switching, which makes a single training instance contain multiple languages. The result is an improvement in the model's performance for low-resource translation.

In addition, prior works also focus on obtaining synthetic training data by turning monolingual data into parallel data through automatic back-translation (Sennrich et al., 2016a) or by using LLMs such as the gpt-family models (Brown et al., 2020) that have been gaining popularity in recent years in many fields (Lu et al., 2023). While back-translation has evolved, becoming a prominent method in the field of NMT (Artetxe et al., 2018; Conneau and Lample, 2019), using LLMs to generate synthetic data has yet to be thoroughly explored. This trend of using generative AI to generate synthetic training data displays initial potential, considering their remarkable performances compared to the state-of-the-art in machine translation (Zhu et al., 2023). However, further research with ablation studies and the inclusion of more language coverage is still needed.

3 Methodology

In this section, we outline our methodology for creating a replicable NMT benchmark for four Indonesian languages: Javanese (jv), Sundanese (su), Minangkabau (min), and Balinese (ban). We aim to systematically explore different training approaches and paradigms for NMT while maintaining a consistent base architecture (XLM), fixed hyperparameters, and controlled computing environment. Our compute environment is given a strict upper bound, in which a total of 48 GPU Hours from a single GPU for each model training, totaling up to 96 GPU Hours for NMT systems utilizing pre-trained language models. We also limit the memory of the GPU used to a maximum of 48 GB.

3.1 Training Approaches

We employ three primary training approaches to build our NMT models:

From Scratch (Scratch): In this approach, models are trained from the ground up without any reliance on pre-existing pre-trained language models. This approach acts as a baseline and allows us to gauge the performance of the models when trained from scratch.

Pre-trained Cross-Lingual (PreXL): Here, an NMT model utilizes a pre-trained cross-lingual model (XLM) (Conneau and Lample, 2019) on two sets of monolingual data. One of the sets is the Indonesian monolingual data, and the other is the low-resource local language monolingual data. This provides a strong starting point for the NMT by initializing the model with knowledge from the target and source languages. Therefore, each language pair in this work is given its own respective model. The number of pre-trained models for **PreXL** equals the number of language pairs in our work, which is four.

Code-switched Pre-trained Cross-Lingual (CodeXL): This approach involves pre-training the language model using additional augmented data from the two sets of monolingual data and a bilingual dictionary through code-switching, explained later in section 3.6. Code-switching allows for a bilingual context within each training instance. The pre-trained model is then fine-tuned for translation. The tasks used to fine-tune **CodeXL** and **PreXL** depend on the training paradigm used (section 3.2. The number of pre-trained models for **CodeXL** is the same as **PreXL**, which is four.

We chose the XLM architecture due to its modest compute resource requirements and its capability of cross-lingual language modeling. Moreover, the architecture is widely used for many low-resource language pairs and shows impressive results despite its modest size (Wang et al., 2019). We use Masked Language Modeling (MLM) (Devlin et al., 2019) to pre-train all the XLM models.

3.2 Training Paradigms

Additionally, we also explore two training paradigms, each influencing how the NMT models learn and what data are used for training:

Unsupervised NMT (Unsup): This paradigm trains the NMT system using only monolingual data of the source and target language. Utilizing both denoising-autoencoding (Vincent et al., 2010) and automatic back-translation (Sennrich et al., 2016a) to train the NMT system. Note that even though **CodeXL** utilizes a bilingual dictionary, it does not use any parallel data during pre-training.

Semi-supervised NMT (Semisup): This paradigm trains the NMT system using both monolingual data and parallel data of the source and target language. Monolingual data are utilized for training NMT by automatic back-translation.

We employ these shortened terms throughout our experiments to refer to the respective training approaches and paradigms. Our results indicate that the performance of each combination of approaches and paradigms on the evaluation dataset depends heavily on the amount of available data for the language: **Unsup** paradigm works better for very low-resource languages. In contrast, **Semisup** paradigm performs better when at least 10K parallel data is available (Artetxe et al., 2018). We do not conduct training using a strictly **Supervised NMT** paradigm because prior work has shown automatic back-translation's undeniable impact in improving low-resource NMT systems performance (Sennrich et al., 2016a).

3.3 Training with Synthetic Data

Following recent trends of using generative AI to generate synthetic training data (Lu et al., 2023; Zhu et al., 2023), we explore the impact of synthetically generated data on low-resource language NMT systems. We define two main approaches to generating synthetic data: (1) generating parallel data using generative AI and (2) translating monolingual data using an existing model.

To gauge the impact of the synthetically generated training data, we train NMT systems with these additional data using the **Scratch** and **CodeXL** training approaches. **Scratch** is also used in our preliminary experiments to identify the synthetic data generation approach that would yield the best empirical results. Once we identify the best approach, we apply the same synthetic data generation approach to all our language pairs and use the generated data to augment the training of our NMT approach with the **Semisup** paradigm.

Through the preliminary experiments (reported in Appendix C), we find that synthetic data generated using generative AI (gpt-3.5-turbo) has the most positive impact on training NMT systems. We generate 5000 parallel sentences for each language pair via a zero-shot prompt[2]: ***"Generate a long parallel sentence in SRC and TGT"***, where **SRC** and **TGT** is the pair of language we want to generate the sentences in. Appendix C provides justifications for these choices.

3.4 Fine-tuning Objectives

Denoising autoencoding **(DAE)** (Vincent et al., 2010) is a popular training objective for fine-tuning pre-trained LM for unsupervised MT tasks (Lample et al., 2018b; Wang et al., 2019) for its ability to increase the robustness of NMT models.

By utilizing the XLM architecture, our NMT system can perform multi-way translation. Thus, we also utilize automatic back translation **(BT)** (Sennrich et al., 2016a) during fine-tuning of our NMT models with **Unsup** and **Semisup** paradigms. By performing back translation using the same model that is being trained, synthetic parallel data is obtained and used automatically during training.

3.5 Training Data

Lang	Mono	Para
jv	1.6M	14.3K
su	550K	13.2K
min	282K	17.2K
ban	60K	0.9K

Table 1: Total number of monolingual sentences (**Mono**) and parallel sentences paired with Indonesian (**Para**) per language

We obtain our monolingual data from multiple publicly available sources. For Indonesian (id), we use the 201M monolingual sentences available from the Indo4B curated dataset (Wilie et al., 2020). We obtain monolingual data for the local languages through publicly available data such as Wikidumps[3], cc100 (Conneau et al., 2020), imdb-jv (Wongso et al., 2021), jadi-ide (Hidayatullah et al., 2020), and su-emot (Putra et al., 2020). The amount of monolingual sentences used to train each language is available in Table 1, with further breakdown available in Appendix A.

[2]Repository of the data we generate using zero-shot prompting

[3]Wikidumps Page

All parallel data we use to train the model are also publicly available from the NusaCrowd repository (Cahyawijaya et al., 2022). We scan the repository for datasets that contain parallel data of the local language paired with Indonesian. The amount of parallel sentences used to train each language pair is available in Table 1. Our largest language in terms of monolingual and parallel sentences, Javanese, is a tiny fraction (almost a 20th and a 500th, respectively) of NLLB-200 reported sentences for Javanese. From publicly available resources in Table 1, we can see that these four languages represent low-resource languages. A further breakdown is available in Appendix B.

The sentence counts in Table 1 are after we perform filtering on both monolingual and parallel data. For monolingual data, we remove sentences that contain less than three words or more than 250 words. We also perform simple filtering for sentences obtained from Wikipedia, including deduplication, removing HTML tags, removing sentences with only numbers, removing sentences that do not start with an alphabet, and removing metadata, bulletin points, or number ordering from sentences. For parallel data, we remove sentences that contain less than three words or more than 250 words and remove sentence pairs whose source sentences have a word count ratio above 1.5 of their translations following the setup of Ghazvininejad et al. (2023).

3.6 Code Switch

Bilingual Dictionary				
	id	A1	B1	C1
	x	A2	B2	C2

Mono_{id}	A1	C1	Y	Z
Mono_{cs} 1	A2	C1	Y	Z

Mono_{x}	B2	L	M	N
Mono_{cs} 2	B1	L	M	N

Figure 1: Illustration of generating synthetic data using code-switch. Using a bilingual dictionary, some words in each monolingual sentence are translated (i.e., blue and orange words). The candidate word for translation is chosen randomly, and not all words will be translated (green box).

In this paper, code-switching is done by utilizing the system made by Kuwanto et al. (2021)[4]. Code-switching is used to create synthetic training data by utilizing a bilingual dictionary. The generated data is used only during pre-training and is treated as a third language (labeled **cs**), where each training instance contains tokens from the other two languages. Results obtained by Kuwanto et al. (2021) imply that this method helps the model by giving stronger cross-lingual signals, which helps translation tasks during fine-tuning.

Lang	$\textbf{Mono}_{id}$	$\textbf{Mono}_{x}$	$\textbf{Mono}_{cs}$
{id, jv, cs}	201M	1.6M	209M
{id, su, cs}	201M	550K	208M
{id, min, cs}	201M	282K	208M
{id, ban, cs}	201M	60K	207M

Table 2: Total number of monolingual training instances for each language in each NMT system. $\textbf{Mono}_{id}$, $\textbf{Mono}_{x}$, $\textbf{Mono}_{cs}$ denotes the size of training instance for Indonesian, regional, and the third language, respectively.

Creating synthetic training data through code-switching utilizes training data from monolingual datasets from both languages in the system. By utilizing a bilingual dictionary, obtained and parsed from Winata et al. (2023)[5], each instance of training data from both monolingual datasets is augmented. Figure 1 illustrates this process, while Table 2 shows how much augmented training data is available for each NMT system.

4 Experiment Results

We concentrate our efforts on four language pairs: **id-jv**, **id-su**, **id-min**, and **id-ban**. Indonesia (**id**) is spoken by approximately 198 million people worldwide, whereas Javanese (**jv**), Sundanese (**su**), Minangkabau (**min**), and Balinese (**ban**) are spoken by roughly 68.2 million, 32.4 million, 4.8 million, and 3.3 million people, respectively, according to (Eberhard et al., 2023). Unsurprisingly, monolingual and parallel data availability for these four local languages in Indonesia generally follows a similar pattern. Javanese boasts the most extensive corpus of monolingual text data, while Balinese has the smallest. Regarding parallel data, Sundanese leads the way, closely followed by Javanese, while Balinese trails behind. Due to the substantial variation in training data availability, we present our findings for each local language separately. This approach allows us to assess the impact of different

[4]Code Switch-based Curriculum Training

[5]NusaX's bilingual dictionary

Translation	Paradigm	Turbo	Scratch	Scratch$_{AUG}$	PreXL	CodeXL	CodeXL$_{AUG}$
`id-->jv`	Zero shot	18.91	–.–	–.–	–.–	–.–	–.–
	Unsup	–.–	12.06	–.–	16.94	*17.90*	–.–
	Semisup	–.–	13.50	18.29	19.31	***21.32***	21.18
`jv-->id`	Zero shot	**29.97**	–.–	–.–	–.–	–.–	–.–
	Unsup	–.–	08.11	–.–	13.73	*20.93*	–.–
	Semisup	–.–	12.18	21.36	18.88	26.17	*26.23*
`id-->su`	Zero shot	16.39	–.–	–.–	–.–	–.–	–.–
	Unsup	–.–	10.42	–.–	*14.69*	10.68	–.–
	Semisup	–.–	13.19	15.33	16.22	***18.91***	18.90
`su-->id`	Zero shot	**30.71**	–.–	–.–	–.–	–.–	–.–
	Unsup	–.–	08.07	–.–	*13.62*	10.68	–.–
	Semisup	–.–	13.55	20.72	21.68	28.06	*28.40*
`id-->min`	Zero shot	13.71	–.–	–.–	–.–	–.–	–.–
	Unsup	–.–	10.18	–.–	16.03	*18.37*	–.–
	Semisup	–.–	22.33	22.59	23.83	***26.04***	25.18
`min-->id`	Zero shot	28.27	–.–	–.–	–.–	–.–	–.–
	Unsup	–.–	07.88	–.–	12.00	*19.43*	–.–
	Semisup	–.–	17.48	25.27	20.93	29.83	***30.06***
`id-->ban`	Zero shot	**14.94**	–.–	–.–	–.–	–.–	–.–
	Unsup	–.–	08.28	–.–	11.03	*12.70*	–.–
	Semisup	–.–	00.22	00.30	02.63	06.36	*09.51*
`ban-->id`	Zero shot	**26.93**	–.–	–.–	–.–	–.–	–.–
	Unsup	–.–	07.13	–.–	10.34	*18.05*	–.–
	Semisup	–.–	00.30	00.36	05.35	11.16	*17.34*

Table 3: Performance of NMT systems for Indonesian (**id**), Javanese (**jv**), Sundanese (**su**), Minangkabau (**min**), and Balinese (**ban**) translations. **Turbo** refers to gpt-3.5-turbo's zero-shot translation performance. **Zero shot** paradigm indicates translation without training. **AUG** denotes models trained with synthetic data generated by gpt-3.5-turbo. Bold values represent the best overall performance, while italicized values indicate the best performance within each paradigm.

training methods and paradigms while assessing the influence of training data size.

We conduct experiments using three training approaches (**Scratch**, **PreXL**, **CodeXL**) and two training paradigms (**Unsup**, **Semisup**). For each combination of these approaches and paradigms, four NMT systems are trained (one of each language pair mentioned above). In total, there are 24 different NMT systems trained this way.

In addition, we conduct experiments using synthetic parallel datasets. We only generate parallel training data, so these data do not affect the **Unsup** training paradigm. To evaluate the impact of these synthetic datasets, we employ two distinct training approaches: **Scratch** and **CodeXL**. We denote the process of training NMT systems with additional synthetic parallel training data as **Scratch**$_{AUG}$ and **CodeXL**$_{AUG}$, respectively. These comprise the remaining 8 NMT systems created in this work, totaling 32. Since we use gpt-3.5-turbo to generate our synthetic parallel data in a zero-shot manner, we also benchmark the zero-shot translation performance of gpt-3.5-turbo (**Turbo**) on our evaluation dataset.

The results of these experiments (all metrics are in spm200BLEU, shown in Table 3), reveal a consistent trend: **CodeXL** approach results in a significantly better performing NMT systems compared to **Scratch** and **PreXL**. An exception to this pattern is noted in the **id-su** language pair when employing the **Unsup** training paradigm.

4.1 Javanese

The **id-jv** language pair is particularly significant due to its relevance in Indonesia, where approximately 198 million people speak Indonesian (id), and Javanese (jv) is spoken by roughly 68.2 million (Eberhard et al., 2023).

Looking at Table 3, we observe a substantial gap in translation performance between **id**→**jv** and **jv**→**id**, emphasizing the performance asymmetry. Notably, when training NMT systems using the **Unsup** paradigm, **CodeXL** consistently outperforms other approaches for both translation directions, reinforcing the findings of Kuwanto et al. (2021), which highlight the generalization capability of this approach.

Surprisingly, when we train NMT models using additional parallel data generated by gpt-3.5-turbo (**CodeXL**$_{AUG}$), we notice a slight decline in performance for **id→jv** translation compared to our best-performing model (**CodeXL**). A more detailed comparison is discussed in the next section.

4.2 Sundanese

Table 3 shows where **id-su** differs from the **id-jv** language pair. For **id-su** language pair, the **Unsup** paradigm shows a different trend where **CodeXL** has a slightly worse performance compared to **PreXL** in the **id→su** translation. However, this trend shifts when using the **Semisup** paradigm, with **CodeXL** regaining its superiority.

Similar to **id-jv** language pair, an intriguing phenomenon arises when we train NMT models using additional parallel data generated by gpt-3.5-turbo (**CodeXL**$_{AUG}$) for the **id-su** language pair. While this approach does not create a better performing model in **id→su** translation, it does result in a slightly better model for **su→id**. This trend indicates that the generated synthetic parallel data's impact heavily depends on the generative AI's translation performance. For both **id-jv** and **id-su** language pairs, gpt-3.5-turbo's zero-shot translation performance on **id→x** is worse than **CodeXL** for each respective language pair, therefore **CodeXL**$_{AUG}$ does not result in improved performance. Meanwhile, the reverse is true, gpt-3.5-turbo's **x→id** translation performance is better than **CodeXL** in **x→id** direction, hence **CodeXL**$_{AUG}$ has a better performance in this direction.

4.3 Minangkabau

The results we obtained for **id-min** follow a similar pattern as **id-jv**. The trend where **CodeXL** models performed better than **Scratch** and **PreXL** continues for **id-min** for both translation directions.

However, unlike **id-jv** and **id-su**, using synthetically generated parallel data to train NMT systems for **id-min** (**CodeXL**$_{AUG}$) performed better than **CodeXL** on the **min→id** translation. This is surprising because **CodeXL** performed better than **Turbo** on **min→id**, yet the parallel data generated by **Turbo** was able to create **CodeXL**$_{AUG}$, which is a better performing NMT system. This breaks the previous trends set by **id-jv**, **id-su**, and even **id-ban** in the later section.

4.4 Balinese

id-ban continues the trend set by the majority of previous language pairs. Following **id-jv** and **id-min** language pairs, **CodeXL** consistently has superior performance compared to **Scratch** and **PreXL**.

Additionally, **id-ban** follows the trend set by **id-jv** and **id-su**, where the use of synthetically generated parallel data from **Turbo** creates a better NMT system compared to others that do not use them. For **id-ban** language pair specifically, **Turbo**'s translation performance is much higher than **CodeXL**, and the data **Turbo** generated has a significant impact during training, as seen in **CodeXL**$_{AUG}$. The difference in score for **CodeXL** and **CodeXL**$_{AUG}$ differs by **3+** and **6+** spm200BLEU for **id→ban** and **ban→id** respectively. This performance difference is much more significant compared to **id-jv**, **id-su**, and **id-min**, where the performance difference is less than **1** spm200BLEU. This finding supports the idea that the generated synthetic parallel data's impact heavily depends on the generative AI's translation performance. Moreover, if the initial parallel data is limited, like in the case of **id-ban** (only 0.9K), the addition of synthetic data can greatly improve performance.

However, Table 3 shows that **Unsup** training paradigm created the best performing NMT system for **id-ban** language pair. While it would not be surprising for **Scratch** due to the limited amount of parallel training data, it is surprising that **Scratch**$_{AUG}$ does not result in a considerably better NMT system, as the parallel training data size becomes 6x its original size (i.e., from 0.9K to 5.9K). This indicates that **denoising-autoencoding** plays a more significant role in model performance than parallel data when the training parallel data is limited.

5 Conclusion

In this work, we create a replicable NMT benchmark under low-resource settings. We comprehensively train and analyze NMT systems for four low-resource Indonesian local languages: Javanese, Sundanese, Minangkabau, and Balinese. Our experiments shed light on the impact of different training approaches, paradigms, data sizes, and generated synthetic parallel data in low-resource local languages in Indonesia. In conclusion:

We observe that the **CodeXL** training approaches generally create NMT systems with better performances compared to **Scratch** and **PreXL** approaches. This further strengthens the robustness of the approach suggested by Kuwanto et al. (2021), where code-switching is used to give a stronger cross-lingual signal during model pre-training. Code-switching more positively impacts translation performance for **x→id** more than **id→x**. For reference, NMT systems created using the **CodeXL** training approach and **Semisup** paradigm have an average performance of **23.80** and **18.15** spm200BLEU for **x→id** and **id→x** respectively.

Furthermore, even after pre-training a language model using the MLM objective, fine-tuning the model using the denoising autoencoding objective might play a more prominent role in extremely low-resource NMT than just training the model to be more robust for the translation task. This is shown in the **id-ban** language pair NMT systems, where **Unsup** created better NMT systems than the **Semisup** training paradigm. It is noteworthy that the addition of 5000 synthetic parallel training data might not be enough to significantly improve NMT system performance, as visible in the **CodeXL-Unsup** entry compared to **CodeXL**$_{AUG}$**-Semisup** entry in Table 3, since the resulting parallel data is still very limited (i.e., less than 6K sentences).

Lastly, we also observe a trend in which generative AIs can help augment the training process by generating synthetic parallel data. In most cases, excluding the **id-min** language pair, the parallel data generated by generative AI can impact the performance of NMT systems to approach or even outperform the performance of the generative AI's translation performance with much less compute and data resource.

6 Future Work

Along with the above conclusions, our work also opens several venues for future research. Further ablation studies are needed to fully understand the impact of denoising-autoencoding on translation tasks. Our results indicate that the denoising-autoencoding objective not only increases model robustness but may also play a role in cross-lingual language understanding in extremely low-resource NMT.

In addition, further investigations into synthetically generated parallel data quality and diversity are crucial. We observe a trend where synthetically generated parallel data from gpt-3.5-turbo impact the training of NMT systems such that its performance approaches or even outperforms gpt-3.5-turbo's zero-shot translation performance.

7 Limitation

While our work has given insight into NMT systems for low-resource local languages in Indonesia, it is essential to note that we have utilized different GPUs (TitanV, RTX8000, RTX6000, A6000, A40) with a maximum memory capacity of 48GB for different experiments. These GPU architectures and memory capacity variations may have influenced the observed performance. However, it is crucial to recognize that hardware differences alone cannot fully account for all the performance gaps observed. Future research should conduct experiments using a more standardized GPU setup to understand the impact of hardware variations better.

Additionally, all of our experiments that include the utilization of gpt-3.5-turbo are problematic as it is a closed-sourced model. This causes problems such as transparency and reproducibility in the future. Future work should continue performing ablation studies on open-sourced LLMs.

8 Acknowledgement

Authors from Indonesia are supported by the MoE-CRT ACE Open Research program. The authors also thank the Indonesian government for their funding and Boston University for providing essential computing resources. We also thanks Garry Kuwanto from Boston University for his help in utilizing his Code-switching system.

References

Steven Abney and Steven Bird. 2010. The human language project: Building a universal corpus of the world's languages. In *Proceedings of the 48th annual meeting of the association for computational linguistics*, pages 88–97.

Alham Fikri Aji, Genta Indra Winata, Fajri Koto, Samuel Cahyawijaya, Ade Romadhony, Rahmad Mahendra, Kemal Kurniawan, David Moeljadi, Radityo Eko Prasojo, Timothy Baldwin, Jey Han Lau, and Sebastian Ruder. 2022. One country, 700+ languages: NLP challenges for underrepresented languages and dialects in Indonesia. In *Proceedings of the 60th Annual Meeting of the Association for Computational Linguistics (Volume 1: Long Papers)*, pages 7226–7249, Dublin, Ireland. Association for Computational Linguistics.

Farhad Akhbardeh, Arkady Arkhangorodsky, Magdalena Biesialska, Ondřej Bojar, Rajen Chatterjee, Vishrav Chaudhary, Marta R. Costa-jussa,

Cristina España-Bonet, Angela Fan, Christian Federmann, Markus Freitag, Yvette Graham, Roman Grundkiewicz, Barry Haddow, Leonie Harter, Kenneth Heafield, Christopher Homan, Matthias Huck, Kwabena Amponsah-Kaakyire, Jungo Kasai, Daniel Khashabi, Kevin Knight, Tom Kocmi, Philipp Koehn, Nicholas Lourie, Christof Monz, Makoto Morishita, Masaaki Nagata, Ajay Nagesh, Toshiaki Nakazawa, Matteo Negri, Santanu Pal, Allahsera Auguste Tapo, Marco Turchi, Valentin Vydrin, and Marcos Zampieri. 2021. Findings of the 2021 conference on machine translation (WMT21). In *Proceedings of the Sixth Conference on Machine Translation*, pages 1–88, Online. Association for Computational Linguistics.

Rohan Anil, Andrew M. Dai, Orhan Firat, Melvin Johnson, Dmitry Lepikhin, Alexandre Passos, Siamak Shakeri, Emanuel Taropa, Paige Bailey, Zhifeng Chen, Eric Chu, Jonathan H. Clark, Laurent El Shafey, Yanping Huang, Kathy Meier-Hellstern, Gaurav Mishra, Erica Moreira, Mark Omernick, Kevin Robinson, Sebastian Ruder, Yi Tay, Kefan Xiao, Yuanzhong Xu, Yujing Zhang, Gustavo Hernandez Abrego, Junwhan Ahn, Jacob Austin, Paul Barham, Jan Botha, James Bradbury, Siddhartha Brahma, Kevin Brooks, Michele Catasta, Yong Cheng, Colin Cherry, Christopher A. Choquette-Choo, Aakanksha Chowdhery, Clément Crepy, Shachi Dave, Mostafa Dehghani, Sunipa Dev, Jacob Devlin, Mark Díaz, Nan Du, Ethan Dyer, Vlad Feinberg, Fangxiaoyu Feng, Vlad Fienber, Markus Freitag, Xavier Garcia, Sebastian Gehrmann, Lucas Gonzalez, Guy Gur-Ari, Steven Hand, Hadi Hashemi, Le Hou, Joshua Howland, Andrea Hu, Jeffrey Hui, Jeremy Hurwitz, Michael Isard, Abe Ittycheriah, Matthew Jagielski, Wenhao Jia, Kathleen Kenealy, Maxim Krikun, Sneha Kudugunta, Chang Lan, Katherine Lee, Benjamin Lee, Eric Li, Music Li, Wei Li, YaGuang Li, Jian Li, Hyeontaek Lim, Hanzhao Lin, Zhongtao Liu, Frederick Liu, Marcello Maggioni, Aroma Mahendru, Joshua Maynez, Vedant Misra, Maysam Moussalem, Zachary Nado, John Nham, Eric Ni, Andrew Nystrom, Alicia Parrish, Marie Pellat, Martin Polacek, Alex Polozov, Reiner Pope, Siyuan Qiao, Emily Reif, Bryan Richter, Parker Riley, Alex Castro Ros, Aurko Roy, Brennan Saeta, Rajkumar Samuel, Renee Shelby, Ambrose Slone, Daniel Smilkov, David R. So, Daniel Sohn, Simon Tokumine, Dasha Valter, Vijay Vasudevan, Kiran Vodrahalli, Xuezhi Wang, Pidong Wang, Zirui Wang, Tao Wang, John Wieting, Yuhuai Wu, Kelvin Xu, Yunhan Xu, Linting Xue, Pengcheng Yin, Jiahui Yu, Qiao Zhang, Steven Zheng, Ce Zheng, Weikang Zhou, Denny Zhou, Slav Petrov, and Yonghui Wu. 2023. Palm 2 technical report.

Mikel Artetxe, Gorka Labaka, Eneko Agirre, and Kyunghyun Cho. 2018. Unsupervised neural machine translation. In *6th International Conference on Learning Representations, ICLR 2018, Vancouver, BC, Canada, April 30 - May 3, 2018, Conference Track Proceedings*. OpenReview.net.

Yuni Azzizah. 2015. Socio-economic factors on indonesia education disparity. *International Education Studies*, 8:218.

Steven Bird and David Chiang. 2012. Machine translation for language preservation. In *Proceedings of COLING 2012: Posters*, pages 125–134.

Tom B. Brown, Benjamin Mann, Nick Ryder, Melanie Subbiah, Jared Kaplan, Prafulla Dhariwal, Arvind Neelakantan, Pranav Shyam, Girish Sastry, Amanda Askell, Sandhini Agarwal, Ariel Herbert-Voss, Gretchen Krueger, Tom Henighan, Rewon Child, Aditya Ramesh, Daniel M. Ziegler, Jeffrey Wu, Clemens Winter, Christopher Hesse, Mark Chen, Eric Sigler, Mateusz Litwin, Scott Gray, Benjamin Chess, Jack Clark, Christopher Berner, Sam McCandlish, Alec Radford, Ilya Sutskever, and Dario Amodei. 2020. Language models are few-shot learners. In *Advances in Neural Information Processing Systems 33: Annual Conference on Neural Information Processing Systems 2020, NeurIPS 2020, December 6-12, 2020, virtual*.

Samuel Cahyawijaya, Holy Lovenia, Alham Fikri Aji, Genta Indra Winata, Bryan Wilie, Rahmad Mahendra, Christian Wibisono, Ade Romadhony, Karissa Vincentio, Fajri Koto, Jennifer Santoso, David Moeljadi, Cahya Wirawan, Frederikus Hudi, Ivan Halim Parmonangan, Ika Alfina, Muhammad Satrio Wicaksono, Ilham Firdausi Putra, Samsul Rahmadani, Yulianti Oenang, Ali Akbar Septiandri, James Jaya, Kaustubh D. Dhole, Arie Ardiyanti Suryani, Rifki Afina Putri, Dan Su, Keith Stevens, Made Nindyatama Nityasya, Muhammad Farid Adilazuarda, Ryan Ignatius, Ryandito Diandaru, Tiezheng Yu, Vito Ghifari, Wenliang Dai, Yan Xu, Dyah Damapuspita, Cuk Tho, Ichwanul Muslim Karo Karo, Tirana Noor Fatyanosa, Ziwei Ji, Pascale Fung, Graham Neubig, Timothy Baldwin, Sebastian Ruder, Herry Sujaini, Sakriani Sakti, and Ayu Purwarianti. 2022. Nusacrowd: Open source initiative for indonesian NLP resources. *CoRR*, abs/2212.09648.

Samuel Cahyawijaya, Genta Indra Winata, Bryan Wilie, Karissa Vincentio, Xiaohong Li, Adhiguna Kuncoro, Sebastian Ruder, Zhi Yuan Lim, Syafri Bahar, Masayu Khodra, Ayu Purwarianti, and Pascale Fung. 2021. IndoNLG: Benchmark and resources for evaluating Indonesian natural language generation. In *Proceedings of the 2021 Conference on Empirical Methods in Natural Language Processing*, pages 8875–8898, Online and Punta Cana, Dominican Republic. Association for Computational Linguistics.

Alexis Conneau, Kartikay Khandelwal, Naman Goyal, Vishrav Chaudhary, Guillaume Wenzek, Francisco Guzmán, Edouard Grave, Myle Ott, Luke Zettlemoyer, and Veselin Stoyanov. 2020. Unsupervised cross-lingual representation learning at scale. In *Proceedings of the 58th Annual Meeting of the Association for Computational Linguistics*, pages 8440–8451, Online. Association for Computational Linguistics.

Alexis Conneau and Guillaume Lample. 2019. Cross-lingual language model pretraining. In *Advances in Neural Information Processing Systems 32: Annual Conference on Neural Information Processing Systems 2019, NeurIPS 2019, December 8-14, 2019, Vancouver, BC, Canada*, pages 7057–7067.

Marta R. Costa-jussà, James Cross, Onur Çelebi, Maha Elbayad, Kenneth Heafield, Kevin Heffernan, Elahe Kalbassi, Janice Lam, Daniel Licht, Jean Maillard, Anna Sun, Skyler Wang, Guillaume Wenzek, Al Youngblood, Bapi Akula, Loïc Barrault, Gabriel Mejia Gonzalez, Prangthip Hansanti, John Hoffman, Semarley Jarrett, Kaushik Ram Sadagopan, Dirk Rowe, Shannon Spruit, Chau Tran, Pierre Andrews, Necip Fazil Ayan, Shruti Bhosale, Sergey Edunov, Angela Fan, Cynthia Gao, Vedanuj Goswami, Francisco Guzmán, Philipp Koehn, Alexandre Mourachko, Christophe Ropers, Safiyyah Saleem, Holger Schwenk, and Jeff Wang. 2022. No language left behind: Scaling human-centered machine translation. *CoRR*, abs/2207.04672.

Jacob Devlin, Ming-Wei Chang, Kenton Lee, and Kristina Toutanova. 2019. BERT: pre-training of deep bidirectional transformers for language understanding. In *Proceedings of the 2019 Conference of the North American Chapter of the Association for Computational Linguistics: Human Language Technologies, NAACL-HLT 2019, Minneapolis, MN, USA, June 2-7, 2019, Volume 1 (Long and Short Papers)*, pages 4171–4186. Association for Computational Linguistics.

David M. Eberhard, Gary F. Simons, and Charles D. Fennig, editors. 2023. *Ethnologue: Languages of the World*, 26 edition. SIL International, Dallas, Texas.

Angela Fan, Shruti Bhosale, Holger Schwenk, Zhiyi Ma, Ahmed El-Kishky, Siddharth Goyal, Mandeep Baines, Onur Celebi, Guillaume Wenzek, Vishrav Chaudhary, et al. 2021. Beyond english-centric multilingual machine translation. *The Journal of Machine Learning Research*, 22(1):4839–4886.

Marjan Ghazvininejad, Hila Gonen, and Luke Zettlemoyer. 2023. Dictionary-based phrase-level prompting of large language models for machine translation. *CoRR*, abs/2302.07856.

John Hewitt, Daphne Ippolito, Brendan Callahan, Reno Kriz, Derry Tanti Wijaya, and Chris Callison-Burch. 2018. Learning translations via images with a massively multilingual image dataset. In *Proceedings of the 56th Annual Meeting of the Association for Computational Linguistics (Volume 1: Long Papers)*, pages 2566–2576.

Ahmad Fathan Hidayatullah, Siwi Cahyaningtyas, and Rheza Daffa Pamungkas. 2020. Attention-based cnn-bilstm for dialect identification on javanese text. *Kinetik: Game Technology, Information System, Computer Network, Computing, Electronics, and Control*, pages 317–324.

Alexander Jones and Derry Tanti Wijaya. 2021. Majority voting with bidirectional pre-translation for bitext retrieval. In *Proceedings of the 14th Workshop on Building and Using Comparable Corpora (BUCC 2021)*, pages 46–59.

Tom Kocmi, Rachel Bawden, Ondřej Bojar, Anton Dvorkovich, Christian Federmann, Mark Fishel, Thamme Gowda, Yvette Graham, Roman Grundkiewicz, Barry Haddow, Rebecca Knowles, Philipp Koehn, Christof Monz, Makoto Morishita, Masaaki Nagata, Toshiaki Nakazawa, Michal Novák, Martin Popel, and Maja Popović. 2022. Findings of the 2022 conference on machine translation (WMT22). In *Proceedings of the Seventh Conference on Machine Translation (WMT)*, pages 1–45, Abu Dhabi, United Arab Emirates (Hybrid). Association for Computational Linguistics.

Muhammed Kocyigit, Jiho Lee, and Derry Wijaya. 2022. Better quality estimation for low resource corpus mining. In *Findings of the Association for Computational Linguistics: ACL 2022*, pages 533–543.

Philipp Koehn and Rebecca Knowles. 2017. Six challenges for neural machine translation. In *Proceedings of the First Workshop on Neural Machine Translation*, pages 28–39, Vancouver. Association for Computational Linguistics.

Fajri Koto and Ikhwan Koto. 2020. Towards computational linguistics in Minangkabau language: Studies on sentiment analysis and machine translation. In *Proceedings of the 34th Pacific Asia Conference on Language, Information and Computation*, pages 138–148, Hanoi, Vietnam. Association for Computational Linguistics.

Garry Kuwanto, Afra Feyza Akyürek, Isidora Chara Tourni, Siyang Li, Alexander Gregory Jones, and Derry Wijaya. 2021. Low-resource machine translation training curriculum fit for low-resource languages.

Guillaume Lample, Alexis Conneau, Ludovic Denoyer, and Marc'Aurelio Ranzato. 2018a. Unsupervised machine translation using monolingual corpora only. In *6th International Conference on Learning Representations, ICLR 2018, Vancouver, BC, Canada, April 30 - May 3, 2018, Conference Track Proceedings*. OpenReview.net.

Guillaume Lample, Myle Ott, Alexis Conneau, Ludovic Denoyer, and Marc'Aurelio Ranzato. 2018b. Phrase-based & neural unsupervised machine translation. In *Proceedings of the 2018 Conference on Empirical Methods in Natural Language Processing, Brussels, Belgium, October 31 - November 4, 2018*, pages 5039–5049. Association for Computational Linguistics.

Yingzhou Lu, Minjie Shen, Huazheng Wang, and Wenqi Wei. 2023. Machine learning for synthetic data generation: A review.

Oddy Virgantara Putra, Fathin Muhammad Wasmanson, Triana Harmini, and Shoffin Nahwa Utama. 2020. Sundanese twitter dataset for emotion classification. In *2020 International Conference on Computer Engineering, Network, and Intelligent Multimedia (CENIM)*, pages 391–395.

Mohammad Sadegh Rasooli, Chris Callison-Burch, and Derry Tanti Wijaya. 2021. “wikily” supervised neural translation tailored to cross-lingual tasks. In *Proceedings of the 2021 Conference on Empirical Methods in Natural Language Processing*, pages 1655–1670, Online and Punta Cana, Dominican Republic. Association for Computational Linguistics.

Rico Sennrich, Barry Haddow, and Alexandra Birch. 2016a. Improving neural machine translation models with monolingual data. In *Proceedings of the 54th Annual Meeting of the Association for Computational Linguistics, ACL 2016, August 7-12, 2016, Berlin, Germany, Volume 1: Long Papers*. The Association for Computer Linguistics.

Rico Sennrich, Barry Haddow, and Alexandra Birch. 2016b. Neural machine translation of rare words with subword units. In *Proceedings of the 54th Annual Meeting of the Association for Computational Linguistics, ACL 2016, August 7-12, 2016, Berlin, Germany, Volume 1: Long Papers*. The Association for Computer Linguistics.

Herry Sujaini. 2020. Improving the role of language model in statistical machine translation (indonesian-javanese). *International Journal of Electrical and Computer Engineering*, 10(2):2102.

Arie Ardiyanti Suryani, Dwi Hendratmo Widyantoro, Ayu Purwarianti, and Yayat Sudaryat. 2015. Experiment on a phrase-based statistical machine translation using pos tag information for sundanese into indonesian. In *2015 International Conference on Information Technology Systems and Innovation (ICITSI)*, pages 1–6.

Zilu Tang and Derry Wijaya. 2022. Knowledge based template machine translation in low-resource setting. *arXiv preprint arXiv:2209.03554*.

C Tho, Y Heryadi, L Lukas, and A Wibowo. 2021. Code-mixed sentiment analysis of indonesian language and javanese language using lexicon based approach. *Journal of Physics: Conference Series*, 1869(1):012084.

Pascal Vincent, Hugo Larochelle, Isabelle Lajoie, Yoshua Bengio, and Pierre-Antoine Manzagol. 2010. Stacked denoising autoencoders: Learning useful representations in a deep network with a local denoising criterion. *J. Mach. Learn. Res.*, 11:3371–3408.

Rui Wang, Haipeng Sun, Kehai Chen, Chenchen Ding, Masao Utiyama, and Eiichiro Sumita. 2019. English-Myanmar supervised and unsupervised NMT: NICT's machine translation systems at WAT-2019. In *Proceedings of the 6th Workshop on Asian Translation*, pages 90–93, Hong Kong, China. Association for Computational Linguistics.

Haryo Akbarianto Wibowo, Made Nindyatama Nityasya, Afra Feyza Akyürek, Suci Fitriany, Alham Fikri Aji, Radityo Eko Prasojo, and Derry Tanti Wijaya. 2021. IndoCollex: A testbed for morphological transformation of Indonesian colloquial words. In *Findings of the Association for Computational Linguistics: ACL-IJCNLP 2021*, pages 3170–3183, Online. Association for Computational Linguistics.

Derry Tanti Wijaya, Brendan Callahan, John Hewitt, Jie Gao, Xiao Ling, Marianna Apidianaki, and Chris Callison-Burch. 2017. Learning translations via matrix completion. In *Proceedings of the 2017 Conference on Empirical Methods in Natural Language Processing*, pages 1452–1463.

Derry Tanti Wijaya and Tom Mitchell. 2016. Mapping verbs in different languages to knowledge base relations using web text as interlingua. In *Proceedings of the 2016 Conference of the North American Chapter of the Association for Computational Linguistics: Human Language Technologies*, pages 818–827.

Bryan Wilie, Karissa Vincentio, Genta Indra Winata, Samuel Cahyawijaya, Xiaohong Li, Zhi Yuan Lim, Sidik Soleman, Rahmad Mahendra, Pascale Fung, Syafri Bahar, and Ayu Purwarianti. 2020. Indonlu: Benchmark and resources for evaluating indonesian natural language understanding. In *Proceedings of the 1st Conference of the Asia-Pacific Chapter of the Association for Computational Linguistics and the 10th International Joint Conference on Natural Language Processing, AACL/IJCNLP 2020, Suzhou, China, December 4-7, 2020*, pages 843–857. Association for Computational Linguistics.

Genta Indra Winata, Alham Fikri Aji, Samuel Cahyawijaya, Rahmad Mahendra, Fajri Koto, Ade Romadhony, Kemal Kurniawan, David Moeljadi, Radityo Eko Prasojo, and Pascale Fung. 2023. Nusax: Multilingual parallel sentiment dataset for 10 indonesian local languages. In *Proceedings of the 17th Conference of the European Chapter of the Association for Computational Linguistics, EACL 2023, Dubrovnik, Croatia, May 2-6, 2023*, pages 815–834. Association for Computational Linguistics.

Wilson Wongso, David Samuel Setiawan, and Derwin Suhartono. 2021. Causal and masked language modeling of javanese language using transformer-based architectures. In *2021 International Conference on Advanced Computer Science and Information Systems (ICACSIS)*, pages 1–7.

Zhen Yang, Bojie Hu, Ambyera Han, Shen Huang, and Qi Ju. 2020. CSP:code-switching pre-training for neural machine translation. In *Proceedings of the 2020 Conference on Empirical Methods in Natural Language Processing (EMNLP)*, pages 2624–2636, Online. Association for Computational Linguistics.

Bing Zhao and Stephan Vogel. 2002. Adaptive parallel sentences mining from web bilingual news collection.

In *2002 IEEE International Conference on Data Mining, 2002. Proceedings.*, pages 745–748. IEEE.

Wenhao Zhu, Hongyi Liu, Qingxiu Dong, Jingjing Xu, Shujian Huang, Lingpeng Kong, Jiajun Chen, and Lei Li. 2023. Multilingual machine translation with large language models: Empirical results and analysis.

A Monolingual Training Data Breakdown

Lang	wikidumps	cc100	imdb-jv	jadi-ide	su-emot	Total	Filter
jv	382K	1.41M	100K	16K	0	1.91M	1.6M
su	220K	387K	0	0	2K	610K	550K
min	282K	0	0	0	0	282K	282K
ban	60K	0	0	0	0	60K	60K

Table 4: Monolingual training data breakdown. **Lang** denotes the language identifier, **Total** denotes the total monolingual sentences for each language, and **Filter** denotes how many monolingual sentences remain after filtering, as listed in our Methodology section.

The monolingual data of local languages in Indonesia are obtained from multiple sources, including parsed wikidumps, cc100 (Conneau et al., 2020), imdb-jv (Wongso et al., 2021), jadi-ide (Hidayatullah et al., 2020), and su-emot (Putra et al., 2020). Excluding wikidumps monolingual data, which was taken in December of 2022, all of these sources are obtained from the compilation done by Cahyawijaya et al. (2022) and was taken in January of 2023. The breakdown for these monolingual data of local languages in Indonesia is found in Table 4

For the monolingual data of the Indonesian language, we use the Indo4B curated dataset (Wilie et al., 2020). Excluding the data obtained from Twitter, the number of monolingual Indonesian sentences is 201 million. No sentences were filtered out due to the high quality of the dataset.

B Parallel Training Data Breakdown

Lang	su-id	min-nlp	code-mixed	bible	nusantara	nusax	Total	Filter
jv	0	0	977	7958	6000	1000	15935	14395
su	3616	0	0	7957	1699	1000	14272	13269
min	0	16371	0	0	0	1000	17371	17260
ban	0	0	0	0	0	1000	1000	997

Table 5: Parallel training data breakdown of the language pair Indonesia and the local language denoted by **Lang** (i.e., the entry **jv** list how much parallel data of the pair **ind, jv** are obtained from each source). **Total** denotes total parallel sentences for each pair of Indonesian and local languages, and **Filter** denotes how much remains after filtering, as listed in our Methodology section.

As with our monolingual data breakdown, all of our parallel data were obtained from the NusaCrowd repository in January 2023. The datasets we use include su-id (Suryani et al., 2015), min-nlp (Koto and Koto, 2020), code-mixed (Tho et al., 2021), bible (Cahyawijaya et al., 2021), nusantara (Sujaini, 2020), and nusax (Winata et al., 2023).

C Ablation of Different Methods in Generating Parallel Data

Model	id→jv	jv→id
text-davinci-003	17.95	26.26
gpt-3.5-turbo	19.10	30.19

Table 6: Zero-shot translation spm200BLEU score of generative AIs on the FLORES200 test set. Results indicate that gpt-3.5-turbo performs significantly more than text-davinci-003 on zero-shot translation.

We performed exploratory experiments regarding different methods of generating parallel data. As mentioned in our methodology, we define two main approaches to generating synthetic data: (1) Generating parallel data using generative AI and (2) Translating monolingual data using an already trained model.

The models we use to generate the parallel data in approach (1) are gpt-3.5-turbo and davinci-text-003. We limit our exploratory experiment to the **id↔jv** translation direction. First, we compare the zero-shot translation performance of these models on the FLORES200 test set, where gpt-3.5-turbo achieved a considerably higher spm200BLEU score. The full breakdown is available in Table 6. We give each model

Model	Approach	id→jv	jv→id
Baseline	-	12.99	12.29
text-davinci-003	zero-shot	14.86	16.88
	ten-shot	14.40	16.82
gpt-3.5-turbo	zero-shot	14.95	**17.10**
	ten-shot	**15.04**	16.87

Table 7: Performance of NMT systems trained from scratch using a **Semisup** paradigm when the original parallel data is mixed with synthetically generated data from gpt-3.5-turbo or text-davinci-003. The first row is the baseline model performance. All BLEU scores are from XLM's automated BLEU scoring. Bolded entries indicate the model with the best performance.

the prompt to generate these parallel data: **"Generate a long parallel sentence in SRC and TGT"**. Our internal experiments show that without the keyword **"long"**, the model will generate short and simple parallel sentences consisting of regularly occurring words.

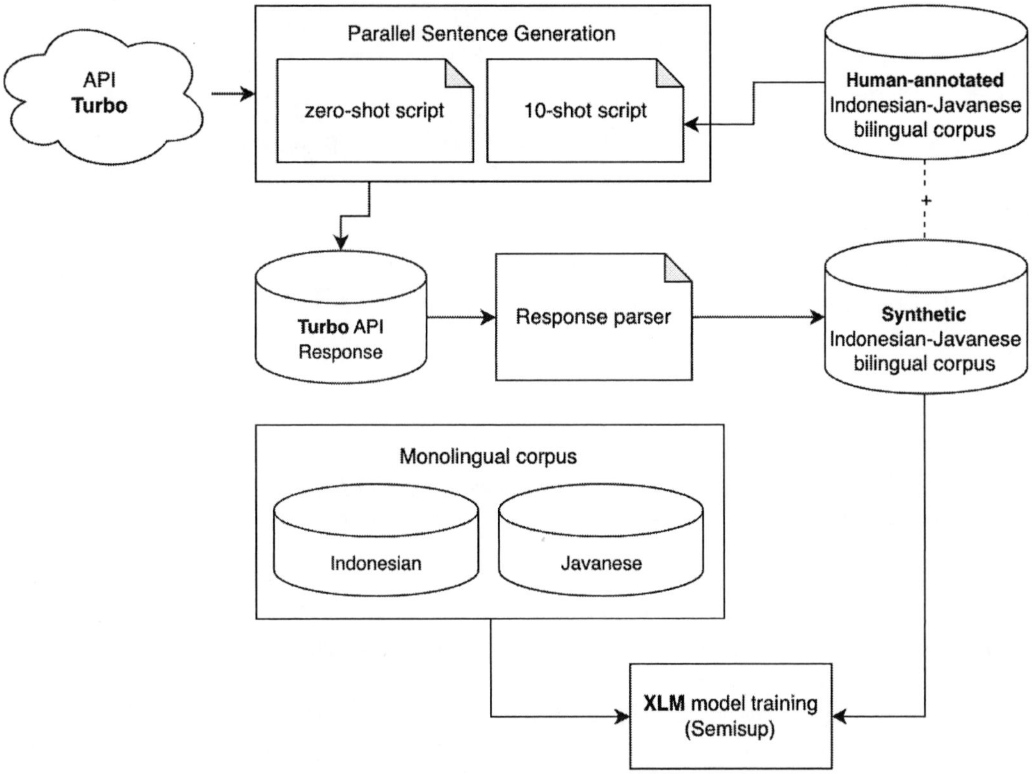

Figure 2: Illustration of using LLMs to generate synthetic parallel data. First tested on **id-jv** language pair, we use the same pipeline to generate synthetic parallel data for the other language pair.

We conduct these experiments using two approaches: zero-shot generation and ten-shot generation. We give the model the prompt above without additional context in zero-shot generation. We then parse the text that has been generated and split it into Indonesian sentences and Javanese sentences. In the ten-shot generation, we sample 10 parallel sentences in our original training data to feed it as examples to the model. Figure 2 illustrates this process. The impact these generated synthetic data have on training is found in Table 7. These performances align with the benchmark results in Table 6, where gpt-3.5-turbo is better at both translation directions than text-davinci-003. The results in Table 7 show that zero-shot generation of gpt-3.5-turbo creates parallel data with the most positive impact on NMT system training. The results shown in Table 7 indicate that few-shot may not have a considerable difference in performance compared to zero-shot for LLMs on translation tasks.

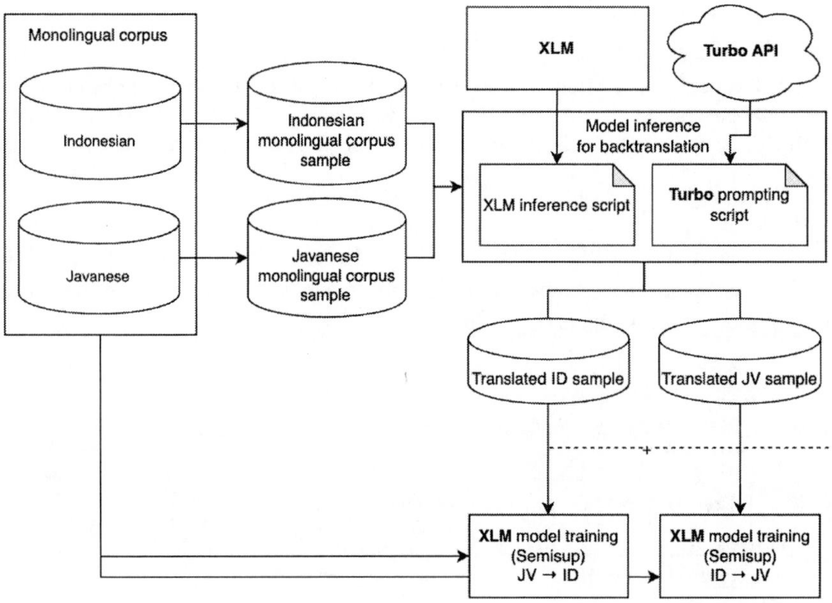

Figure 3: Illustration of translating monolingual data using an already trained model. In this work, we choose gpt-3.5-turbo and our NMT model trained on id-jv language pair using **Scratch** approach and **Semisup** paradigm.

Method	id→jv	jv→id
BT (baseline XLM)	10.35	12.29
BT (gpt-3.5)	13.22	13.80

Table 8: Comparison of additional data generation techniques. BT is for Back translation, in which we sample sentences from external monolingual corpora and translate them using the model indicated in the parentheses.

Besides prompting gpt-3.5 to generate parallel sentences directly, we also compared it with generating additional data from translating existing monolingual datasets. We use gpt-3.5 and the baseline XLM model to translate Wikipedia monolingual sentences. gpt-3.5-turbo is used instead of text-davinci-003 based on the results of the experiments shown in table 6. Our findings show that additional data from translating monolingual corpus using the baseline XLM model does not yield any significant performance increase or even hurts it, as shown in Table 8, whereas monolingual corpus translated using gpt-3.5 yields over 1 BLEU score on the Javanese to Indonesian translation direction.

However, this increase is modest compared to the results shown by directly generating parallel sentences from gpt-3.5-turbo as additional parallel data. Therefore, we move forward with approach (1). We apply the same procedure to the remaining language pairs: Sundanese, Minangkabau, and Balinese. Synthetic data generation is a promising research avenue in which both approaches (1) and (2) should still be included.

D Hyperparameters

In this work, there are a total of ten combinations of training approaches and paradigms which are:

- **Scratch** - **Unsup**
- **Scratch** - **Semisup**
- **Scratch**$_{AUG}$ - **Semisup**
- **PreXL** - Pre-training Language Model

- **PreXL** - **Unsup**
- **PreXL** - **Semisup**
- **CodeXL** - Pre-trained Language Model
- **CodeXL** - **Unsup**
- **CodeXL** - **Semisup**
- **CodeXL**$_{AUG}$ - Semisup

Across all of these models, nine hyperparameters are shared among them:

- `emb_dim`: 1024
- `n_layers`: 6
- `n_heads`: 8
- `dropout`: 0.1
- `attention_dropout`: 0.1
- `gelu_activation`: true
- `batch_size`: 32
- `bptt`: 256
- `epoch_size`: 200000

Models that are training using the **Unsup** training paradigm sets the hyperparameter **lambda_ae** to ***0:1,100000:0.1,300000:0***.

The hyperparameter **max_vocab** is set to ***200000*** for all models trained except models in **CodeXL** - Pre-trained Language Model, which uses the default values.

The hyperparameter **optimizer** is set to ***adam_inverse_sqrt, beta1=0.9, beta2=0.98, lr=0.0001*** for all models trained except models in **CodeXL** - Pre-trained Language Model and "**CodeXL** - **Unsup**" which set the value to ***adam, lr=0.0001***.

The hyperparameter **tokens_per_batch** is set to ***2000*** for all models excluding all models in **CodeXL** and **Scratch**$_{AUG}$ which set the value to ***4000***.

Association for Computational Linguistics
209 N. Eighth Street
Stroudsburg, Pennsylvania 18360

ISBN 978-1-7138-9008-9

9 781713 890089

CURRAN ASSOCIATES INC.
proceedings.com